COMPLETE
COCKNEY RABBIT

COMPLETE COCKNEY RABBIT

RAY PUXLEY

BOOKS

First published in Great Britain in 2008 by
JR Books, 10 Greenland Street, London NW1 0ND
www.jrbooks.com

A catalogue record for this book is available from the British Library.

ISBN 978-1-906217-64-8

1 3 5 7 9 10 8 6 4 2

Printed in the UK by CPI Bookmarque, Croydon, CR0 4TD

INTRODUCTION

Down the years much has been written by philologists and socio-linguists, all eminently better qualified than I in sweeping the gutters of the past to trace the origins of a form of speech that was born there. I don't pretend to be a slang historian – I leave that to those who have the time, resources and inclination to peer into the mouth that houses 'the vulgar tongue' – so when I'm asked about the origins of rhyming slang I have to say: I don't know. But then nobody does.

The most popular belief is that it began as a secret language of the underworld, formed in the mid-19th century as a means of confusing the constabulary and the casual eavesdropper who could be a 'nark'. That it was used by the lowlife of the day is undoubted, but they may well have been contributors rather than founding fathers. It has been suggested the seeds were planted earlier that century during the major reconstruction of London's infrastructure, when the foundations of a modern capital were being laid with the building of main roads, railways and the docks. The main workforce for these great undertakings was made up of local men and Irish immigrants and to perplex their 'foreign' counterparts the cockneys are said to have invented rhyming slang.

Another theory is that it came from the fertile imaginations of street chanters. These nomadic wanderers would travel from market to market (which at the time were known as 'fairs'), telling stories, reciting ballads and informing the populace of the news of the day. Because there were so many of these itinerant spielers, each had to develop their own style of patter which they embellished with colourful phrases and pieces of slang, some of which rhymed.

Although I have never made any attempt to research its history, with the aid of the Internet I have delved into the origins of many previously unrecorded terms. A look through these pages is like viewing a potted history of our recent past, via the people and events that our forbears threw into their speech. The earliest influences are the music hall and the Victorian stage, from where we find terms based on popular songs such as 'The Ratcatcher's Daughter' and 'Burlington Bertie'. Comedians, singers, actors and other assorted turns are well to the fore with the likes of Lionel (Lal) Brough, R.G. Knowles, Harry Tate, Dan Leno, Jenny Lind and George Bohee. Early sportsmen are also on the mark – particularly boxers – including Jem Mace and Darky Cox, plus a jockey Tod Sloane and cricketer Charlie Pope thrown in for good measure. Various Victorian and Edwardian noblemen and women (the Duke and Duchess of Teck, for example) and politicians (Charles James Fox and Charlie Dilke) are also on show and then a few social reformers (Mrs Chant and Angela Burdett-Coutts) just to add a bit of class. The beginnings of institutions such as The Salvation Army and The Scout Association are noted by the inclusions of General Booth and Robert Baden-Powell and writer Sir Arthur Conan-Doyle makes an appearance on the back of his creation, the ever-popular Sherlock Holmes.

World War I could provide a book of slang on its own with numerous rhyming examples that reflect the horror of the conflict, often with the gallows humour made famous by the British. 'Dig my Grave' was a shave, whilst 'Stand at Ease' referred to the infernal fleas. 'Muddy Trench', 'Pork & Beans' and 'Terrible Turk' are just a few others. With the advent of film after the war, it was the turn of the stars of the day to get into the spotlight with Tom Mix, Anna May Wong, Mae West among others and later William Powell, Myrna Loy and Bob Hope. 1930s' boxers Jack Doyle and Elky Clark entered the ring whilst jockeys Harry Wragg and Charlie Smirke were also on parade. British variety is well catered for with all the members of The Crazy Gang on show, along with Max Miller and northern comic Sandy Powell.

World War II came and went, leaving a smattering of terms in its wake: 'Eisenhower', 'Lord Lovat' and 'Benghazi', to name but three. The late 1940s/early 1950s was the age of the crooner, with American singers Johnnie Ray, Frankie Laine and Doris Day among others all adding to the list, along with Brits such as Vera Lynn and Frankie Vaughan. Footballers the calibre of Tom Finney and Frank Swift rub shoulders with the likes of Prime Ministers Harold McMillan and Edward Heath, both of whom had apparently taken to crime.

The late 1950s was the age of rock'n'roll when the likes of Big Bopper, Buddy Holly and Adam Faith took to the stage and many more climbed aboard during the 1960s, including George and Ringo, Acker Bilk and Manfred Mann. This was the age of TV and now celebrities from that medium entered the building with shows such as *Doctor Who*, *Take Your Pick* and *Dad's Army*, plus names like Benny Hill, Frankie Howerd and Cilla Black all getting in on the act. The triumphant World Cup side of 1966 is represented by skipper Bobby Moore, Geoff Hurst, Nobby Stiles and Roger Hunt, whilst 'Man on the Moon' is a nod towards the 1969 moonwalk.

The 1970s witnessed the battle between Margaret Thatcher and Arthur Scargill, both to be found here, along with entertainers as diverse as Peters & Lee and Lou Reed. TV presenter Bill Grundy represents the punk era, indirectly at least, having lost his career after a disastrous interview with the Sex Pistols.

And so to the 1980s when the Royal ups and downs of Princess Diana, Camilla Parker-Bowles and Sarah, Duchess of York are on display as is the television revolution with the mention of Kerry Packer. The 1990s saw the invasion of the foreign footballer into the English league and names such as Ruud Gullit, Gianfranco Zola and Gianlucca Vialli entered the game (and the rhyming slang). And the rise of New Labour is noted with the inclusion of Tony and Cherie Blair, plus John Prescott. 'Popney', a type of slang based entirely on celebrity came onto the scene at this time and the likes of George Michael, Tom Hanks, Brad Pitt, Belinda Carlisle and more recently Axl Rose, Sinead O'Connor and Simon Cowell have helped swell the ranks. Modern technology, such as mobile phones, pagers, scanners, printers, DVDs, etc., all have their own terms and when one considers how such things were beyond science fiction when cockney rhyming slang first started, it's an indication of how far we've come in relatively few pages.

Although I have tried not to take the work too seriously, I have in most cases attempted to age and to explain the terms behind the phrases; I have also raised one or two questions and thrown in a few theories for good measure. Rhyming slang (RS) is by its nature a fun thing that's meant to be light-hearted and humorous and this is how I hope it will come across to the reader and why, when asked, I refer to the book as a 'sort of dictionary'.

In the years since *Cockney Rabbit* was first published in 1992 there has been a tremendous upsurge in the use of rhyming slang, its popularity no longer arising out of a necessity for a secret language but as a way of brightening up the English language. Many would argue that our tongue is bright enough and in the hands of our great pencil-wallahs past and present I would not disagree but the everyday speech of the common man is in the main unexceptional, though functional. The use of a colourful word substitute livens things up a bit and seldom fails to amuse: there is nothing funny about a bout of diarrhoea, for example, but reduce it to 'a touch of the Eartha's' and even if your rear exit currently resembles a Ford Mondeo's brake light, the misery of it is lightened. At the opposite end of the scale, constipation becomes less of a bind when referred to as 'having a bung in the bottle' and as a remedy, a 'bottle opener' sounds like a far better treatment than anything with 'lax' in the name. No one really wants to hear about lavatorial afflictions – or any other ailments come to that – but a well-chosen piece of RS can bring a smile.

Another great thing about rhyming slang is that it's a great leveller: the rich and powerful rub shoulders with the lowly and all treated with equal disrespect. George the Third might have been a great monarch but in this book…well, let's just say you wouldn't want him on your carpet! Stephen Fry may occupy a place on the top table in the acting and writing professions but in this production he must settle for a place on the table in a pie and mash shop. Other strange bedfellows include Donald Trump, Brad Pitt and Egon Ronay who take their business to weird mother Frank Zappa or ex-tennis menace Ille Nastase. Country singer Patsy Cline and racing driver Niki Lauder manage to get up people's noses and the least said about James Blunt and Paul Anka, the better!

Like everything else, rhyming slang suffers the ravages of time and as people become forgotten, in most cases their place in slang disappears to be replaced by modern characters. These days who tells 'Binnie Hales' or drinks 'Ralph Lynn'? Who plays 'Wilkie Bards' or goes on their 'Edna May'? Dead people, dead terms, but their names live on in these pages, so anyone offended by their role in RS should take comfort in the fact that they've also achieved a kind of immortality. Although known as the 'London Slang', it's no longer exclusive to the capital. RS has been picked up and carried on the airways of TV and radio to the four corners of the UK. The boot of any Briton, not just a Cockney's, can deliver a 'kick up the Khyber'. Indeed, the cockney is no longer confined to London either. As the boundaries of Greater London expand to accommodate more and more people, so successive generations of Londoners have spilled over into surrounding areas, especially Essex, with Barking and Dagenham becoming the new East End. In towns slightly further afield, such as Harlow, Basildon and Canvey Island, more and more people can trace their roots back to the capital and as folk move, so the language follows and funnels its way into fresh ears, urging new mouths to repeat it. And as Britain gets smaller, the landlord of a hostelry in Devon is as likely to come from Bow as Bodmin, thus everyone, from doctors to dustmen and taxi drivers to tax inspectors all over the country gets to know a term or two of RS and drops it into conversation for comic effect.

As already stated, rhyming slang was originally the jargon of the lowlife and many of the terms and meanings have not risen above ankle level, but I have left nothing out on the grounds of bad taste. Had I omitted examples relating to taboo words, this work would have been considerably shorter, but incomplete. And a complete dictionary demands the inclusion of the unpalatable, the objectionable and the downright offensive. It is not the intention or wish of myself or the publisher to cause offense to anybody but merely to repeat established terms of slang, most of which were coined before the working man knew that words like sexism or racism existed.

Backslang

'Backslang', a form of slang that originated with 19th-century costermongers and was mastered by subsequent workers in the meat, fish and fruit markets, was another form of speech prevalent in London. Its original use was to bamboozle customers by talking backwards but as with rhyming slang, once the customers caught onto it, it blossomed into yet another weird and wonderful language. Soon drinkers were going to the 'bup' for a 'teenip o' reeb' or a 'slag o' nig'. The 'retchub' sold 'kayrop' and 'feeb', the 'neergresorg' sold 'elpas' and 'eganaros' and 'shif and piches' was a cheap supper. Smokers stuffed 'occabot' into their 'eepips' and rolled it into 'gaffs' whilst others shoved 'funess' up their 'eesons' rather than lines of 'eekoc'. I have included some examples in this book, but a careful study will show the reader how to compose their own terms, should they so wish. You will note that in many cases I have added the backslang variation to the rhyming slang definition. For example, Abraham's Willing, a shilling, is 'Nillish'.

I became aware of slang from an early age – 'course I didn't know it was slang, I took it for granted that the 'reekab posh' and the baker shop were the same place, that 'uncle fred' and bread were the same thing and the 'carsey' and the lavatory occupied the same spot in the back yard wherein was kept a 'box o' lights' and an 'andlekay' which served two purposes: (a) you could see what you were doing in the dark and (b) you could keep an eye on what the spiders were doing in the dark!

My grandmother Liz Pyne was the backslang speaker, a true daughter of the East End, who would apparently converse with neighbours almost entirely in a language that her daughters at first found unintelligible My father was (in order): a layabout, snooker hustler, moody bookmaker and all-round dodgepot before he was found and conscripted. After the War he became a dock worker by day and a 'tic-tac' man by night, working at nearly all the dog tracks in the capital, of which there were a great many in the 1950s and 60s. Drawing from all the different avenues his varied career had taken him along, his slang vocabulary was considerable in all its forms.

Mother, God bless her, had a breathtaking array of words and phrases. To a child with a busy finger up its nose she'd say, 'Don't pick your nose, love, you'll go bandy.' Of anyone with a shocked expression she would say, 'He looks like he's seen one and don't like the shape' and if a film plot was unbelievable, it was 'like shit from China' (far-fetched). Her version of 'death before dishonour' was 'I'd rather be blown up than shown up' and her favoured form of slang was pig-latin or 'igpay atinlay' so I knew what 'amscray' meant before I could 'alkway'.

To the loud clanging of bells in 1948, I made my entry into the world at a hospital in Bow. Not the famous Bow Bells, of course – they are to be found in the church of St Mary-le-Bow in

Cheapside, a few miles away in the City of London. My delivery room was directly opposite the hospital bar and I arrived at the same time as they rang the bell for last orders. This apparently had a terrifying effect on me – which would explain the chronic aversion I later developed towards closing time! The 1950s was a great time to be a kid, especially in Poplar where I grew up. Being near the docks it was a regular target for the Luftwaffe during the Blitz and almost every street bore the scars of that one-sided encounter. Vast tracts of rubble-strewn wastelands, where once stood homes, long overgrown with a multitude of weeds, wild flowers and stinging nettles that I swear used to reach out to deliver their spite to the backs of little bare legs, remained throughout that decade and into the next.

The 'debris' or 'debrys' as we called them were our play-grounds. Health and Safety? Ha! The potholes, brick mountains and loose footings all added to the fun and the frequent cut knees didn't warrant sympathy from your mum – you got told off for using another plaster! Each child belonged to a gang and each gang had a debry, where we would build little huts out of whatever we could find and campfires on which we would roast potatoes. When it was raining we'd sometimes light a fire inside the hut – never a great idea as no one knew how to build a chimney. It wasn't long before a bunch of smoky-flavoured urchins poured out, coughing their offal up, and if the last one out didn't put out the fire, then up would go the roof (usually a piece of tarpaulin or an old door dug out of the ruins).

Most of the time there was no animosity between rival gangs: they played together, sat next to each other in class and were school football and cricket team-mates. But once a year came the wood war season. This occurred in the week leading up to 5 November when all gang members would scour the streets for bonfire wood and inter-gang rivalry became intense. At that time the neighbourhood had a profusion of bombed houses, the ruins of which contained a plentiful supply of wood and other combustibles. But that wasn't good enough. What we had, they wanted and what they had, we had to have. Raids into 'enemy territory' were mounted. This usually happened around five or six o'clock when your scouts came back and reported that all enemy personnel had gone for their teas. There was always a guard, but he didn't count – he was often the youngest member of the gang. He would stand resolutely at his post, a saucepan on his head and a stick carried sentry-like against his shoulder, his heart full of valour. At the first sight of a bunch of screaming, club-wielding yahoos charging towards him he'd be off in the opposite direction to raise the alarm. As if synchronised, nearby doors would open in unison and the opposing army spilled out onto the street to begin the battle. Boys would trade blows over a rotted piece of linoleum, an old rafter would become the prize in a splintery game of tug o' war and perfectly good friends fought over a piece of wood they had stepped over 365 times since last year. Eventually the raiders would retreat, taking with them whatever spoils they could get away with and knowing full well that the next night they would have to defend their own territory.

With no television to keep us indoors and hardly any traffic to present a danger, the street had everything we needed. It was our football pitch in winter, our cricket pitch in summer (the two never crossed) and our permanent racetrack. On long summer nights everyone, children and adults alike, would be out playing, talking and sometimes arguing until dark. Those streets are not there any more – they were pulled down at the end of the 1960s to make way for a housing estate. In dreams I often return.

My first ambition was to be a footballer. At 8 years old the school sports master told me that I had the ability of an 11-year-old. Unfortunately when I was 15, I still had the ability of an 11-year old! So that was that. At 13 I got a Saturday job in the new betting shop industry and I was paid the staggering amount of £2/10 shillings (£2.50) to file away the 'sloshers' (losing bets). Bookmaking, I decided, was a good way to make money so I made my own book at school on the 1963 Grand National. This was not a success. The race was won by a 66/1 chance called Ayala and two people backed it. One was a spotty fat kid whom I had **never** liked and the other was the school hardnut from the fifth form, who insisted on immediate payment. Pleadings of insolvency were met by my being dangled upside-down from a railway bridge. Needless to say, I found their money. But they bashed me anyway. Many years later, I bumped into spotty fatty wotssname – I still didn't like him.

My bookmaking career in ruins, I decided to venture into the world of rock'n'roll. The Beatles and the Stones were in the ascendancy and I would be a great guitarist; I would dethrone George Harrison. I bought a cheap, second-hand guitar and took it to my room, along with a Bert Weedon instruction book called *Play in a Day*. This was going to be easy. Ah, the sweet naïvety of youth!

I nailed a notice on my door saying 'DO NOT INTERRUPT UNTIL I AM A GREAT GUITARIST'. This was the first indication I'd ever had that my mother could read – she followed the instructions to the letter and I emerged a week later, an emaciated, skeletal figure with sore fingers and a total inability to even tune the bloody thing. Play in a day be-bollocks! Somehow I persevered, and after a few weeks' practice, I managed to string a few chords together. Great, I thought, I'm on my way. My father, though, had other ideas and took to clouting me round the ear and then taking himself off to the pub whenever I picked up my instrument. One terrible day I came home to find a demolished guitar; it had been trodden on. The old man maintained it was an accident, but I had reason to doubt this as I used to keep it on top of my wardrobe. Thus my strumming career was consigned to the dustbin of broken dreams and all I had to show for putting my fingers through a contortional hell was a busted guitar, a cauliflower ear and a parent with a drink problem. And George Harrison was still top banana.

Never a great scholar, I was more interested in climbing the Tree of Life than carving my initials on the Tree of Knowledge and at 15 I decided to drop out. With a courage I never knew I had, I marched into the school principal's office and told him that I was leaving and he couldn't stop me. He didn't try.

So there I was, fresh out of school and fresh out of work, but not for long. Through an old family friend I got a full-time job with East London's biggest bookmaking firm at the time, William Massey Ltd., where I learned all the aspects of bookmaking. Eventually I became a 'settler', and later, when I was old enough, a shop manager. It was during this time that I first became interested in rhyming slang, picking up bits and pieces from both sides of the counter. I worked in shops all over the East End and the City, from the Docklands (before dockers became an endangered species) to market sites and all stops in between. And my vocabulary blossomed.

At 21 my feet started to get itchy – there had to be more to life than 5/4 the field and *The Sporting Life* – so I set out to find it. The next few years saw me drifting in and out of a variety of jobs, from a council building site to a Post Office parcel depot. Driving a lorry for a carpet firm and labouring in a saw-mill, where missing fingers were an occupational hazard. Not to mention that last refuge of the unemployed (and often unemployable): mini-cabbing. Everywhere I worked, I picked up a snippet or two of slang – even in a car showroom-cum-garage in Jersey, where I befriended an ex-pat Poplar boy.

In the early 1970s whilst watching a dire sitcom on TV, I just knew I could write a funny script. I now had a wife and a young son and this career move would make me rich. Move over Galton & Simpson, Speight and the rest, I was coming through! I wrote a comic masterpiece called *Worms Up a Lamppost*, for which I received a bucketful of rejection slips. Philistines! Heads of TV comedy departments wouldn't know a funny script if it crept up behind them in a clown suit and tickled them. Heeding the family motto: 'If at first you don't succeed, pack it in', I watched sadly as another dream bit the dust.

In 1977 I took a job driving a lorry for the City and East London Health Authority (as it was then) and found that being alone in my cab allowed my words and thoughts to emerge in tune. Could songwriting be my forte? Played in my head, they sounded great but I also discovered that I have a voice a bit like a 'nanny goat shitting on tin' (another of my mother's little eloquences) and I soon realised that a singer-songwriter I would never be. But a songwriter, maybe, if only I could get someone else to sing them. With luck I might be up there with Dylan, Lennon, McCartney, Jagger, Richards et al. Ah, sweet naivety of middle-age!

Of course, not being able to write music or play any form of musical instrument was a potential drawback, but a chance meeting with Lyndon Bournon, a brilliant, undiscovered guitarist from Romford, led to a collusion which enabled me to commit my 25 compositions to tape. I liked them, Lyndon (a special needs teacher by day and musician at night) also liked them and used several of them in his act. He now lives in Canada and still uses them, so they can't be all that bad. Considering the time and effort I put into producing them, it still amazes me what little energy I put into getting them published or even heard. A couple of knockbacks sapped my confidence, I guess, and the tape marked 'Raysongs' occupies a place in a drawer somewhere. I still like the songs that remain unpublished and largely unheard so if anyone is interested, get in touch.

In 1989, whilst working as a courier in my own van, a large Northern driver of a large Northern lorry tried to fit his vehicle into the back of mine but failed abysmally. All he managed to do was to write off my van and put me out of work for six months with a back injury. To pass the time during this spell of enforced idleness I began toying with the idea of an up-to-date book on rhyming slang and *Cockney Rabbit*, published in 1992, was the result. The effect was startling, with books and websites devoted to the subject springing up all over the place. My term, 'cockney rabbit', seems to have become the established synonym for 'cockney rhyming slang' – just Google it and see. There was even a show of the same title.

Fresh Rabbit followed in 1998 and *Britslang*, a dictionary of general British slang, hit the shelves to widespread acclaim in 2003. And now *Cockney Rabbit* hops again. You will notice the size of the work: this is a result of me scouring every book and website I could find on the subject and even then I have still had to edit it. Soppy terms made up just to effect a rhyme on a famous name have been ignored. Lester Piggott (bigot)? Kevin Keegan (vegan)? No! Who would use them? And I regret ever including Germaine Greer (beer) in a previous book so I refuse to involve Britney Spears (beers) in this one. I have also tapped into the memories of some older people and found terms from the 1950s and 60s undocumented until now due to a lack of books on the subject and I have pestered younger people to see if anything new has entered the arena. Of course I accept that I may have bought a few dummies but if they tickled me or sounded genuine enough, then I have incorporated them amongst the old, the established and the obsolete, making this the most comprehensive 'dick'n'arry' of rhyming slang ever.

My thanks to friends, relatives, strangers and all the unwitting contributors to this work and a special thanks to Fred the Ted for his list of forgotten terms of his 1950s' youth. Thanks also to Jeremy Robson for his backing over the past 15 years. And to computer wizard, Andy of EasyPC Systems in Dagenham for his help and advice on all things computorial.

This book is dedicated to the memories of John Skeels, a great pal, and Sylvia Reeves, a wonderful sister-in-law. Heaven's a nicer place for their being there.

A to Z   **Shed**
Probably after the roadmap people. Many men seek refuge and solitude in their 'ada'. A backslang shed is a 'desh'.

Abel & Cain   **Rain**
The biblical brothers get together to give the English something to moan about. When it's raining cats and dogs in backslang, it's 'nyaring tacks and gods'.

Aberdeen(s)   **Beans**
Mainly applies to baked beans but also serves as a spoonerism on 'ad a bean', whereby a hungry spoonerist may claim they haven't 'aberdeen' all day. A 'nit of neabs' – a backslang tin of beans.

Abergavenny   **Penny**
Originally a pre-decimal penny, which was handy for buying things with, not like today's model. 'Yannep' – a backslang penny.

Abraham   **Sham**
Pronounced 'abram', this applies to getting out of something by feigning illness. Known today as 'pulling a sickie'.

Abraham's Willing   **Shilling**
A piece that was defunct long before Britain's previous currency. 'Nillish' – a backslang 'deaner' (see Riverina).

Ace of Spades   **Aids**

The traditional card of misfortune is said to have been drawn by sufferers of the disease.

Ache & Pain   **Rain**

Reduced by 'aching' or stretched to 'ache & paining', either way it's time to don your 'titfer'; a term never more apt than during the washout summer of 2007 when torrential downpours brought floods, chaos and misery to thousands. See 'Tit for Tat'.

Acker Bilk   **Milk**

An early 1960s piece based on an English clarinetist, who, along with his Paramount Jazz Band, was a regular chart-occupant during the Trad Jazz boom of the period. From Somerset, the man is more cider apple than cow juice. A 'slag of kaylim' – a backslang glass of milk.

Adam & Eve   **(a) Believe**

Very old, very common and often an expression of disbelief – but I can't adam & eve you didn't know that.

(b) Leave

When it's time to go, it's time you were 'adam & eveing'.

Adam Ants   **Pants**

Underpants from the 1980s, when this British singer was frequently in the charts. His trademark was his flamboyant dress. We can only wonder at the state of his 'adams'. 'Teenaps' – backslang pants.

Adam Faith   **Safe**

A piece employed by betting office managers of the early 1960s based on a British singer, actor and later newspaper columnist advising on matters financial (1940–2003). No doubt he had an 'adam' of his own, but the term never got the better of the more widely used 'peter'. 'Eefas' – a backslang safe.

After Eight Mint   **Skint**

What the 'after-dinner bachelor' is by Monday morning. When you're broke, in backslang you are 'teenicks'.

AGGRAVATION

Aggravation   **Station**
A term from the 1920s that suggests the arsehole-ache of rail travel is nothing new.

Ain't it a Treat?   **Street**
A 19th-century term probably used ironically to describe a slum.

Ain't She Sweet?   **Seat**
Before it became a sexist thing to do, gentlemen used to give up their 'ain't she's' to standing ladies.

Airs & Graces   **(a) Braces**
Support for this term was suspended with the popularity of the belt.

(b) Faces
If there's some dodgy-looking 'airs & graces' in the pub, go elsewhere!

(c) Races
An early 20th-century term no longer in the running.

Ajax   **Tax**
Based on the name of the ancient Greek warrior who later became a scouring powder and a Dutch football team. Now in the shape of a disc, he is to be seen on a car windscreen – or should be! 'Exat' – a backslang burden.

Al Capone   **Phone**
An old, seldom-used piece that's probably as dead as the notorious American gangster himself (1899–1947). 'Eenophe'/'Eenof' – a backslang blower.

Al Murray   **Curry**
An early 21st-century piece that fits in nicely with this British comedian's alter ego, the Pub Landlord, who would no doubt order a vindaloo for the lads and a korma for the ladies.

Alabama   **Hammer**
Heard as an 'ala' on a 1990s building site.

Alabaster   **Plaster**
Always said as 'ala', this is the bottom rung of the most

3

convoluted ladder of rhyming slang. When you reach the top, you'll find yourself at the bottom. See also 'Plaster of Paris'.

Alan Brazzle   Razzle

On the razzle, that is. On a spree, bender, booze-up, pub crawl…whatever keeps your glass full. Coined with more than a passing nod to Scottish football international and later successful broadcaster and wine-taster Alan Brazil, who you may well bump into somewhere when you're out on the 'Alan'.

Alan Ladd   Sad

As well as a sense of dejection, this may also be used to describe people with mundane interests. Anyone who by choice knows the difference in width between any two given railway tracks in the world is laughed off as being 'a bit alan ladd'. Based on the American film star (1913–64).

Alan Minter   Splinter

Based on the Crawley-born boxer who in 1980 became a World Middleweight champion; the term was briefly used by woodworkers when tree slivers invaded their fingers, thumbs, etc.

Alan Whicker   Nicker (£1)

A 1990s piece of youthspeak based on a British TV personality, which sees the Pound Shop become the 'alan whicker' shop. 'Reckin' – a backslang nicker.

Alan Whicker's   Knickers

A piece from the late 1960s, when boys 'on the pull' sought to get into a girl's 'alan whicker's'.

Albert Hall   Wall

Harassed parents are driven 'up the albert' by their troublesome offspring. Based on the Royal Albert Hall, Kensington, West London.

Alderman's Nail   Tail

A very old term concerning an animal's tail, which may have originated in the meat industry. Most commonly associated with a dog's wag-piece, 'nail' was a 19th-century term for an arrest. So could a bent official of yore be in the frame here?

Aldershot Whore   Four

A piece of army slang; Aldershot, Hampshire has been an army training centre since 1854. 'Rofe' – 'four' in backslang.

Aldgate East   Priest

Based on a London Underground station, this is how the 'sky pilot' became an 'aldgate'.

Aldgate Pump   Hump

To be displeased or fed up is to have the 'right aldgate'. Based on an ancient City of London water pump no longer in use, although it remains a city landmark.

Alf Garnett   Barnet (Hair)

English actor Warren Mitchell's alter ego provides us with an example of how, when a term becomes as common as 'barnet fair' (qv), it acquires a piece of RS of its own.

Alf Tupper   Supper

A 1950s example based on a British comic character; a working-class athlete who took on all-comers in a strip called 'The Tough of the Track' in *Rover* and *Wizard* comics between 1949 and 1992. He trained on beer and fish and chips, so an 'alf tupper' is often a fish supper.

Alfie Bass   Gas

A term relating to the natural resource that's been on the back burner since the early 1960s when the British comedy actor (1920–87) was seldom away from our TV screens.

Alfred the Great   Weight

Always reduced to 'alfred' by those wishing to decrease their waistlines. Based on the old King of Wessex (849–99), who was famous for burning cakes, not calories.

Alhambra   Camera

A rarely-heard piece based on the name of a theatre built in London's Leicester Square in 1854 and demolished in 1936. Coined before anyone knew what 'digital' meant and the thought of putting an 'alhambra' in a 'dog' was pure sci-fi. 'Aramac' – a backslang snap-taker (see Dog & Bone).

Ali G   Pee/Wee

This recent term sees the owners of overflowing bladders nipping out for an 'ali'. Based on the comic creation of British comedian Sacha Baron Cohen.

Alive or Dead   Head

A 19th-century piece kicked into obsolescence years ago. 'Deeache' – a backslang napper.

All Afloat   Coat

A 19th-century term long consigned to the ragbag of discarded RS, it may have lasted longer had it applied to a 'floater' (boat).

All Behind   Blind

Applies sympathetically to those who can't see, but angrily to those who can, but don't. 'What d'you mean, you didn't see me? What are you, all behind?'

All Complain   Rain

Appropriate since bad weather brings out the moaner in all of us. Come to think of it, so does good weather!

All Forlorn   Horn (Erection)

The dictionary describes 'forlorn' as 'sad, abandoned and lonely'. This may then relate to waking up with an 'alfor' and having no one to share it with. 'Enroh' – a backslang hard-on.

All Night Rave   Shave

A modern piece in current use by young shavers. 'Eevash' is the backslang for shave.

All Quiet on the Western Front   Cunt

An overlong term used when Mr Unpopular, possibly a police officer, is about to join a group: 'Look out, all quiet!' 'Teenuc' – an unpopular person in backslang.

Allan Border   Order

Based on an Australian cricket captain whose success depressed many an Englishman. He now frustrates still more at closing time when the barman calls 'last allan borders'.

Allez/Ali Oop   Poop (Excrement)
The phrase commonly associated with stage acrobats at the performance of a feat. It may be used when a piece of 'hard-baked' excrement is finally ejected after a long and bitter teethmarks-on-the-lavatory-door struggle.

Allied Irish Bank   Wank
A 1990s term for an act of masturbation. It's a bit of a mouthful, which is why it's generally reduced to an 'allied irish'. 'Kaynaw' (caner) – one off a backslang wrist.

Alligator   Later
A 1950s piece inspired by the rock'n'roll song, 'See You Later, Alligator' – a hit for US band Bill Haley & His Comets.

Almond Rock   Cock (Penis)
The male member is well-represented in RS and many descriptions, like this one, take the form of long, suckable confectionery.

Almond Rocks   Socks
Old, common and always worn as 'almonds'.

Alphonse   Ponce
Applies not only to a pimp, but also a 'sponger', someone who deliberately goes out with nuppence in his pockets and exploits the generosity of others.

Alton Towers   Flowers
Based on a leisure resort in Staffordshire, a bunch of 'altons' may bring pleasure to a recipient. They won't always get the giver out of trouble, though!

Amos & Andy   (a) Brandy
A term based on an American radio and TV series broadcast in the UK during the 1950s. The radio show was to political correctness what Vlad the Impaler was to humanitarianism. A and A were two black men played by white actors Freeman Gosden (1899–1982) and Charles Correll (1890–1972). After a furore, black actors Alvin Childers (1907–86) and Spencer Williams (1893–1969) took the TV roles. 'Yadnarb' – a backslang inhabitant of the top shelf.

7

(b) Shandy

Following the introduction of the breathalyser in the 1960s, 'shandies' became a common member of a round of drinks and so the term began its confusing merger with (a). 'Yadnash' – a backslang soft drink.

Amsterdam   Jam

No matter what fruit it's made from, it's all 'amster'. A 'raj of madge' – backslang for a jar of jam.

Anchors Away!   Gay

'Anchors' is one of a kotchel of terms to spring up since 'gay' became a widely accepted word to describe homosexuality. In backslang, it's 'yag'.

Andy Cain   Rain

A 19th-century term for cloud juice that seems to have disappeared down the RS drainhole.

Andy Capp   (a) Crap 1

One of many terms to describe defecation and excretia: one goes for an 'andy' and flushes the resultant produce away – unless it's a 'double-flusher', which is harder to shift. For a 'bog-blocker' you may need the help of Dyno-Rod

Crap 2

Rubbish, spoken or otherwise, whereby tall stories, cheap goods and no-star rated entertainment is a load of 'andy'.

(b) Tap (Borrow)

Fittingly based on a British cartoon character who is permanently skint and so forever 'on the tap'.

Andy McGinn   Chin

An example from the 1930s that was subsequently KO'd by 'Errol Flynn' (qv). May be based on Andrew McGinn, an early Highland Games participant, the first and only exponent of 'catching the caber'. Being the first and only fatality in the first and only contest, it was decided that simply 'tossing the caber' was the safer option. The original now occupies a place on the dangerous sports list, along with 'catching the javelin' and 'nutting the shot'. A backslang chin is a 'nitch'.

Andy McNish   **Fish**

Applies to a swimmer in its role as food, anglers don't go 'andy mcnishing'. 'Shif'n'Piches' – backslang fish'n'chips.

Andy Pandy   **(a) Brandy**

An ingredient in the hot toddy that brings relief to those with a touch of the 'loo-be-loo' (qv) – those of a certain age will spot the connection.

(b) Shandy

Based on a TV puppet that everyone Watched with Mother in the 1950s. A pint of 'andy pandy' is a common order from those with a driving licence to protect.

Anna Maria   **Fire**

Applies to the domestic coal-fire of yore rather than anything the Fire Brigade would be called out to. 'Eerif' – a backslang roary.

Anna May Wong   **Pong**

Reduced to 'anna may', this early 20th-century piece is based on a Chinese-American film actress (1907–61), who may or may not have suffered from reeking armpits.

Anthea Turner   **Earner**

A 1990s term, an 'anthea' represents wages, usually for a cash-in-hand, no-questions-asked job. Based on a TV personality of the period.

Apple & Pip   **Sip**

An uncommon example of a piece of RS for a term of backslang, 'sip' is a back formation of piss, therefore to 'go for an apple' is to urinate.

Apple Cider   **Spider**

The only multi-legged 'apple' you'll ever see – unless it's a crab apple.

Apple Core   **Score (£20)**

Always shortened to the first element, whereby an 'apple' each-way double could prove fruitful.

Apple Fritter   **Bitter (Ale)**

An early 20th-century example, making it the oldest term of RS for this type of larynx lubricant.

Apple Pie   **Sky**

Shepherd's delight in a red 'apple' at night.

Apple Pips   **Lips**

An old term for the kissers, trappy types may be told to watch their 'apples'.

Apple Sauce   **Horse**

Often the racehorse that trailed in last or 'ran like a pig'. Hence apple sauce. 'Esroch' – a backslang gee-gee.

Apple Tart   **Fart**

A disgusting stench often follows a dropped 'apple' – or in backslang a 'traff'.

Applejack   **Crack**

A 1980s term for this form of cocaine based on a brandy distilled from cider apples.

Apples & Pears   **Stairs**

The one piece of rhyming slang everyone knows…but hardly anyone uses.

Apples & Rice   **Nice**

Generally shortened to the first element when describing anything pleasant – a sunny day may be 'apples' – but said in full when used ironically of something amiss: 'Oh that's very bloody apples and rice' means it isn't.

Apricot & Peach   **Beach**

A trip to the 'apricot' to soak up the 'currant' may prove treble fruitful if it's 'full of lemons'. See also 'Currant Bun' and 'Lemon Curd' (a).

April Fool   **(a) Stool**

Most commonly applies to a bar stool, on which to park one's 'april in paris' (qv).

(b) Tool

Originally a tool of the housebreaking trade, it now applies to any tool of any trade.

April Fool's   **Pools**
In Pre-National Lottery days it was everyone's dream to win the 'april's' but only a fool ever believed that they actually would.

April in Paris   **Aris**
An example three times removed from its meaning, namely the backside. Aris – Aristotle (bottle). Bottle & Glass – arse.

April Showers   **Flowers**
One of the most common terms to pass between two lips; also applies to this brand of beer as a pint of 'april'. A 'reewolf' is a backslang bloomer.

Arabian Nights   **Shites**
Diarrhoea courtesy of an ancient book containing a collection of tales of old Arabia; a major symptom of the hospital superbug. C-Diff is a prolonged attack of the 'arabians'.

Archbishop Laud   **Fraud**
A piece from the fictional underworld of novelist Robin Cook *The Crust On Its Uppers* (1962) and based on William Laud (1573–1645), an Archbishop of Canterbury.

Aristotle   **Bottle**
Always shortened to 'aris', this applies to any bottle but is mainly heard as slang for slang reference to the backside. See also 'Bottle & Glass'. Named after the Greek philosopher (384–322BC). The term is responsible for the backside being known as as the 'Rolf' (Rolf Aris). Geddit? Of course you get it!

Arm & Leg   **Egg**
What a chocolate one can cost at Easter. 'Googy and nocab' – a backslang breakfast of egg and bacon.

Army & Navy   **Gravy**
An example first dished up and splashed on soldiers' dinners in World War I field kitchens.

Army Rocks   **Socks**
A WWI version of 'almond rocks' (qv).

Army Tank Yank

An American, originally a GI, coined by British soldiers during 'the second lot', i.e. World War II.

Arnold Palmers Farmers

A piece of twice-removed slang based on an American golfer. 'farmers' is short for 'farmer giles' (piles) (qv), so if your 'grapes' are the size of golf balls you've got a nasty case of 'arnolds'.

Arnold Schwarzenegger Beggar

A 21st-century example used for humorous effect. It relates to professional 'mumpers' (beggars) who ride the London Underground in search of handouts. Based on the Austria-born film star elected Governor of California in 2003.

Arrivederci Roma Coma

An underworld term from the 1950s, based on a popular song title, used in connection with rendering someone unconscious; putting them in an 'arrivederci' which is Italian for goodbye.

Artful Dodger Lodger

An oft-used term when it was common for householders to take in lodgers; based on the Dickensian thief in *Oliver Twist*. 'Regdol' – a backslang boarder, said as 'Reg Doll'.

Artful Fox Box

A theatrical expression from the 19th century regarding a box in that establishment.

Arthur Ashe Cash

A piece from the used car trade based on an American tennis player (1943–93), the Wimbledon champion of 1975. 'Shack' – backslang readies.

Arthur Bliss Piss

The act of urination is to 'go for an arthur'. Also to 'take the arthur' is to assault verbally; to take the proverbial piss. Based on the knighted English composer (1891–1975).

Arthur Scargill Gargle (Drink)

Beer normally, courtesy of an English trade unionist who from

1981–2002 was president of the National Union of Miners (NUM).

Artichoke   **Smoke**
A piece that also works as a pun, suggesting its originator was coughing his offal up at the time; i.e. having a hearty choke.

Artichoke Ripe   **Pipe**
From a time when pipe-smoking was common practice, but has now run out of puff.

Arvy Mariah   **Fire**
An infrequent mispronunciation of 'ave maria' rarely heard since the demise of the coal fire but those in a hurry may be told to: 'Slow down. Where's the arvy mariah?'

Ascot Heath   **Teeth**
Based on an English racecourse and as actor Hugh Grant might have remarked of prostitute Divine Brown (qv): 'You don't come across ascots like her's every day.'

Ascot Races   **Braces**
Known as 'ascots' but probably not to the 'titfer and tails' brigade who gather there during 'The Season'.

Ash & Oak(s)   **Smoke(s)**
Commonly associated with telling someone to hand round their cigarettes: 'Come on, it's your turn to flash the ash.'

Aston Villa   **Pillow/Pillar**
Since both words are pronounced the same, an 'aston' is equally at home as a headrest or a view-obstructer at a football ground.

Aunt Annie   **Fanny (Vagina)**
The aunt you don't want to visit if she's unwell.

Aunt Lil   **Pill**
Usually something from the chemists, as in 'Don't feel well?' 'Send for aunt lil.' Kipper – a sleeping pill, it makes you kip.

Aunt Lily   **Silly**
Rarely heard and possibly based on someone's dopey relative who may have been 'as silly as a bunch of lights'.

Aunt Maria   **Fire**

A 19ht-century piece, which went out of fashion when old king coal ceased to rule the fireplace.

Aunt Nell   **(a) Gel**

Hair-slick, a 2000s example that saw people walking about with heads full of 'aunt nell'.

(b) Smell

Said as: 'It don't half aunt nell in here!' Possibly based on someone's redolent relative.

Auntie Ella   **Umbrella**

An infrequent term for a 'mush', 'auntie ella' was once a vital part of the on-course bookmaker's paraphernalia.

Auntie Ena   **Cleaner**

Refers to a charlady and appears in a rhyme:

> Have you seen my auntie Ena?
> In the City she's a cleaner
> Met a bloke from Bethnal Greena
> Since then Uncle hasn't seen 'er.

Auntie Nellie   **Belly**

Often used in relation to an upset stomach, when your 'auntie nellie' might be playing you up, making you feel 'uncle dick' (qv).

Auntie Ruth   **Tooth**

A recently acquired gap in your dental collection will prompt questions as to the whereabouts of your 'auntie ruth'.

Auntie Vi   **Anti-bi(otic)**

Heard in a chemist's shop in Barking, much to the bemusement of the Asian pharmacist on duty.

Auntie's Ruin   **Gin**

Old alternative to 'mother's ruin' (qv) in a family of female boozers; 'Esslag of nig' – a backslang glass of gin.

Aunt's Sisters   **Ancestors**

More of a pun than RS...but relative.

Autumn Leaf   **Thief**

'Autumn leaves' may be thick on the ground down Hooky Street.

Ave Maria   **Fire**

See also 'Arvy Mariah'.

Axl Rose   **Nose**

A piece of 2000s popney which sees an American musician, the frontman with the band Guns N' Roses, on stage as a schnozzle. 'Eeson' – a backslang for the shonk (nose).

Aylesbury Duck   **Fuck**

Only used in the sense of not caring, the insensitive 'won't give an aylesbury'; 'Kaycuff' – how the f-word, in backslang becomes a k-word.

Ayrton Senna   **Tenner**

An 'ayrton' has become a common expression for £10 in the years since the death of this Brazilian racing driver in 1994 (b. 1960). Two backslang fivers make a 'rennet'.

Baa Lamb   **Tram**

A term that was widely used when trams were.

Babbling Brook   **(a) Cook**

Originally, a 'babbler' was an army cook from the 'first lot' (World War I) but later applied to anyone who could wield a tin-opener.

      (b) Crook

Any rogue, villain or conman can be a 'babbler'.

Baby's Cries   **Eyes**

Rarely-used example for the peepers.

Baby's Pap   **Cap**

First recorded in the mid-19th century when the working man was particularly adept at turning out children and wearing flat hats, often at the same time. Hence the connection with nipper food, I suppose.

Baby's Pram   **Jam**

The integral part of a continental breakfast and nothing to do with traffic chaos – except maybe in shops. It's a sign of the times that mothers are too scared to leave prams outside anymore.

Bacardi & Coke   **Bloke**

How 1990s man became a 'bacardi'...

Bacardi Breezer   **Geezer**

...And how 21st-century man became likewise. This one based on a popular alcopop.

Back Porch   **Torch**

Cockney dwellings tended not to have back porches so possibly from the music-hall song 'Last Night On The Back Porch'.

Backseat Driver   **Skiver**

Someone who doesn't want to do the work but will tell you how it should be done; a person said to work fewer hours than Father Christmas.

Back-Wheel Skid   **Yid (Jew)**

A 'back-wheeler' is sometimes used as an alternative to the more common 'front-wheel skid' (qv). Same meat, different gravy really...

Bacon & Egg(s)   **Leg(s)**

Fat, thin, shapely or corned beefish, they are all 'bacons'.

Bacon Bonce   **Nonce**

Late 20th-century prison slang for a child molester.

Bacon Lardon   **Hard-On**

A recent term for an erection, one that grew in the suburbs.

Bacon Rind   **Blind**

Always sliced to the first element whereby the short-sighted are said to be 'as bacon as a bat'.

Bacon Slicer   **Shicer**

A name given to anyone who will 'carve you up'; a 'bacon' will swindle, cheat or welsh on you.

Baden-Powell   **Trowel**

The original scoutmaster Robert Baden-Powell (1857–1941) has been a bricklayer's tool for a century or so.

Bag of Coke   **Poke (Sexual Intercourse)**

An old term, possibly from the allusion that coal was often paid for in kind, as in the saying: 'Never be unfaithful with the coalman when it's the milkman you owe money to.'

Bag of Flour   **Shower**

After a match, cricketers may jump in the 'bag of flour' – unless, of course, play was stopped by one.

Bag of Fruit   **Suit**

An example that only fits properly when it isn't shortened; you're always cased up in your best 'bag of fruit'.

Bag of Sand   **Grand**

A 'bag' is a 1990s term from the City of London in relation to £1,000.

Baked Bean   **Queen**

An unflattering term for Queen Elizabeth II and possibly a blinding hand at poker, as in four 'baked beans'.

Baked Beans   **Jeans**

A term from the 1960s mirroring the rise in popularity of both products.

Baked Potato   **Waiter**

One of several examples rhyming the restaurant worker with 'potater'. See also 'Hot', 'Cold' and 'Roast Potato'.

Baker's Dozen   **Cousin**

Relating to your relation, 'baker's' is an old expression based on a term for 13.

Bakewell Tart   **Fart**

Drop a 'bakewell' in the bath and someone is likely to bring you a hot-water bottle.

Balaclava   **Charver**

A sinister term for sexual intercourse, 'charver' comes from the Romany word for the taking of a woman and a balaclava has become the symbol of a rapist.

Bald Head   **Red**

Heard only in the snooker hall for that coloured ball, possibly from the expression 'bald as a billiard ball'.

Ball & Bat   **Hat**
Although an ancient piece, it has always been shaded by the famous 'tit for tat' (qv). 'Tattah' – a backslang titfer.

Ball & Chain   **Strain**
Used sarcastically when a job is being done with the minimum of effort: 'Don't you ball & chain yourself!'

Ball of Chalk   **Walk**
Has tirelessly stridden the road of RS for generations, often as a 'ball-y'.

Ball of Fat   **Cat**
Descriptive of many a pampered puss.

Ball of Lead   **Head**
A piece first fired in World War I, when many a head was pierced by an enemy bullet.

Balloon Car   **Saloon Bar**
Always known as the 'balloon', this is an unusual example in that it effects a rhyme on both elements.

Ballroom Blitz   **Shits**
An attack of the squirts courtesy of a 1973 top ten hit by British band, Sweet. Fluid faecal fallout has been known as the 'ballrooms' ever since.

Balmy Breeze   **Cheese**
Any type, texture or colour, it's all 'balmy breeze' – even the stuff you have to stand downwind of. 'Eseech' – backslang mouse-bait.

Banana Fritter   **Shitter (Lavatory)**
The place to accommodate someone suffering from a case of the 'banana splits' (qv).

Banana Split(s)   **Shit(s)**
Either you go for a 'banana' or have a touch of them in an outpouring of diarrhoea.

Band of Hope   **Soap**
An apt example since it's based on an old organisation that preached clean living to juveniles.

Bang & Biff **Syph(ilis)**

Two slang terms for the sexual act get together to give the result of a bad one.

Bangers & Mash **(a) Slash**

A 'bangers' is one of many terms for urination on stream.

(b) Cash

Rarely heard, but the potless are 'out of bangers'.

Bar of Soap **(a) Dope 1**

An old example from the world of drugs.

Dope 2

A dimwit, half-wit or a witless walloon. Any fool can be a 'bar o' soap'.

(b) Pope

A term that serves to prove that cleanliness is next to Godliness.

(c) Rope

An old piece from the docks that was cast off when that industry died in London.

Barbecue Griddle **Piddle**

Going for a 'barbie' is another means of 'giving a water sample'.

Barbie Doll **Moll**

A term from the underworld to describe a gangster's girlfriend.

Barcelona **Moaner**

An habitual grouch; someone who could moan for England – or Spain.

Barclays Bank **Wank**

One of many banks connected with the 'wringing of the richard'.

Barclays Banker **Wanker**

An unpleasant or useless person; often a football referee, depending on which side he refused a penalty to. 'Reknaw' (reckner) – a backslang tosser.

Bargain Hunt **Cunt**

Not necessarily one for sale in a cheap brothel. This mainly applies to a fool or a despicable person, so if someone tells you that you are a 'bargain', make sure it's in jest. Based on the popular 'noughties' TV show. 'Teenuc' – a backslang scrote.

Barge & Tug　　　　　**Mug**
Old dockworkers would have a 'barge o' rosie' when the tea van came round. See also 'Rosie Lee'.

Bark & Growl　　　　　**Trowel**
An archaic piece that has laid its last brick.

Barnaby Rudge　　　　　**Judge**
A Dickens of a title for a legal big-wig. 'Egdudge' – 'M'lud' in backslang.

Barnacle Bills　　　　　**Pills (Testicles)**
A 'pill' is an old slang term for a ball which has evolved quite happily into a reference to a man's tender dangly bits. Reduced to 'barnacles', from the song about a sailor of this name.

Barnet Fair　　　　　**Hair**
Applies to a head of hair en masse, or lack of mass when referring to a bloke 'Who's got no barnet'. Based on an event dating back to medieval times. There's a story of two Limehouse policemen who came upon the body of a tramp. 'Any sign of life?' Asked one: 'Only in his barnet,' came the reply. 'Riah' – backslang hair. 'Nanty riah' – no hair.

Barney Moke　　　　　**Poke**
A 'poke' is a wallet and its contents; a term used by those that would dip into a pocket and separate a 'barney' from its owner.

Barney Rubble　　　　　**Trouble**
Not to be confused with the longstanding 'barney' meaning a fight. Fred Flintstone's pal lends his name to a worrying situation, a spot of bother, etc. When you're low on petrol and miles from the next garage, you're in 'barney rubble'.

Barry McGuigan　　　　　**Big 'Un**
Heard in a baker's shop: when asked which of the three remaining loaves he wanted, the customer replied: 'The barry mcguigan.' Ironic since the Irish boxing pundit is a former World Featherweight champion and therefore more of a little 'Un.

Barry White **Shite**

An American soul singer (1944–2003), whose name is now lent to anything considered rubbish. Heard on a bus: '*Big Brother*? You don't watch that barry white, do you?'

Bash Street Kid **Yid (Jew)**

A 1960s term that sees a Jew become a 'bash street'. Based on the anarchic gang of kids from the *Beano* comic, now fast approaching their old-age pensions.

Basil Brush **Thrush**

Applies to the fungal infection that can be sexually transmitted and leaves male sufferers with an 'itchy richie'. Based on a TV puppet.

Basil Fawlty **Balti**

Carry-out curry, courtesy of John Cleese's classic comic creation.

Basin of Gravy **Baby**

A leaking, bawling, sleep reducing, time-consuming, stress inducing, pocket-emptying bundle of happiness: that's a 'basin'.

Bat & Ball **(a) Stall**

As trundled out on market day when barrow-boys come out to play.

(b) Wall

What prisoners 'have it over' and the tormented are 'driven up'.

Bat & Wicket **Ticket**

Any ticket, be it train, theatre or test match.

Bath Bun **Son/Sun**

Not often used either way.

Battle Cruiser **Boozer**

Post-war term for a pub that's usually known as a 'battle'. Ironic that many a 'battle' has called its final 'last orders' due to the rise of the booze cruiser.

Battleship & Cruiser **Boozer**

A rare alternative to the above.

Battleship(s)   **Lip(s)**

Apart from the mouth-edges, this applies to insolence: 'Let's have a little less battle' or 'button your battle' are warnings against further argument.

Bazaar   **Bar**

Long-serving reference to the saloon, public, spit & sawdust, snug, etc. Sometimes given as 'Bizarre', depending on the pub.

Bazooka   **Snooker**

An example from the 1970s, when the game became one of televised sport's big guns.

Beano & Dandy   **Shandy**

Based on the popular kids' comics and formed when people began to take drink and drive laws more seriously.

Bear's Paw   **Saw**

Maybe it's sharpness that connects Bruin's claws with this carpentry tool.

Beatie & Babs   **Crabs**

Refers to an infestation of crab lice in the pubic area. Based on a music-hall duo, the sisters Bertha and Hilda Samuels – who probably deserve better than to be remembered as 'bollock-jockeys'.

Becher's Brook   **Look**

A rival to the renowned 'butcher's hook' (qv); one that is based on a fence at Aintree racecourse and heard once every Grand National day.

Beechams Pill   **(a) Bill 1**

Applies to the police and based on the name of an old brand of laxative. Aptish, as just a glimpse of a police car in the rear-view mirror can have exactly the same effect, even though you've done nothing wrong.

Bill 2

Between the wars a bill was a notice carried by ex-servicemen unable to work either through circumstance or injury. The 'beechams' stated their 'qualifications' for begging, busking, selling bootlaces, matches or the like in the streets of the 'land fit for heroes'. A typical notice would read: 'Wounded at Ypres' or simply 'Blind'.

Bill 3

Any type of bill or receipt although doubtful whether anyone asks for a 'beechams' with their petrol these days.

(b) Still

A still photograph; a piece from the film and TV industry. Outside of that the term stands motionless.

Beef & Mutton   **Glutton**

A cow and a sheep get together to make a pig. A 'noshbag' – someone said to have a 'mouth like a musket'.

Beef Heart   **Fart**

An offering from the offal counter for back-end backfire.

Beehive   **(a) Dive**

Cheating footballers take a 'beehive' to gain an advantage. I blame Johnny Foreigner.

(b) Five

Chiefly a bingo term sometimes heard as a 'beehiver' – fiver.

Bees & Honey   **Money**

A 19th-century term for 'spending' that still has a currency. Coins and notes may change but some terms of RS go on forever. 'Yenom' – backslang dosh.

Bees' Knees   **Business**

More of a pun than RS and a reference to 'the business', an old expression for the best; could also be a fitting complaint for a Brentford footballer – like a West Ham player with a hammer-toe, a Crystal Palace player with an eagle-eye or an Arsenal man with gunner-ear.

Bees' Wingers   **Fingers**

Never actually heard this one in action so I don't know if it is based on flying insects or wide players at Barnet FC.

Beeswax   **Tax**

Refers to Income Tax and is a cleverly composed play on 'bees' whacks' – or money one gets whacked for. See also 'Bees & Honey'.

Beetles & Ants   Pants
Underwear, once commonly dropped to 'beetles'.

Beg Your Pardon   Garden
In a previous book I wrote that this was a post-war term but apparently it's older. In which case I beg your pardon.

Beggar Boy's Ass   Bass (Beer)
It's a common sight nowadays to see a beggar with a sleeping dog. Maybe they had sleeping donkeys 100-odd years ago when this was coined.

Beggar Boy's Arse   Brass (Money)
Always short-changed to 'beggar boys', the phrase is ancient and apt. 'Brass' is what the poor little sod would have been after and a kick up the jacksie is all he might have received.

Beggar My Neighbour   Labour
'On the labour' was another expression for being on the dole, hence 'on the beggar' is to be out of work.

Behind With the Rent   Bent/Homosexual
A piece which may allude to the male prostitute, if so it cleverly reflects the nature of his business in that his rent money is in the rear of his customer.

Belinda Carlisles   Piles
An example of 'popney' that may catch on, it's based on a late 20th-century American singer, which sees those afflicted with haemorrhoids suffering from 'belindas'.

Bell Ringers   Fingers
Try ringing a bell without them!

Belt & Braces   Races
A piece that begs you to be double careful about what you place your hard-earned on.

Ben Flake   Steak

An example cooked up in the 19th century and no longer on the nosh-up chart.

Ben Gunns   Runs

Diarrhoea, thanks to the fictional pirate in *Treasure Island*; a spell of the 'bens' means multiple trips to the 'ben'. See also 'Benghazi'.

Ben Hur   Stir

A term for a spell in prison first coined in the late 1950s after the success of a film of the same name.

Bended Knees   Cheese

Always grated down to a 'piece of bended', the answer to the prayers of a hungry church mouse.

Bengal Lancer   Chancer

A 2000s term for an opportunist, often a conman. Based on a member of the British Cavalry in 19th century India.

Benghazi   Carsey

Refers to a lavatory and is often truncated to 'the ben'. Said to have been originated by World War II soldiers after the Battle of Benghazi in Libya during the North Africa Campaign.

Benny Hill   (a) Drill

A carpenter, asked why his Black & Decker had become identified with this British comedian (1926–92), replied: 'They both bore a bit' – obviously not a fan.

(b) Till

A 1990s term for a cash register based on the man whose comic persona would have enjoyed having his buttons pushed by a young woman at the checkout.

Berkeley Hunt   Cunt

A different version of 'berkshire hunt' (qv) and sometimes a fool is known as 'sir berkeley'.

Berkshire Hunt   Cunt

It is well documented that in its shortened form of 'berk', the term has become accepted in all circles and many who use it would be shocked learn of its origin. Never used anatomically, a 'berk' is always a fool and never said as 'barkshire'.

Bernhard Langer　　　**Banger**
Based on a champion German golfer in regard to a sausage. Not necessarily a champion German one, though. 'Edgasos' – a backslang sausage.

Berni Flint　　　**Skint**
Empty pockets, courtesy of a British singer who peaked in the 1970s.

Bertie Mee　　　**Pee/Wee**
To urinate; in the early 1970s Arsenal supporters, in deference to their then manager (1918–2001), would nip out at half-time for a 'bertie'.

Bertie Woofter　　　**Poofter**
A homosexual, and always a 'bertie', based on a pun or a lisped version of the upper-class twit of P.G. Wodehouse's imagination, Bertie Wooster.

Beryl Reid　　　**Lead**
Probably greyhound track inspired, but if the sign says 'Keep Dogs On A Leash', put it's 'beryl' on! Based on the British actress and comedienne (1920–96).

Bessie Braddock　　　**Haddock**
A fish-porter's term broadly based on a broadly-based British politician (1899–1970).

Betty Boop　　　**Soup**
A tasty dish, based on an early cartoon one, and served as a bowl of 'betty'.

Betty Grable　　　**Table**
Named after a Hollywood actress (1916–73) noted for having a great pair of legs. Now she has two pairs. 'Elbat and Ryach' – a backslang table and chair.

Bexley Heath　　　**Teeth**
An area in South-East London provides a rare term for the 'chomping gear'.

Bicycle Lamp   **Tramp**

Applies to tramps and scruffbags in general and would appear to come from a time when cyclists bothered to have lights on their bikes.

Big Bass Drum   **Bum**

Reduced to 'big bass', this applies to the posterior of portly proportions.

Big Ben   **Ten**

The clock at Westminster strikes a reference to £10 (formerly 10 shillings). 'Net dunops' – 10 pounds of backslang.

Big Bloke   **Coke**

First recorded in the 1940s as a reference to cocaine and still to be found in the toilet of a pub or club near you.

Big Bopper   **Copper**

A police officer of course, from the late 1950s. This was a time when bopping criminals with a truncheon wouldn't land the assailant in court. Based on an American singer-songwriter of the period, J.P. Richardson (1932–59). 'Reepock' – a backslang rozzer.

Big Dipper   **Slipper**

An old piece of schoolboy jargon from the days when corporal punishment often came in the shape of a plimsoll (or carpet slipper) – which would come down like a white-knuckle fairground ride onto clenched buttocks.

Big Ears   **Cheers**

Used jocularly when raising a glass and formed on the name of an Enid Blyton character. See next entry.

Big Ears & Noddy   **Body**

Based on the names of Toytown's most prominent citizens, it is often said in admiration of a well-shaped female torso and dwarfed to 'Look at the big ears on that!' The shell-likes won't come into it. Created by British writer Enid Blyton (1897–1968).

Big Mac   **Sack**

Dismissal from work may come in the form of a McDonald's

hamburger. May also be used for a bed, whereby the tired and exhausted may 'hit the Big Mac'.

Bill & Ben   **Pen**
Based on the names of the world's most prominent flowerpot men, the term was commonly heard in betting shops in the 1960s.

Bill Grundy's   **Undies**
Underwear, courtesy of a TV presenter; Grundy (1923–93) had a successful career during the 1960s and 70s until an infamous interview with the punk band The Sex Pistols during which he goaded them into swearing on tea-time television, causing several TV chiefs to crap their 'bill grundy's'.

Bill Murray   **Curry**
An early 20th-century example based on an American film actor who makes an entrance as a rival to his established namesake Ruby but has so far failed to upstage her. 'Wyruc' – a backslang ring-burner.

Bill/Billy O'Gorman   **Foreman**
A 19th-century term said to be based on a real-life Irish navvy who couldn't possibly have imagined he would achieve a kind of immortality in RS.

Bill Stickers   **Knickers**
Said in the form of a name rather than the illegal occupation of those who will be prosecuted.

Billy Bunter   **(a) Punter**
An old bookmaker's term for his client based on the most famous fat boy in English literature as created by British novelist Frank Richards (1875–1961). A 'two-bob billy bunter' – a small punter.

                         (b) Shunter
A term from the steam railways industry to describe an engine that pushes rather than pulls.

Billy Button   **Mutton**
The slang term for a tailor serves up this old term for sheep-meat.

Billy Cotton   **Rotten 1**

Based on a British bandleader (1899–1969), this is what disgruntled kids called their old man if he didn't come across with a tanner for an ice-cream. Now he's called much worse if he doesn't weigh in with a week's wages for a pair of trainers.

Rotten 2

Foodstuff that has gone off – anything rank, rancid or garrotty has gone 'billy cotton'.

Rotten 3

What the leglessly drunk are said to be. When you're 'drunk in 14 languages' you're 'billy cotton'.

Billy Goat   **Coat**

Rarely heard alternative to the female of the species (see also Nanny Goat). 'Tayoc' – a backslang 'smother'.

Billy Liar   **Tyre**

Based on the name of a 1960s film, this is quite fitting as a flat 'billy' is often a moody excuse for being late.

Billy Smart   **Fart**

When the question 'Who let billy smart in here?' is asked it's usually the one with the smug grin on their face who did it. Based on a British circus proprietor (1893–1966).

Billy The Kid   **Yid**

How a Jew became a 'billy'. Based on the infamous outlaw of the American Wild West, (William Bonney 1859–81). Had he lived to a ripe old age, he would presumably have grown into Billy the Goat.

Billy Whizz   **Quiz**

A modern piece based on a character in the *Beano* comic that generally relates to a pub quiz.

Billy Wright   **Tight**

A 1950s piece used by the Teddy Boy generation in relation to ill-fitting attire – when their drainpipe trousers and winklepicker shoes began to pinch, they were 'too billy wright'. Based on an enduring England football captain of the period (1924–94).

Binnie Hale   Tale
An oldish term for a con-man's sob story current during this British actress's lifetime (1899–1994).

Birch Broom   Room
An ancient term for living quarters that's rarely visited nowadays.

Birchington Hunt   Cunt
A seldom-heard, but old example used both anatomically and condescendingly for a fool or ne'r-do-well. A hunt saboteur's idea of a huntsman, in fact.

Birdcage   Stage
Where entertainers put themselves on display – or datplay. Or any play really.

Birdlime   Time
Widely and most commonly employed as 'bird', meaning a prison sentence. 'Doing bird at one of Her Majesty's hotels' – serving time.

Bird(s) & Bee(s)   Knee(s)
An injured 'bird' is the mid-leg crisis much dreaded by sporting folk.

Bird's Nest   (a) Pest
Chiefly applies to a child with a God-given talent for driving adults potty.

                                   (b) Chest
A human chest, especially a hairy one – therefore probably a male one.

Biscuits & Cheese   Knees
An example that shouldn't be used in the singular, but is nevertheless. Which is how a knee turns into a 'biscuit'.

Bishop of Norwich   Porridge
Formed on the name of a pub that once existed in Shoreditch, East London. Breakfasting on 'bishop' was a localised thing.

Bit & Piece   Niece
Affectionately known by uncles as a 'little bit', which separates her from the 'bit' that goes to an hotel with her 'uncle'.

Bites & Scratches　　　**Matches**
A smoker's term for a 'box of lights'.

Black & Blue　　　**Cue**
A pool or snooker cue. Used as a club by the sound of it.

Black & Decker　　　**Pecker (Penis)**
Formed on the name of a company that produces power tools, so a sexual marathon man may come to mind. Of course the name is also synonymous with DIY. This is pecker in its American form and it shouldn't be confused with the British version meaning the nose. 'Keep your pecker up' conveys a whole different message in the States.

Black & White　　　**(a) Night**
Descriptive of the night sky with a full moon – in the middle of the 'black' pretty well sums up darkness.

(b) Tight
Refers to meanness and short-armed, long-pocketed people.

Black Bess　　　**Yes**
A definite affirmative is a 'big black bess'. Based on an early rifle or Dick Turpin's horse.

Black Eye　　　**Pie**
A piece that possibly came about when a hungry customer asked a barman for a 'smack in the eye' (qv).

Black Man Kissed 'er　　　**Sister**
A piece from less enlightened times. Based on a juvenile taunt: 'Know your sister? A black man kissed her.'

Black Mariah　　　**Fire**
Applies to a burn-up the Fire Brigade need to deal with, rather than a domestic one.

Blackadder　　　**Ladder**
Formed on the name of a British comedy series, the fiercely ambitious will climb the blackadder of success two rungs at a time. No matter who those rungs happen to be. Heard on a 1980s building site.

Blackbird & Thrush — Brush

A late 19th-century term for a shoebrush, hence to 'blackbird one's boots' was to shine 'em up.

Blackheath — Teeth

Heard outside a Soho cinema: 'Call that porn? I've seen dirtier films on my brother's blackheath!' It's the teeth of the dentally careless.

Blackpool Rock — Cock (Penis)

One of a shedload of terms for the piddle-pipe, this one was probably inspired by the title of a song made famous by the English comedian George Formby (1904–61).

Blackwall Tunnel — Funnel

A term to describe part of a ship's chimney from the time when London had a docks industry. The Blackwall Tunnel runs underneath the Thames between Poplar and Greenwich and is known locally as the 'pipe' or 'conduit'. At peak times it's a motorist's nightmare and so has collected a few other names as well – usually two words, the first beginning with F.

Bladder of Fat — Hat

An out-of-date example probably referring to the greasy headwear that sat on greasy heads of yore.

Bladder of Lard — (a) Card

A playing card and also a World War I bingo card which, on its formation, would have been a housey-housey card. 'Dracks' – backslang cards.

(b) Yard

The 'bladder' was a 1920s reference to Scotland Yard, the old headquarters of the Metropolitan Police.

Blaydon Races — Braces

Based on the famous song of Geordieland, 'blaydons' have long held up the trousers of bonny lads of the North-East.

Blindman's Buff — Snuff

An obsolete piece as cocaine has replaced snuff in the nose-powder stakes. Based on the name of a party game. A 'Chinp o' funess' – a backslang pinch of snuff.

Block & Tackle   Shackle

Originally referred to fetters when to 'put the block on' something was to stop it. Sometime in the 20th century it was hoisted up from the ankles to the wrists to become handcuffs.

Block of Ice   (a) Dice

Presumably one that is running cold.

(b) Shice

An old racing term that relates to welshing. To 'shice' someone is not to pay them out on a winning bet. Many a hooky bookie 'had it over the wall' when his bag was full.

Blood Red   Head (Fellatio)

Hence a 'blood donor' is someone who performs oral sex, i.e. she 'gives blood'. And if she goes down on a first date, she gets the nickname 'Titanic'.

Blue & Grey   Day

An obvious allusion to the colours of the sky: another 'blue', another 'oxford' – another day, another dollar. See 'Oxford Scholar'.

Blue Moon   Spoon 1

Applies to the utensil that makes eating soup a simple task.

Spoon 2

Spoon is an old fashioned word for romancing and because no one does it any more the term is obsolete in this sense.

Blue Peter   Heater

Mainly applies to the heat source of a motor vehicle. Most likely after the long-running children's TV programme rather than the naval flag, which indicated a ship was ready to sail.

Blueberry Hill   Bill (Police)

Based on American singer Fats Domino's hit record of the 1950s, the 'blueberry' is a 1980s example heard in a TV cops and robbers drama – possibly *The Bill*.

Bo Peep   Sleep

A well-known term based on the famous, though inept sheep minder.

Board & Easel   **Diesel**

An example first chalked up in the transport industry at a time when you could buy a new car for what it now costs to fill a lorry with 'board & easel'. For younger readers, the term refers to a blackboard and its stand that was used in early- to mid-20th-century classrooms.

Board & Plank   **Yank**

An American – a term that just has to be connected with the wooden actors in those dire American soaps hidden away on afternoon satellite TV stations.

Boat & Oar   **Whore**

Not exactly a rhyme, but since the 1950s prostitutes have been known as 'boats'.

Boat-hook   **Book**

How the British Library came to be full of boat hooks; a 1950s piece from the docks.

Boat Race   **Face**

The annual University race along the Thames provides us with the most common piece of RS for the face. Heard at a grab-a-granny do: 'She's got some form on her.' 'Yeah. Dodgy boat, though.'

Bob & Dick   **Sick**

Uncommon alternative to 'tom & dick' (qv). It seems bob fills in when tom's not feeling well.

Bob & Hit   **(a) Pit (Vagina)**

A 19th-century term from the boxing arena meaning to punch and move gives rise to a slang-for-slang term for the dark hole of womanhood.

(b) Shit

What one can pass or step in, i.e. to defecate or the matter involved in it. 'Tish' – backslang caca.

Bob & Weave   **Leave**

Time to 'bob & weave' or time we were 'bobbing and weaving', either way it's time to go.

Bob Dylan   **Villain**

Based on the legendary American singer whose biggest act of villainy is impersonating a singer. Love the songs though, Bob.

Bob, Harry & Dick   **Sick**

Take a week off work with an illness and you're on the 'bob harry'.

Bob Hope   **(a) Dope**

The English-born American comedian (1903–2003) lends his name to drugs and an idiot. Somehow it's easy to connect both.

     (b) Soap

People have been bathing with 'bob hope' and passing him around in the shower since the 1950s at least.

Bob Marley   **Charlie (Cocaine)**

The availability of cocaine nowadays is reflected in the number of terms that have sprung up for it. This one is based on the Jamaican reggae star who died in 1981, aged 36.

Bob McNab   **Cab**

An Arsenal and England footballer hit the road as a taxi in the 1970s as a rival to the older 'sandy mcnab' (qv).

Bob Squash   **Wash**

An old term that applies to a public washroom. People using this facility do so at their peril as it's often a haven for pickpockets 'working the bob'.

Bobbing & Weaving   **Breathing**

A reply to the question: 'How are you?' is 'Oh you know, bobbing and weaving.' It means getting by, jogging along, etc.

Bobby Moore   **(a) Door**

A late 1990s term coined by football fans too young to have seen the legendary captain of West Ham and England (1941–93).

     (b) Score

A 'bobby' is an expression for £20.

Boiled Beef & Carrot   Claret

Nothing to do with wine, reduced down to the first two elements it refers to blood. 'There was boiled beef all over the place.' May refer to the aftermath of a fight, accident or the first day of the Harrods sale.

Boiled Carrot   Parrot

Never shortened, as in a conversation overheard in a pub, where a parrot was a feature of the saloon bar:
Customer: What does your boiled carrot keep saying?
Publican: Iggle oggle wiggle woggle woo
Customer: Why does he keep saying that?
Publican: Oh it's just a silly phrase he's going through.

Boiled Sweet   Seat

Heard in a café: 'You get the teas and I'll find us some boiled sweets.'

Bolt the Door   Whore

A time-ravaged prostitute, one you wouldn't want to be caught with. So bolt the door!

Bonnie & Clyde   Snide

Applies to designer gear what ain't. Imitation watches, perfume, clothes, etc. are 'bonnies'. Based on the US gangsters of the 1930s, Bonnie Parker (1910–34) and Clyde Barrow (1909–34), whose exploits were made into a successful film in 1967.

Bonnie Dundee   Flea

Elderly and once-common term for the scourge of heads, dogs and sporrans, it's based on a popular song about the Scottish rebel and Jacobite commander John Graham. The term was his nickname.

Boo & Hiss   Piss

These sounds of disapproval would be apt if you caught someone having one in your doorway although these days stopping him would probably land you in court for interfering with his Human Rights. 'Sip' – a backslang drain-off.

Boom & Mizen   **Prison**

Parts of a sailing ship shouldn't conjure up visions of convicts being transported to the colonies because the term isn't very old. More likely a sailing holiday for a young offender c. 2000.

Bootlace   **Suitcase**

To prevent a calamitous trip, secure your 'bootlace'.

Bootsie & Snudge   **Judge**

A TV comedy of the early 1960s gave rise to His Lordship being called a 'bootsie' for a while around that period.

Boracic Lint   **Skint**

Very old and very familiar as 'brassic', it was commonly heard outside dog-tracks of yore as potless punters began the slow walk home:

When boys have money they think they're men
But when they're brassic they're boys again.

Borrow & Beg   **Egg**

An old piece – and probably now an empty shell.

Botany Bay   **(a) Hay**

'Hitting the botany' is an ancient form of 'getting some sleep'. Based on the Australian landing site of Captain Cook in 1770, later to become a penal colony for transported convicts.

(b) Run Away

To abscond is to 'do a botany'.

Bottle & Glass   **Arse**

A well-known example only ever used in its first element; the lethargic often need a kick up the 'bottle' to get them going. The main usage however is in connection with courage or 'arse-hole'. The brave and bold may have a 'lot of bottle' and a coward may 'bottle it' or 'bottle out' of a confrontation forever to become known as a 'bottler'.

Bottle & Stopper   **Copper**

Arrested at the first element for a police officer, as in 'So I said to these three bottles, "'Ello, 'ello, 'ello!"'

Bottle Bank   **Wank**
A noughties example of DIY sex.

Bottle of Beer   **Ear**
Always used in full, e.g: 'A word in your bottle of beer'. 'A word in your bottle' takes on an altogether different and unsavoury meaning. See also 'Bottle & Glass'.

Bottle of Booze   **(a) News**
How the 9 O'Clock News became the 9 o'clock bottle.
     (b) Twos (odds of 2/1)
There seems to be some contention as to whether this or 'bottle of spruce' (qv) is responsible for the familiar expression 'bottle' in this sense. Odds on 'spruce', I think.

Bottle of Drink   **Stink**
A nasty 'bottle' could mean someone's 'bottle' needs a cork in it. See 'Bottle & Glass.

Bottle of Fizz   **Whizz**
To 'whizz' or 'bottle' someone is to pick their pocket.

Bottle of Kola   **Bowler**
This old term for the once-traditional headwear of the city gent is now old hat.

Bottle of Pop   **Wop (Italian)**
Possibly based on that well-known Italian soft drink, Pop Sicola.

Bottle of Sauce   **Horse**
Refers to one that pulls a cart rather than a racehorse.

Bottle of Scent   **Bent**
Refers to homosexuality and is from a time when men were considered fey if they smelt of anything other than soap or sweat.

Bottle of Scotch   **Watch**
So old it first alluded to a pocket watch.

Bottle of Spruce   **Deuce**
Originally applied to two pence in old money but is more readily associated with £2. Also used for the playing card and

odds of 2/1 is known as 'bottle'. Formed on the name of a cheap and nasty concoction known as 'spruce beer'.

Bottle of Water   **(a) Daughter**
When daddy hears he's got a little girl for a daughter, is this what he 'wets the baby's head' with? I don't think so.

                              (b) Quarter
In the dingy world of drugs this is a quarter of an ounce.

Bottle of Wine   **Fine**
Piece laid down some years ago that refers to the punishment as poured out by a magistrate.

Bottle Top   **(a) Cop 1**
This is about value, anything that's 'not much bottle' isn't very good.

                              (b) Cop 2
To catch, receive or take hold of. The prisoner at the bar may 'cop for a twelvemonth' or 'bottle for a year's nick'.

Bottles of Booze   **Shoes**
In vogue since Elvis sang about his 'Blue Suede Bottles' in 1956.

Bouncy Castle   **Parcel**
Dropped to a 'bouncy' by some careless workers in the parcel delivery industry, where 'bounce the bouncy' would appear to be a popular game, especially if the package is labelled 'Handle With Care'.

Boutros-Ghali   **Charlie (Cocaine)**
A late 1990s piece based on the Egyptian diplomat Boutros Boutros-Ghali, who served as general secretary of the United Nations (1992–6).

Bow & Arrow   **(a) Barrow**
A piece from a late 20th-century building site, obviously a reputable one – you never see cowboys with bows and arrows.

                            (b) Charra
When the early form of motor coach was known as a charabanc it soon got reduced to a 'charra', only to make a further transition to a 'bow & arrer'.

(c) Sparrow

The bird much in the affections of Londoners which, much like the cockney, seems to be leaving the East End for the suburbs.

Bow & Quiver　　　　　　**Liver**

Refers to the human organ and that on the offal counter, but mainly applies to feeling liverish or irritable. On cold and damp mornings in Sherwood Forest, Robin Hood would have had a bow and quiver.

Bowler Hat　　　　　　**Rat**

Applies to either the rodent or an untrustworthy person, someone thought to be 'lower than Old Nick's basement'. An informer is a 'bowler'.

Box of Toys　　　　　　**Noise**

Since kids + toys = a racket, this is a well-fitting term. Especially to those of us who think that no noise is good noise. Back-chatting people may be warned to 'hold their box o' toys'.

Box of Tricks　　　　　　**Flicks**

The 'flicks' is an old slang term for the cinema and when this was formed it would have been very apt.

Boy & Girl　　　　　　**Twirl**

Another example of slang for slang, a 'twirl' is a key, especially a skeleton key. To a thief, the tools of his trade are his 'boys and girls'.

Boy Scout　　　　　　**Shout 1**

To talk loudly, like the British abroad in an attempt to make foreigners understand them.

Shout 2

It's your turn to get the drinks in when it's your 'boy scout'.

Boy Scouts　　　　　　**Sprouts**

A greengrocer's term for Brussels sprout, whereby 'boy scouts' are traditionally eaten with the Christmas dinner.

Boys in Blue　　　　　　**Stew**

Nothing to do with food, to be in a 'right boys in blue' is to be in a state of agitation.

Brace & Bit   Shit
Reduced to 'brace' or 'braces' if the said brace comes loose and often. Tish – backslang poop.

Braces & Bits   Tits
Known as 'braces', which is apt enough since breasts come in pairs.

Brad Pitt   Shit
A late 20th-century piece based on a Hollywood actor who is flushed with success.

Bradford City   Titty
Reduced to 'bradford' or 'bradfords' if we are talking pairs – which we generally are.

Brahms & Liszt   Pissed
A famous piece from the theatre based on a pair of well-known composers who may or may not have been well-known drunks. Johannes Brahms (1833–97) and Franz Liszt (1811–86).

Brands Hatch   Scratch
The Kent motor-racing circuit takes a turn for getting rid of an itch and a slight injury is: 'Nothing, just a brands hatch'.

Brandy Butter   Nutter
A 'brandy' is one of several terms for someone who might be otherwise known as a 'loon'. Someone also known as 'East Ham' as they are one stop short of Barking. (See the London Underground map.)

Brass Band(s)   Hand(s)
One of several musical combos making the same connection.

Brass Monkey   Dunkie (Condom)
So-called because it offers no protection from frost, so be careful when making love in the open on a cold night.

Brass Nail   Tail (Prostitute)
An example of secondary slang, a 'tail' is an old term and 'brass' is a familiar piece. A woman who dresses gaudily is likely to be called 'brassy' – now you know why.

Brass Tack(s)   **Fact(s)**

A piece of RS that has now joined the ranks of standard English. Everybody 'gets down to brass tacks'.

Brave & Bold   **Cold**

To be 'bloody brave' is to be freezing, like Sir Ernest Shackleton on both counts. 'Deloc' – 'baltic' in backslang.

Bread & Butter   **(a) Gutter**

A very old example when used in relation to being down and out, those in the 'bread & butter' can't sink any lower.

(b) Nutter

A well-known piece from the 1980s – most of us know at least one 'headcase'.

(c) Putter

A piece from the golf course probably coined by a club-wielding cab driver.

(d) Shutter

Reflective of the inner city High Street, where shop windows are protected by 'bread & butters'.

(e) Stutter

A term not easily said by one with this speech impediment.

Bread & Cheese   **Sneeze**

The result of the nose itch.

Bread & Honey   **Money**

World-famous as 'bread' and used by many who are unaware that it's RS.

Bread & Jam   **(a) Pram**

Late 20th-century rival to the older 'jar of jam' in the baby-carrier stakes.

(b) Tram

A piece that's as old and outmoded as this form of transport.

Bread & Lard   **Hard**

Used sarcastically to anyone complaining unnecessarily: 'So your dishwasher's broke and you had to wash up by hand? Well, how bread and lard for you!'

Breadcrumbs   **Gums**
Those with their mouths full of 'breadcrumbs' where once there were teeth are those most likely to hold the world peanut-sucking record.

Breadknife   **Wife**
One of a drawerful of terms connecting she of the sharp tongue with a cutter.

Brenda Frickers   **Knickers**
A late 20th-century term based on a film and TV actress from Ireland, where smooth-talking Romeos are said to be able to 'talk a nun out of her brendas'.

Brewer's Bung   **Tongue**
Old term for a 'licker'. A crawler may have his 'brewers' firmly stuck up his bosses' 'khyber' (qv).

Brian O'Flynn   **Gin**
A distortion of the next example.

Brian O'Linn   **Gin**
Victorian sots were partial to a drop of 'brian' or 'bri'. Based on the eponymous hero of a traditional Irish folk song.

Bricks & Mortar   **Daughter**
Possibly based on the old joke: She was only a bricklayer's daughter but she never went up the wall. Then again, perhaps not.

Bride & Groom   **(a) Broom**
Whereby a new 'bride' sweeps clean.
          (b) Room
Coined when a room was all working-class newlyweds could expect to move into.

Bright & Breezy   **Easy**
May be used in full or reduced to 'bright'n'. See? 'brighton' when you know how.

Bright & Frisky   **Whisky**
In short, 'brighton'.

Brighton Line   **Nine**
An old 'un from the bingo hall.

Brighton Pier   **(a) Queer**
In early RS this applied to feeling unwell and later to anything strange or odd. Nowadays a 'brighton' is a homosexual.
                 (b) Disappear
An early 20th-century term meaning to run away or leave. When the police sirens can be heard, you know it's time to 'brighton'.

Brighton Rock   **(a) Cock (Penis)**
Long, hard and sucked at the seaside, that's a rock and the connection is there for all to see.
                 (b) Dock
The 'brighton' is the part of the courtroom where the accused learns whether or not he is to spend some time at one of Her Majesty's guesthouses.

Brig's Rest   **Vest**
A rough, itchy undergarment worn by convicts and named by convicts – but not recently.

Bristol City   **Titty**
Commonly known and accepted as 'bristols'.

British Rail   **Stale**
An obvious allusion to the infamous Intercity sandwich.

Brixton Riot   **Diet**
Following the disturbances of April 1981 when the youth of Brixton, South London, waged war with the police, overweight people began their battles of the bulge by going on 'brixtons'.

Broken Heart   **Fart**
Probably from the old rhyme scrawled on many a lavatory wall:
Here I sit, broken hearted
Spent a penny and only farted.

Bromley-By-Bow   **(a) Dough**
A cab driver's term for money that is short-changed to 'bromley', after an area of East London.

(b) Toe

A broken 'bromley' is an injury much-dreaded by athletes.

Broncho Layne　　　　**Pain**

An early 1960s piece based on a popular TV Western series of the period when a pest was a 'broncho' in the arse.

Bronze Figure　　　　**Kipper**

An imperfect rhyme that finds itself cut up by the more common 'jack the ripper' (qv).

Brother & Sister　　　　**Blister**

As seen on the hands after a rare burst of hard graft – or on the feet as a result of ill-fitting shoes.

Brother Bung　　　　**Tongue**

Whereby 'don't be an arse-licker' becomes 'don't bung your brother up your boss's backside'. The term, which was the name of a pickle company, was an old slang term for a brewer, who was a 'Brother of the Bung'. Other examples in the same vein are Brothers of the Blade (soldier), String (fiddler), Gusset (pimp) and Brush (painter).

Brown & Mild　　　　**Wild**

A loss of temper; angry – possibly as a result of mixing drinks like these two ales: 'Don't make me get my brown & mild up. You wouldn't like me if I get my brown & mild up' – The Incredible Cockney Hulk.

Brown Bess　　　　**Yes**

The same as 'black bess' (qv), in that they were both early rifles.

Brown Bread　　　　**Dead**

Old and most common term for the 'popping of the clogs', an extension of which is 'hovis'. Heard on a bus: 'I don't know why they still call it Taggart, he's been hovis 10 years.'

Brown Hat　　　　**Cat**

An old term for that which chases a 'bowler hat' (qv).

Brown Joe　　　　**No**

The equally aged and unused opposite of 'brown bess' (qv).

Brown Paper   **Caper**

Asked of anyone doing something they shouldn't in a place where they shouldn't be doing it: 'What's your brown paper then?'

Bruce Lee   **Pee/Wee**

The American-born but Hong Kong-raised martial arts expert (1940-73) who brought his full repertoire of skills to television and the cinema, now brings a full bladder to RS and then empties it.

Bruce Forsyth   **Knife**

A late 20th-century piece based on a well-known London born entertainer whose catchphrase is 'knife to see you. To see you, knife' – or something very similar. 'Eefin & Kayrof' – a backslang knife and fork.

Brussels Sprout   **(a) Scout**

A boy scout that is, and the term is nearly as old as the Boy Scout Movement itself.

                              (b) Tout

Originally used on the racecourse concerning tipsters but now relates to the ticket tout.

Bryan Ferry   **Sherry**

Another British rock star apparently turns to drink. 'Wyresh' – as used in a backslang toast.

Bryant & Mays   **Stays**

Now that women no longer case themselves up in these old-fashioned corsets, the famous matchstick men strike a light no more in RS.

Bubble & Blister   **Sister**

Closely related to 'skin & blister' (qv) but not as common.

Bubble & Squeak   **(a) Beak**

Those up before a magistrate are up before the 'bubble', beak being an old slang term for a judge.

                              (b) Greek

Very familiar in the shortened form of 'Bubble'. When a Greek football team play at West Ham, the fans are 'forever booing Bubbles'.

(c) Leak

A plumber's term for a leak in a pipe; also, to urinate is to go for a 'bubble'.

(d) Speak

Most frequently used in terms of informing either to the police or somebody in authority like the boss or the wife. Grasses will 'bubble up' or 'put the bubble in'. Anatomically 'bubbling (speaking).

(e) Weak

A sure sign of the flu is when you come over 'all bubble & squeak'.

(f) Week

Seven days a 'bubble' make. 'Bubble and Squeak' is a dish of fried leftovers, generally served on Monday from what's left of the Sunday dinner.

Bubble Bath   Laugh

The bane of the Peeping Tom is a sign that everyone else is happy. Also used as a term of disbelief: 'You're having a bubble' translates to 'You must be joking'.

Bubble Gum   Bum

Bottom fetishists are partial to a 'lovely bubble'.

Buccaneer   Queer

Homosexuality has long gone hand in hand with sailors and the dictionary describes this early seaman as: 'A pirate, an unscrupulous adventurer'. Well, boys will be boys.

Buck & Doe   Snow

Said with a heavy emphasis on the first element, it creates an impression of an expletive as in 'Look at the buck'n'doe out there.'

Bucket & Pail   Gaol

For a shorter sentence, say 'in bucket'.

Bucket & Spade   Maid

Generally applies to a barmaid but a spinster of the parish may be an 'old bucket'. 'Delo diam' – a backslang old maid.

Bucket & Well   Hell

Was said in full to replace the F-word in fucking hell, as in

'What the bucket & well are you on about?' Rarely heard now as no one is shocked by bad language any more. So bollocks to it!

Bucket Afloat   **Boat**
An old piece with nautical connections, a bucket being an old slang term for a ship. Soldiers of World War I changed it to 'Bucket & Float'. Same shoes, different laces really. 'Tayob' – a backslang floater.

Bucket of Sand   **Grand**
A late 20th-century term from the City of London regarding £1,000.

Buckle My Shoe   **(a) Jew**
An early example but Jews are rarely heard of as 'Buckles' these days. 'Wedge'/'Wej' – a brace of backslang Jews.

                                     (b) Two
Buckle my shoe, the number two – a bingo call. 'Owt'/'Oat' – a pair of backslang deuces.

Bucks Fizz   **Quiz**
A popular pastime based on a favourite cocktail. A piece heard in 2007 on a cruise ship en route to the Baltic.

Bucks Hussar   **Cigar**
A piece that seems to have been stubbed out in the ashtray of obscurity: 'Close, but no bucks hussar' may have been an early piece of fairground banter. 'Ragick' – a backslang smoke.

Buckshee   **Free**
British troops serving in 19th-century Persia heard the word 'baksheesh' meaning a tip or a gift, brought it back to Blighty and adapted it to a slightly different meaning. That's the history, the reality is 'buckshee' beer is the best beer.

Buddy Holly   **(a) Volley**
A footballer's term for kicking the ball in mid-air based on the legendary American rock musician of the 1950s, who kicked the bucket in mid-air when the plane in which he was travelling crashed in 1959. Buddy was 22 when he died, but his music lives on.

(b) Wally 1
How a pickled cucumber sold in fish and chip shops became a 'buddy'.

Wally 2
'Wally' is a modern reference to a fool, someone thought to be 'about as much use as a railway timetable to Prince Andrew'.

Buffalo Bill Till
1960s betting shops had employees working the 'buffalo'. Based on the name used by William F. Cody (1846–1917), legendary American Indian fighter, army scout and buffalo slaughterer.

Bug & Flea Tea
First brewed by itching, trench-bound soldiers of World War I. A 'Puck of Ate' – a backslang cup of tea.

Bugs Bunny (a) Funny
As said by the butt of a practical joke: 'You think you're bugs bunny, don't you? Well, I got news for you. You ain't!'
(b) Money
Based on the carrot-crunching cartoon rabbit and may be known as 'bugs' or 'bugsy' as in: 'I fancied the first two winners but I didn't have the bugsy to back 'em.'

Bugsy Malone Phone
Made a swift call in the mid-1970s when this award-winning film caused a bit of a stir but was chased off by the 'dog'.

Bull & Bush Push
Getting dismissed from work is known as 'getting the old bull & bush'. Based on a music-hall song about a pub in Hampstead, North-West London.

Bull & Cow Row
An argument that often occurs between the male and female of the species, i.e. man and wife.

Bulldozer Poser
A vain exhibitionist, one who forces attention on himself for

effect; someone who tries to bring the house down based on something that can.

Bullock's Heart   Fart

Seldom heard nowadays – the term, that is.

Bullock's Horn   Pawn

Archaic example that is always cut down to the first element. Many a wedding ring has been put in and got out of 'bullocks'.

Bullock's Liver   River

An old example from the butcher's shop that dried up years ago.

Bully Beef   (a) Chief

An old convict's term for the chief officer in prison.

                                       (b) Deaf

Piece from the North of the English border unlikely to be heard or understood South of it.

Bulrush   Brush

Refers to a paintbrush and is from the painting and decorating trade. These days it pays to be choosy about who you get in to do your place up as the world is awash with ne'er-do-well decorators. In our multi-racial society, even Indians can be cowboys.

Bumblebees   Knees

In RS, a 'bumblebee in the flowers' takes on a new and eye-watering meaning. See 'Flowers & Frolics'.

Bung It In   Gin

A gin-drinker may simply hold up his glass and tell the barmaid to 'bung it in'.

Bunsen Burner   (a) Earner

A nice little tickle that brings some bunce in, that's a 'bunsen'.

                                       (b) Turner

A 'bunsen' is a cricketing term for a pitch that's beneficial to spin-bowlers.

Burdett-Coutts   Boots

Outmoded piece based on the philanthropic Baroness Angela Burdett-Coutts (1814–1906), whose acts of charity must have included putting footwear on impoverished Victorian feet.

Burglar Alarm(s) Arm(s)

One of several terms rhyming on 'alarm' that send out warning signals to the long dominant 'chalk farm' (qv). 'Emras' – backslang cuddlers.

Burke & Hare Chair

Based on the infamous 19th-century Scottish murderers who donated their own bodies as well as those of their victims to medical science. Had they been Americans they would have died in the electric 'burke'. William Burke (1792–1829) and William Hare (1790–1860).

Burlington Bertie Thirty

Another piece from the bingo caller's handbook, this one based on the famous shirtless toff from Bow. TV racing expert John McCrirrick uses the term for odds of 100/30.

Burlington Hunt Cunt

A widely ignored version of 'berkshire hunt' (qv) in reference to a fool, someone thought to be 'about as much use as a black light-bulb'.

Burn(s) & Smoulder(s) Shoulder(s)

Apt when you've done the mad dogs and Englishmen bit and your shoulders could stop traffic. 'Redlush' – a backslang shoulder.

Burnt Cinder Window

Or 'winder' as spoken and always reduced to the first element. Old-time smash 'n grab merchants would throw a brick through a jeweller's 'burnt' and scarper with the loot. Now they drive motors through them.

Burton-On-Trent (a) Rent

It may be no coincidence that the name of this famous brewery town should be used when very often a landlord's money was blown on its product. Also a male prostitute, a rent-boy is a 'burton'.

(b) Went

Offered by some as the origin of the phrase 'gone for a burton', but I'm not convinced.

Bus & Tram   **Jam**

Apt if referring to snarled-up traffic but less so if the sweet stuff is involved. In fact, not at all.

Bushel & Peck   **Neck**

An old term that's got the measure of both the inside and outside of the neck. You can wear a scarf round it or get a pint down your 'bushel'. 'Kayken' – a backslang 'bushel'.

Bushel of Coke   **Bloke**

An early 20th-century term that never made the 21st. But a geezer used to be a 'bushel' and in backslang he's an 'ecklob'.

Bushfire(d)   **Tire(d)**

Sits alongside that well-known expression 'bushed' but probably isn't connected.

Bushy Park   **Lark**

One of several parks (this one by Hampton Court) to make the link, parks being synonymous with messing about.

Butcher's Hook   **Look**

Widely used and always in the first element. Take a 'butcher's' at its rival, 'docker's hook' (it's in the D section). 'Kool toul' – look out – a warning from a backslang 'kool-toul'.

Butter Churn   **Turn**

A theatrical turn for a theatrical act; when pubs had pianos anyone could get up and do a 'butter'.

Buttercup & Daisy   **Crazy**

Used by a distraught father whose kids were driving him 'buttercup'.

Buttered Bread   **Dead**

One of several terms to link death with the Staff of Life. Heard in an East End tavern:
Man: I see they buried Alfie Smith yesterday.
Pal: (surprised) Is old Alfie buttered bread then?
Man (sarcastic) No, he's the first prize in a treasure hunt.

Buttered Bun   **One**
An alternative to 'kelly's eye' down the bingo hall. 'Eno' – a
backslang one.

Buttered Scone   **One**
An alternative to the previous alternative to 'kelly's eye' down
the bingo hall.

Butterfly   **Tie**
Any form of neck-tie but may relate more easily to a bow-tie.

Buttons & Bows   **Toes**
'Shall we have it on our buttons?' translates as 'Shall we leave?'

By Pass   **Arse**
A kick up the 'by pass' may be just what's needed to get a
layabout moving. 'Esra' – a backslang backside.

C&A   Gay (homosexual)
   Based on a High Street store, which in this case may stand for 'cocks and arses'.

Cab Rank   Bank
   Apt in a money goes to money sense, though taxi drivers will of course deny it. 'Kaynab' – a backslang bank.

Cabin Cruiser   Boozer
   Something to do with pushing the boat out?

Cabman's Rests   Breasts
   Obsolete 19th-century piece which shows that yesterday's cabbies weren't solely interested in tips.

Cadbury's Snack   Back
   Anatomically speaking or referring to the back of a building, this chocolate biscuit gets broken to the 'cadburys'. 'Kaycab' – a backslang 'haystack'.

Cain & Abel   Table
   On which dinners have been served for over a century. Based on the sons of Adam and Eve.

Calamity Jane   Train
   Of modern coinage, a 'calamity' seems about right given the problems and disasters that continually beset our railways. Based on the nickname of Martha Jane Canary (1852–1903), legendary US frontierswoman and famed driver of the Deadwood Stage.

Calcutta   **Butter**
A term that seems to be spreading simply because it rhymes.

Callard & Bowsers   **Trousers**
Usually cut down to 'callard's' and formed on the name of that well-known confectioner. 'Resworts' – backslang leg-holders.

Calvin Klein   **(a) Fine**
The punishment you might receive if caught selling snide designer gear. A 'two-grand eenif' – a £2,000 fine in a backslang court.

     (b) Wine
Red or white, vintage or plonk, it's all 'calvin' and based on an American fashion designer.

Camber Sand(s)   **Hand(s)**
Another resort on the Kent coast (see also Margate and Ramsgate Sands) for what's never out of your pocket when on holiday. 'Deenach' – a backslang 'gripper'.

Camden Lock   **Shock**
A late 20th-century piece, a 'camden' is what an electric bill is designed to do.

Camden Town   **Brown**
Ancient slang for copper coinage and pennies, old and new, are 'camden'.

Camel's Hump   **Dump (Defecate)**
An early 20th-century example whereby to go for a 'camel's' is to take up residence in the 'benghazi' (qv) for a while.

Camerer Cuss   **Bus**
A piece that dates back to the days of the omnibus and is formed on the name of a long-established London company specialising in antique timepieces and jewellery.

Cameroon   **Coon**
Derogatory term for a black person that came into being after the 1990 World Cup, in which the football team of that country did so well.

Camilla Parker-Bowles   **Rolls**
Formed when the current Duchess of Cornwall was the lady friend of the Prince of Wales in reference to the Prince of Wheels, the Rolls-Royce.

Can of Coke   **Joke**
An early 20th-century piece of 'yoofspeak', where the cheapest 'can o' cokes' are usually at someone else's expense.

Can of Oil   **Boil**
Refers to the great pus-filled swelling on the skin and is known as a 'canov'.

Canal Boat   **Tote**
A racecourse term concerning the totalisator: if you don't like the bookies' odds, bet on the 'canal' and hope it doesn't 'do a Bismark' (go down).

Canary   **Fairy**
An effeminate homosexual; an example from the theatre probably for a chorus boy or any gay man who makes a living on the 'birdcage' (qv).

Canary Wharf   **Dwarf**
Ironic piece for a small person, in that the Canary Wharf Tower in London's Docklands was once the tallest building in Britain. A 'canary': one of the seven who go *up* on Snow White.

Candle Sconce/Candle & Sconce   **Ponce**
Either way shortened to 'candle' in reference to a pimp or a generally unpleasant person, one considered to be on a par with a 'spunkstained gusset of a two-bob whore'.

Candle Wax   **Tax**
Heard for the first time in 1960s betting shops after the introduction of the betting tax. Reduced to 'candle', it is likely to burn itself out now that the tax has been abolished.

Candyfloss   **Toss**
Those who don't care 'couldn't give a candy'.

Canoe(s)   **Shoe(s)**
To be kept in good repair – once they get holes in them you're sunk. 'Eeosh' – a backslang 'chimney' holder (see Chimney & Soot).

Can't-Keep-Still   **Treadmill**
A 19th-century term for a type of punishment meted out to criminals may make a comeback now that this piece of equipment has been re-packaged and is now a feature of the modern gym, where people pay to be tortured.

Cape Horn   **Corn**
The most southerly point of South America comes in for the painful condition on the most southerly point of the body.

Cape of Good Hope   **Soap**
Shortened to 'cape', the term has been in existence for a century or so.

Capital City   **Titty**
Breasts, known as 'capitals', may be the talk of the town.

Captain Bligh   **Pie**
After the old salt famous for the mutiny on his ship, *The Bounty*, in 1789. Against the odds he survived to make mincemeat out of the mutineers. William Bligh (1754–1817) later became an admiral before serving as governor of New South Wales and more recently an equal partner on a plate of pie and mash. Or in backslang 'Ipe and Sham'.

Captain Cook   **(a) Book**
Applies to any book, including the one made by bookies. Inspired by the English explorer and navigator James Cook (1728–79).

                    (b) Look
Not very common but 'give us a captain cook' means 'let's see'.

Captain Flint   **Skint**
Long John Silver's parrot flies in without any pieces of eight.

Captain Grimes   **Times**
Refers to the newspaper and appears to be based on a

character in Evelyn Waugh's novel, *Decline and Fall*; evidently a piece from suburbia.

Captain Kettle — **Settle**
Based on a comic-book hero of a bygone generation, the term for putting an end to an argument by violent means or otherwise is, like the good captain, retired.

Captain Kirk — **(a) Turk**
A late 20th-century phrase following the rise in popularity of Turkey as a holiday destination.

(b) Work
Coined in the early 1990s when a recession meant that many people had more chance of meeting a Klingon than a job interviewer. Based on the hero of TV's *Star Trek*.

Captain Morgan — **Organ**
Theatrical piece applying to any organ, musical or otherwise. Based on the Welsh pirate Henry Morgan (1635–88), who ended up as Governor of Jamaica. Who says crime doesn't pay?

Captain Scott — **Hot**
Typical East-End humour to use the name of a man who froze to death as a term relating to heat. The weather or a curry can be too 'captain scott'. Robert Falcon Scott (b. 1868) died on an expedition to the South Pole in 1912.

Captain's Log — **Bog (Lavatory)**
When there are rumblings in the 'poop deck' an entry into the 'captain's log' is warranted.

Car Park — **Nark**
An informer – probably because an empty car park is a likely meeting place for a copper and his snout.

Carbuncle — **Uncle**
The dictionary describes a carbuncle thus: 'An extensive skin eruption resembling a boil but much larger and having many openings'. Sounds exactly like one of my uncles!

Cardboard Box   Pox

One of many terms for 'Aldgate ague', the disease you wouldn't tell your mother about – or your partner for that matter. 'Exop' – how the condition looks in backslang.

Careless Talk   Chalk

A post-war term employed by darts players and based on a wartime slogan: 'Careless talk costs lives'. A stick of 'kaylatch' – a backslang scribbling stick.

Carl Rosa   Poser

Based on a German musician (1842–89), who formed a London-based operatic society. Can't imagine this is a piece of cockney RS but it refers to anyone who makes himself out to be something he isn't: 'Operatic Ernie was up the pub last night singing something from a Rembrandt opera. What a carl rosa he is!'

Carlo Gatti   Batty

Mad or eccentric, courtesy of the name of a company supplying ice to restaurants in London before fridges were the norm. Swiss born Gatti (1817–78) was also, at varying times, a restaurateur and café owner specialising in home produced ice cream, as well as a public house and music-hall owner.

Carol Singer   Ringer

Anything or anybody who is not what they appear to be is a 'carol', from a lookalike greyhound to a stolen car with moody number plates.

Carpet Bag   Drag

A 'drag' is a slang term for a three-month prison sentence and is responsible for 'carpet' becoming a common replacement for the number three. £3 is well known as a 'carpet' as are the odds of 3/1. And 33/1 is a 'double carpet'.

Carving Knife   Wife

She of the cutting tongue and sharp glances can be known as a 'carving'.

Casablanca   Wanker

Mainly used in full but a sometimes a 'handshagger', 'tosser' or someone who by any other name is a 'scrote' is reduced to a 'cazza'. Casablanca shake – an abusive hand gesture of contempt.

Cash & Carry   **Marry**
An example that begats two offspring: Cash & Carried and Cash & Carriage.

Castle Rag   **Flag**
One of the oldest examples of RS in that it applied to a slang term for fourpence. Now it quite suitably fits that which is flown, waved or hung from car aerials each time the World Cup comes round.

Castor & Pollux   **Bollocks**
The names of the twins of Gemini are transferred to the twins of the 'ballbag'. 'Kaylobs' – backslang nuts.

Castor Oil(s)   **Royal(s)**
How the royal family became disrespectfully renamed the 'castors'.

Cat & Dog   **(a) Catalogue**
Probably more of a pun than RS but people who do their shopping at home do so often do so with a 'cat & dog' on their lap.

(b) Bog (Lavatory)
Frequent trips to the 'cat & dog may follow a meal at a restaurant selling questionable meat.

Cat & Kitty   **Titty**
As displayed, possibly, by a woman who puts her 'pussy' to work in a 'cathouse'.

Cat & Mouse   **House**
When this was first coined many homes had both. 'Esouch' – a backslang gaff.

Cat's Face   **Ace**
One of four in a pack of cards – perhaps the one that takes the kitty.

Cat's Milk   **Silk**

Relates to smoothness, hence a malt whisky can go down as smooth as 'cat's milk'. 'Cow's Milk' is probably more suitable. After all, how do you milk a cat? Gingerly, I suppose!

Cattle Truck   **Fuck**

Commonly reduced to the first element, mainly in context of being tired or rendered helpless. You're 'cattled' if you get two punctures, for instance. It's also what tends to happen to British tennis players at Wimbledon and the sex act is known as 'cattling'.

Cecil Gee(s)   **Knee(s)**

An example, based on the chain of menswear shops, where the second element is usually discounted.

Celebrity Chef   **Breath**

A 21st-century example whereby someone with a 'reeking celebrity' has probably eaten something that was heavy on the garlic. The term stems from the seemingly never-ending parade of cookery programmes on TV and the glut of pan handlers who have found fame on them.

Cellar Flap   **Tap**

Originally applied to tap dancing but latterly anybody on the 'cellar' wants to borrow some money.

Centre Half   **Scarf**

A neck warmer or 'stook', which fittingly comes from the football terraces since it's based on the player in the Number 5 shirt.

Chain & Crank   **Bank**

A piece that's never generated a lot of interest.

Chain & Locket   **Pocket**

Keep your hands in your 'chains' when thieving 'hooks' are about.

Chalfont St Giles   **Piles**

After the village in Buckinghamshire, 'chalfonts' is a theatrical term for what keeps bums off seats: haemorrhoids.

Chalk Farm   **(a) Arm**

An ancient and still common piece, a gambler will 'chance his chalk'. Chalk Farm is an area of North-West London.

(b) Harm

What a good minder will see doesn't befall his employer.

Chalky White   **Light (Ale)**

A 'chalky' is now a largely unheard-of piece since lager has become the most popular of bottled beers.

Champagne Glass   **Brass**

A twice-removed term for a prostitute (see Brass Nail), which is suggestive of a high-class call girl who entertains visiting nobs.

Chandelier   **Queer**

That which hangs gaily from the ceiling – a chandelier, that is – becomes a 'shandy' in connection with a homosexual.

Channel Fleet   **Street**

Whereby anything agreeable may be 'right up your channel'.

Channel Port   **Short**

A measure of spirit from the 'top shelf', this 1990s term is probably based on cross channel 'booze cruises' on which duty-free bottles of 'channel' are bought in vast quantities.

Channel Ports   **Shorts**

Known as 'channels' in reference to those garments that expose the thin, pale, hairy, knobbly things men call legs.

Charing Cross   **Horse**

In old cockney dialect 'cross' is pronounced 'crorse' and 'charings' are horses. Old carmen would have driven an 'esroch and track' – a backslang horse and cart.

Charles Dance   **Chance**

A meticulous planner leaves nothing to 'charles dance'. This 1990s piece is based on a British actor of the period.

Charles James Fox   **Box**

An ancient piece for a theatrical box that has long been known as a 'charles james'. It is based on Britain's first foreign secretary (1749–1806).

Charley Chase   Race

Originally an Australian term for a contest but occasionally heard here, when a withdrawn horse is 'out of the charlie'. Based on an early American film comedian (1893–1940).

Charlie Brady   Cady

A 19th-century term for a hat long consigned to the hat-stand of obsolescence.

Charlie Brown   Clown

Professional jester or anyone who acts the fool, a joker. A 1950s example based on a hit song by US group, The Coasters.

Charlie Chan   Can

Started with an advertising campaign for canned beer in the 1970s and based on the fictional detective of book and film fame.

Charlie Clore   (a) Floor

Elderly piece from the fight game, where to put an opponent down was to 'put him on the charlie'.

(b) Score (£20)

Based on a millionaire financier (1904–79), who has probably never appreciated the joy of putting on a long-since worn pair of trousers and finding a 'charlie' in the pocket.

Charlie Cooke   Look

A 1960s term based on a Scottish international footballer, who rarely gave opposing full backs a look in.

Charlie Dicken   Chicken

The name of the great author (1812–70) is suggested here, albeit incorrectly but RS isn't that particular. It refers to poultry, not cowardice. 'Neckitch' – a backslang 'chook'.

Charlie Dilke   Milk

A 19th-century example based on the long-departed politician and author Sir Charles Wentworth Dilke (1843–1911).

Charlie Drake   (a) Brake

It would be interesting to see a mechanic's reaction if a woman drove into his garage and asked to have her 'charlies' looked at.

(b) Break

A tea break or rest, courtesy of a British actor and comedian (1925–2006), whose catchphrase on 1950s TV was: 'Is is tea-time yet?'

Charlie Freer   **Beer**
Example from the 'penny a pint' days. A 'teenip of reeb' – a backslang pint of beer.

Charlie Frisky   **Whisky**
Long-standing opponent of 'charlie randy' (qv), both of whom sound as if they're up for a bit of nonsense – after a drop of nonsense. Distiller's droop permitting, of course.

Charlie Howard   **Coward**
Famously to 'turn charlie' is to 'bottle it'. You don't need to be brave to be a coward – a piece of useless advice.

Charlie Hunt   **Cunt**
Widely used in respectable circles by people who know not what they're saying. You may look a right proper 'charlie' in that titfer but until someone tells you, you won't know.

Charlie Lancashire   **Handkerchief**
Doesn't seem much of a rhyme but old cockney dialect heard a 'snotrag' pronounced 'hankershef'.

Charlie Mason   **Basin**
Kitchenware is not necessarily involved here. To have a basinful of something is to have a go at it or get in on it, so the next time there's a tip circulating, you might want to have a 'charlieful of it'.

Charlie Pope   **Soap**
Coined in the trenches of World War I by soldiers who would have been caked in mud. Possibly inspired by Charles Pope (1872–1959), an England cricketer of the period.

Charlie Prescott   **Waistcoat**
An old term for the third part of a three-piece suit which is pronounced 'westcot'.

Charlie Randy   Brandy

A 19th-century term based on a bloke called Randy, whose first name was Charlie.

Charlie Ronce   Ponce

An old term for a prostitute's minder and a shameless sponger. 'Ecnop' – a backslang ponce.

Charlie Smirke   Berk

A fool based on an English jockey (1906–93) and a piece of secondary slang, (see also Berkshire Hunt). Must be used in full to differentiate from 'charlie hunt' (qv).

Charlie Wiggins   Diggings

A theatrical term for the place where actors hang their wigs whilst performing away from home.

Charlton & Greenwich   Spinach

A greengrocer's term for Popeye's favourite that's based on a couple of areas of South-East London.

Charming Wife   Knife

As introduced to enemy soldiers in World War I.

Chas & Dave   Shave

A 1980s term for the cockney musicians that never seemed to do a lot of 'chazzing' themselves. 'Eevash and Riahtuck' – a backslang shave and haircut.

Chatham & Dover   Over

Taken from the old Chatham and Dover railway line, this is used to emphasise finality: 'That's it, finished. All chatham & dover'.

Cheddar Gorge   George

'Cheddar' is a rare appellation given to men, boys and saints of this name. Named after a deep gorge in the Mendip Hills, Somerset.

Cheerful Giver   Liver

Someone who happily carries a donor card although the term somewhat predates transplant technology.

Cheese & Crackers　　　　**Knackers**

The after-dinner course in relation to the testicles, or vegetarian's lunchbox – two veg without the meat.

Cheese Grater　　　　**Waiter**

Fitting example for he who sprinkles the parmesan and acts 'kraftily' till he gets his tip; a piece that renames the head waiter the 'big cheese'.

Cheesy Quaver　　　　**Favour**

Based on a savoury snack, people have been doing 'cheesys' for each other since the early 1990s.

Chelsea Bun　　　　**Son/Sun**

Either way, this early 20th-century term has become stale.

Chelsea Potter　　　　**Squatter**

A 1990s term that's probably based on the pub in Chelsea's King's Road. The last thing you want to find on returning from holiday is a houseful of 'chelseas'.

Cheltenham Bold　　　　**Cold**

An old term based on the home of the National Hunt Festival, where bold jumpers may fall like the temperature. Also given as 'Cheltenham Gold' after the Cheltenham Gold Cup. Either way, when it's freezing, it's 'bloody cheltenham' – or 'Deeloc' in backslang.

Cherie Blair　　　　**Fare**

A piece that came into existence in the late 1990s when the wife of the then Prime Minister hit the headlines by becoming a high-profile fare dodger when she tried to ride the railway without purchasing a ticket.

Cherry Hog　　　　**Dog**

A 'cherry' is a widely used example regarding man's best friend. It is especially common amongst greyhound racing enthusiasts, who may go to the 'cherries'. Cherry 'ogs are the stone of that fruit, which were used as playthings by early 20th-century kids. 'A hair of the cherry' is a cockney hangover cure.

Cherry Picker   **Nicker (£1)**
A 'cherry' is a piece from the 1970s, rarely heard then and now.

Cherry Red   **Head**
The 'cherry' – what centre forwards score with, scientists think with and dirty fighters throw at opponents.

Cherry Ripe   **(a) Pipe**
A term dating back to when smoking a pipe was a common way of making people cough.

                                  (b) Tripe
Written or spoken nonsense: What a load of 'cherry'.

Chevy Chase   **Face**
One of the earliest terms of RS, still common as a 'chivvy'. Based on an ancient ballad about the battle of Chevy Chase, which took place near Otterburn, Northumberland, in 1388. 'Eecaf' – a backslang mug often shortened to 'Eek'.

Chew the Fat   **Chat**
Well-known piece that has transcended the realms of RS to join conventional English.

Chicken & Rice   **Nice**
From the takeaway restaurant comes this modern rival to 'apples & rice' (qv).

Chicken Heart   **Fart**
Used when a fetid fragrance of a faecal nature assails the nostrils: 'Who's chicken-hearted?'

Chicken Perch   **Church**
Known as 'chicken' – as all cockney 'parsons knows'.

Chicken's Neck   **Cheque**
An alternative to 'goose's neck', possibly for a less poultry amount.

Chimney & Soot   **Foot**
The sock-filler, not the measurement; as in the complaint 'athlete's chimney'.

China Plate   **Mate**
Very old and very familiar, whereby your 'toppo oppo' becomes your best 'china'. Seamen use the term for the first officer.

Chips & Peas   **Knees**
Whereby the unfortunate victims of a kneecapping have 'had their chips'.

Chirrup & Titter   **Bitter (Ale)**
Old piece that has sunk to the bottom of the barrel.

Choc-Ice   **Dice**
Mainly those included in board games and probably unheard of in Monte Carlo or Las Vegas.

Chocolate Biscuit   **Risk It**
When you've heavy work to be done, be careful. If you 'chocolate biscuit', you may end up with a dodgy 'cadbury's snack' (qv).

Chocolate Eclair   **Prayer**
Sweet dreams may follow as a result of children saying their 'chocolates' at bedtime.

Chocolate Frog   **Wog**
A non-PC Australian term for a foreigner or immigrant that is unused here, except probably by ex-patriot Aussies. Which kinda makes them 'chocolates' to us.

Chocolate Fudge   **Judge**
How 'M'lud' became known as a 'chocolate'.

Chop/Chopping Sticks   **Six**
A brace of terms from the bingo hall, although £6 is sometimes called a 'chop'; 'Exis' is a backslang half-dozen.

Chop Suey   **Hooey**
An item from a Chinese nosh-up list comes in as rubbish/nonsense/rot/gank. Whatever insults your intelligence is a load of 'chop suey'.

Christmas Card **Guard**
Takes in all types, from a fireguard to a railway worker, to the soldier who minds the Queen.

Christmas Cheer **Beer**
A drunk may truthfully state: 'The last time I was sober was eight christmases ago.'

Christmas Crackered **Knackered**
To be exhausted, broken or in trouble comes down to being 'christmassed'.

Christmas Crackers **Knackers (Testicles)**
The pulling of which is guaranteed to make the eyes water.

Christmas Dinner **Winner**
An old street-corner newsvendor's cry: 'All the christmas dinners' related to the racing results.

Christmas Eve **Believe**
Would you 'christmas eve' it? 'Adam & Eve' (qv) have a rival.

Christmas Log **Dog**
How a poochimutt becomes what, ordinarily, he'd piddle on.

Christmas Shop **Strop (Masturbate)**
Doing your Christmas shopping in the privacy of your home doesn't necessarily mean you have the Argos catalogue in your hands.

Christmas Trees **Knees**
The seasonal indoor toilet that your dog pines for in cold weather represents those known to tremble behind the bike shed. Not necessarily in cold weather.

Christopher Lee **Pee/Wee**
British actor famed for his roles in horror films gets back in character as a 'vampire's kiss' (qv).

Chunk of Beef **Chief**
The top banana has long been known as a 'chunka'.

Chunk of Wood **Good**
A 19th-century term used mainly in the negative sense, i.e.

anything bad was 'no chunka wood' or in backslang, 'On Doog'.

Cigarette Holder   **Shoulder**
Heard at a football match on a freezing day:
Her: Got a hanky? My nose keeps running.
Him: Use your sleeve.
Her: No, this is my new coat.
Him: Well, I've been using your cigarette holder.

Cilla Black   **Back**
More people cry off work with dodgy 'cillas' than anything else these days. Based on a British singer whose voice makes some people wish they had dodgy ears.

Cinderella   **(a) Smeller (Nose)**
People who get on your nerves may get right up your 'cinderella'.

(b) Yellow
Mainly used in connection with a snooker or pool ball of that colour but can also be a nickname for a coward.

Cisco Kid   **Yid**
Old term for a Jew that's based on a Western hero of the 1930s onwards.

City Banker   **Wanker**
Obnoxious person, a 'snotbubble'; courtesy of an office wallah and close rival to 'merchant banker' (qv).

City Tote   **Coat**
When summer heads for sunnier climes for the winter, put on your 'city tote'. Formed in the 1970s from the name of a bookmaking firm.

Claire Rayners   **Trainers**
A 1990s term for the footwear designed for physical activity and formed on the name of an agony aunt, who clearly wasn't!

Claret & Blues   **Shoes**
An early noughties term based on the colours of West Ham United FC and worn as 'clarets'.

Clark Gable   **Table**
American actor (1901–60), known in his time as the King of Hollywood, who still gets laid every mealtime.

Clark Kent   **Bent**
Inspired by the mild-mannered alter-ego of Superman, which makes for an ironic allusion to corruption, the Man of Steel being the ultimate good guy.

Clement Freuds   **Haemorrhoids**
Based on a British writer, TV and radio personality who also sat as a Liberal MP. The condition is painfully known as 'clements'.

Clever Dick   **Brick**
As laid by a 'clever dickie' – brickie.

Clever Mike   **Bike**
An old term possibly based on an early stunt cyclist. Or one who had the sense to have lights fitted on his bike, unlike today's idiots who don't realise they are invisible at night.

Clicketty Clickers   **Knickers**
Ladies underwear. In brief, 'clickettys'.

Clodhopper   **Copper**
Applied to a copper coin of old when a penny was known as a 'clod'. Also a police officer – who may be known as 'Plod the clod'.

Clothes Peg   **(a) Egg**
Formed when bad eggs were common so a clothes peg would have been a handy piece of nosewear.

     (b) Leg
As a footballer was being carried off on a stretcher on Hackney Marshes his opponent protested his innocence: 'But Ref, it was a 50-50 ball.' 'Yes,' replied the official. 'Now he's got a 50-50 clothes peg. Name?'

Cloud Seven   **Heaven**
Where happy people tend to dwell.

Cloven Hoof   **Poof**
A devilish rival to the well-known 'iron hoof' (qv) in the homosexual stakes.

Coachman on the Box   **Pox**
A piece from pre-penicillin days for VD and known as the 'coachman's'. Based on he who drove a stagecoach.

Coal & Coke   **Broke**
Potless, without the proverbial pot to piss in – or to put it the flash way, devoid of the receptacle required in which to urinate.

Coal Heaver   **Stever/Stiver**
Obsolete example for an old slang term for a penny.

Coal Miner   **Shiner (Black Eye)**
A term for a 'mince-noir' that doesn't get shortened; anyone sporting one is likely to be quizzed as to who gave them the 'coal miner'.

Coalman's Sack   **Black**
Applies to being dirty. When your shirt collar becomes 'coalman's', go and wash your neck.

Coat & Badge   **Cadge**
Formed on the name of the Doggetts Coat and Badge, which is the oldest sporting event in Britain. Contested by rowers, the course is the four-and-a-half mile stretch of the Thames between London Bridge and Cadogan Pier, Chelsea. People said to be 'on the scrounge' are on the 'coat & badge' and sometimes on the 'doggetts'.

Coat Hanger   **(a) Banger**
Mainly used to describe an old car but sometimes a sausage.
                    (b) Clanger
It's a mistake to drop a 'coat hanger'.

Cob of Coal   **Dole**
One of the older examples describing unemployment benefit.

Cobbler's Awls   **Balls**
'Cobblers' is probably the most common of all the RS terms for the testicles. It's also an argumentative retort: 'Cobblers! You don't know what you're talking about.'

Cobbler's Stalls   **Balls**
Corruption of the above: 'Slabs pew' – a backslang mistake or 'balls up'.

Cock & Hen   **(a) Pen**
The oldest of terms for a scribbler, which in its day would have been a scratcher, i.e. a nib and inkwell job.
      (b) Ten
A commonish reference to £10.

Cock Linnet   **Minute**
The time people are kept waiting. It may be more or less than a minute but 'I'll be with you in a cock linnet' means 'hang on a while'.

Cock Sparrow   **(a) Arrow**
Old public bar term for a dart, as in a game of 'cock sparrers'.
      (b) Barrow
A market trader's expression for what he wheels to his field of business.

Cock-a-Leekie   **Cheeky**
Time was when children were 'cock-a-leekie', they got their legs smacked. Now they're straight on the blower to a human rights lawyer at the sight of a raised hand.

Cocked Hat   **Rat**
Applies to a human rodent, an informer or someone thought to be 'lower than a traffic warden in a submarine'.

Cockerel & Hen   **Ten**
Always reduced to a 'cockle' (lazy pronunciation of the first element), this originally applied to 10 shillings but has been revalued to become a well-known term for £10. A 'cockle' is also a 10-year stretch in prison and 10 years of marriage.

Cockroach   **Coach**

Long-running term for the 'beano bus' that still travels the highway of RS.

Cod's Roe   **Dough (Money)**

The long-standing moan of the losing punter. When his bet has gone down or 'done a Bismarck', he has 'done his cods'.

Cod's Roe(ing)   **Snow(ing)**

When it's cold enough for 'cod's roe', suck a Fisherman's Friend.

Coffee & Cocoa   **Say So/Think So**

Common but unusual in that it's always reduced to the second element as a term of disbelief or doubt: 'Do you think he'd be selling the car so cheap if it were a good 'un? I should cocoa!'

Coffee & Tea   **Sea**

Nice to get away for a while and dip your feet in the 'coffee', even if it's only Blackpool where the sea resembles tea.

Coffee Stalls   **Balls**

Reduced to 'coffees' in relation to testicles, so chaps beware: steer clear of coffee grinders. 'Esslabs' – backslang gooliboos.

Cold Potato   **Waiter**

If your spuds are 'taters', get the 'cold potater' to get you some hot ones (see Potatoes in the Mould).

Coldstream Guards   **Cards**

Playing cards based on the ace regiment who have long been minding kings and queens.

Collar & Cuff   **Puff**

A homosexual male – a 1950s example – now rarely heard. Derogatory when it was.

Collar & Tie   **(a) Lie**

People were telling 'collars' long before the now common 'porkies' came on the scene. See also 'Pork Pie'.

                          (b) Spy

Usually refers to the workplace snitch, who runs bosswards with tales of everyday shirking folk.

Colleen Bawn **Horn (Erection)**
At a stroke this is reduced to a 'colly' and is based on the name of the heroine of the 19th-century opera, *The Lily of Killarney*.

Colney Hatch **Match**
Based on the name of the Mental Institution in North London in regard to what inmates shouldn't play with.

Colonel Blimp **Shrimp**
Seafood, courtesy of cartoonist David Gill's bumptious creation.

Colonel Gadaffi **Taffy**
How the Libyan leader became associated with the Welsh.

Colonel Prescott **Waistcoat**
Based on an officer and gentleman sportsman whose game, mayhap, was snooker.

Comb & Brush **Lush**
A drink of an alcoholic nature, therefore also a drinker of an alcoholic nature.

Come & Go **Snow**
Vulgarists may enjoy reducing this to the first element, e.g. 'There's no racing at Sandown 'cos there's come on the course.'

Come A-Clover **Tumble Over**
A World War I term that was probably apt when the bullets were flying, it's what too many young men did. It's also an accident waiting to happen: 'Tie your laces or you'll come a-clover'.

Come A-Tumble **Rumble (Find Out)**
An expression that may signify a downfall as in if anyone 'comes a tumble' to your wrongdoing, you've had it.

Comic Cuts **Nuts (Testicles)**
Cut at 'comics' for the region in which a kick is no laughing matter.

Comic Singer(s) **Finger(s)**
As rare today as a comic song in the charts.

Comical Chris   **Piss**

A character from the 1940s radio show *ITMA* comes onstream as an act of urination. Caught short between the pub and home, many a drunk has had a 'comical' up an 'albert hall' (qv).

Comical Farce   **Glass**

Possibly formed on the joke about the Irish glazer who confused dog shit for putty and his windows fell out.

Compact Disc   **Risk**

An early 21st-century term where to chance something risky is known as 'taking a CD'.

Con & Col   **Dole**

What these diminutives of the name Colin have to do with signing-on, I don't know. 'Eelod' – backslang benefit money.

Conan Doyle   **Boil**

Based on the author Sir Arthur Conan Doyle (1859–1930), the large septic beast that appears on the skin is known as a 'conan'. Also to boil, whereby a busy kettle may be 'on the conan'.

Conger Eel (er)   **Squeal (er)**

The slippery fish comes in for a slippery person, as this is what an informer does.

Connaught Ranger   **Stranger**

Based on an old Irish regiment, a 'connaught' is an underworld term for an unknown face, one that might belong to an undercover cop.

Constant Screecher   **Teacher**

Relevant more to 'caners' and 'flaybottomists' of yesteryear than today's teachers who are more likely to be screeched at.

Constipation   **Station**

Probable allusion to motionless trains and hold-ups on the line.

Cooking Fat   **Cat**

Not sure if this is RS or a Brummie spoonerism for a mog that got under someone's feet.

Cool Hand Luke   **Fluke**
Based on a well-known film of the 1960s in regard to a lucky accident, especially in a snooker or pool match, and known as a 'cool hand'.

Corn & Bunion   **Onion**
A couple of foot complaints make for a less than tasty-sounding example from the greengrocers. 'Noino' – a backslang tearjerker.

Corn Flake   **Fake**
Anything that isn't what it appears to be, including funny money, snide jewellery, forged art and 150-year-old mahogany hi-fi cabinets.

Corn-on-the-Cob   **Job**
Piece from the suburbs to describe what's needed to earn one's corn.

Corned Beef   **(a) Chief**
The chief officer in prisons of old.
     (b) Thief
Applies to a petty criminal or one who could break into a tin of meat without a key.

Cornish Pastie   **Tasty**
Used in relation to an attractive and highly fanciable person who may be described as being a bit 'cornish'.

Corporal Klinger   **Ringer**
A piece heard briefly in the 1970s when the TV series *M.A.S.H.*, in which Corporal Klinger was a character, was at the height of its popularity. It concerned unregistered players in amateur football matches. The memorable soldier put in many an appearance on Hackney Marshes of a Sunday morning.

Cotton Wool   **Pull**
The hunt for sexual quarry is known as being on the 'cotton'.

Cough & Choke   **Smoke**
As a noun or verb this could not be more pertinent, as proved

by the sound of smokers coughing up their ribcages in public places.

Cough & Drag   **Fag**

A fitting term for a cigarette, or put another way, a 'cough & drag' for a coffin nail.

Cough & Sneeze   **Cheese**

The 'cough' course doesn't sound a very appetising way to end a meal!

Cough & Splutter   **Butter**

If this comes from the same grocer as the previous entry, shop elsewhere! A 'resorg' is a backslang grocer.

Council Gritter   **Shitter (Anus)**

Based on the vehicle that unloads its brown contents on icy roads.

Council Houses   **Trousers**

Whereby 'gam cases' become 'councils'.

Country Cousin   **Dozen**

An old term largely heard on the racecourse for £12 or odds of 12/1. Also, the number 12 at the bingo hall – a 'neezod' in backslang whilst 12 is 'evlenewt'.

Couple of Bob   **(a) Gob (Phlegm)**

If you saw a 'couple of bob' on the pavement in pre-decimal days it was best left alone. A bob was a shilling.

(b) Job

If a 'couple of bob' is worth doing, it's a good idea to give someone a couple of bob to do it properly. 'Bodge' – backslang employment. Sounds like we're in cowboy country.

(c) Swab

A piece from the pub in connection with the dart team: it's the damp rag used to wipe the scoreboard.

Cousin Ella   **Umbrella**

Probably the only cousin you have who is in any way useful. The daughter of 'auntie ella' (qv), no doubt. 'Allerbum' – a backslang brolly.

Cousin Sis   **Piss**
Old reference to boozing; to go on the 'cousin sis'. Sissy was once a common name for a girl.

Covent Garden   **(a) Farthing**
Long-abandoned piece for a long-forgotten coin. A 'farden' was a quarter of an old penny.

(b) Pardon
Based on an area of London that once housed the central fruit and vegetable market, a 'covent garden' can be begged and granted. And it's what every innocent prisoner craves.

Covered Wagon   **Dragon**
Ugly or disagreeable woman. Said of a man whose address book is full of ugly women: 'He's pulled more covered wagons than a carthorse'. Hence, such a chap is known as a 'carthorse'.

Cow & Calf   **(a) Half**
See 'Cow's Calf'.

(b) Laugh
Heard in a nightclub:
1st man: You cowing at me?
2nd man: Yes
1st man: Why?
2nd man: You're the comedian.

Cow & Gate   **Late**
When a woman is 'cow & gate' for her period it is often a sign that she'll soon be buying baby food, which makes the name of this pap-producing company a suitable term.

Cowdenbeath   **Teeth**
A Scottish term for what fills the 'queen of the south' (qv) until gum rot sets in and the 'gnasher-snatcher' gets his pliers on them.

Cows & Kisses   **Missus (Wife)**
In mid-19th-century parlance a cow was a common but inoffensive reference to a woman so this very old term makes sense when you understand that it means women and kisses. Unless there was some secret perversion that went undocumented…

Cow's Calf   **Half**

Revamped version of 'cow & calf' in that 50p (or half a quid) is universally known as a 'cow's'. As is a six-month (half-a-year) prison sentence. 'Flatch a voss' – half a sov (50p) in backslang.

Cow's Lick   **Nick**

Insider's reference to prison.

Cow's Licker   **Nicker (£1)**

The bovine tongue is used in full so as not to confuse it with a 'cow's calf' (qv).

Cream Bun   **Son**

One of several buns leaving the baker's shelf to make the same connection.

Cream Crackered   **Knackered**

Exhausted, worn-out or broken. 'Creamed', as they say.

Cream Crackers   **Knackers (Testicles)**

A low blow in the 'cream crackers' is liable to drop a man to his 'biscuits & cheese' (qv).

Cream Puff   **Huff**

People in a bad mood will often leave in a 'cream puff'.

Cribbage Peg   **Leg**

One of several terms linking peg with leg, making them close partners in rhyme. 'Gel of beemal' – a backslang leg of lamb.

Crimea   **Beer**

Formed by soldiers of a bygone century – the Light (ale) Brigade, perhaps.

Cripple & Crutch   **Touch**

To touch someone is to borrow money from them so anyone who 'cripples' his mum for a few quid isn't necessarily a bad person.

Crispy Duck   **Fuck**

An early 21st-century term for the sex act – on a table in a Chinese restaurant, by the sound of it. And would they give a 'crispy duck' if they were caught? Probably not.

Crocodile   Smile

An urge to get someone smiling: 'Come on, show us your teeth, give us a crocodile!'

Crocodile Dundee   Flea

Had a slight usage in the 1980s when this film became popular, mainly in connection with a dog's boarders: 'The dog won't bite you but his crocodiles might.'

Crosby, Stills & Nash   Slash

Urination 1970s-style courtesy of a successful rock band of the period made up of Americans David Crosby and Stephen Stills and Englishman Graham Nash. Usually slashed to a 'crosby stills'.

Croûton   Root On

A 1990s term for an erection, this is an example of slang for slang.

Crowded Space   (Suit) Case

A term used by thieves who make a living from stealing luggage from airports, stations or any other crowded spaces.

Crown & Anchor   Wanker

One of many terms used to describe an obnoxious or useless git; also one of the oldest and based on a gambling dice game popular with seamen since the days of sail.

Crown Jewels   Tools

Appropriate since a tradesman's tools are precious to him and do not come cheap. Also, a frequent reference to man's baby-making equipment, especially the main member.

Crust of Bread   Head

Applies physically rather than mentally. You may scratch your 'crust' whilst you use your 'loaf'. See also 'Loaf of Bread'.

Cucumber   Number

Used mainly in connection with a phone number: 'Leave your cucumber and I'll call you back.'

Cuddle & Kiss   (a) Miss

An old and obvious term for a girlfriend, coined when a kiss and a cuddle was all a boy could expect until about their 95th date.

(b) Piss

Quite common when reduced to the first element, full bladders are emptied with a 'cuddle'. Liberty-takers, however, are given to taking the 'cuddle & kiss'.

Cuddled & Kissed   **Pissed (Drunk)**

The frequently 'cuddled' may wind up 'addled' or 'puddled'.

Cufflink   **Drink**

Originally an Aussie term that probably arrived here in a can of Fosters.

Cunning Stunt   **Cunt**

A spoonerism based on the old joke: What's the difference between a circus and a strip club? One has cunning stunts. It's a comical euphemism for a fool or the ineffectual type, someone as useful as a poultice on a wooden leg.

Cup of Tea   **(a) Pee/Wee**

If you hear someone at the pub say he's going for a 'cup of tea', he isn't!

(b) See

Used mainly as a term of farewell: 'I'll cuppa tea ya later'.

Currant Bread   **Dead**

Should be used in full – referring to the passed-on as 'currant' somehow sounds wrong.

Currant Bun   **(a) Nun**

A 1990s term for the woman of habit. 'Nun' – backslang …Oh.

(b) Run

More specifically 'on the run' or 'on the currant'.

(c) Son

The fruit of his father's loins.

(d) Sun 1

The most common use of the term is for the sky-light…

(d) Sun 2

And also well employed for the *Sun* newspaper.

Currant Cakes   **Shakes**

Refers to the DTs, delirium tremens or drinker's trembles. As suffered by those who were not merely 'cut' but 'cut to pieces' or 'ploughed'.

Currant Cakie   Shaky
Descriptive of how you feel the day after a heavy session or any circumstance that makes you wobbly.

Currants & Plums   Gums
'Currants' is a nickname for a 'suckermouth', someone without teeth. People with no teeth suck! – a piece of graffito.

Curry & Rice   Price
An example from the racecourse that may relate to the price of a hot favourite. 'Eecrips' – backslang odds.

Custard & Jelly   Telly
When there's nothing on the 'custard', a lot of people adjourn to the pub and stay for afters. In the newspaper industry, the *Telegraph* (the *Tele*) is also known as the 'custard'. 'Wylet' – a backslang TV.

Custard Cream   Dream
'Bo peep perchance to custard,' as Shakespeare may have scribbled, had he come from Stratford E15. See 'Bo Peep'.

Custard Tart   Fart
To 'drop a custard' is to 'leave one's calling card'.

Cut & Carried   Married
An unusual version of 'cash & carried'. See also 'Cash & Carry'.

Cut(s) & Scratch(es)   Match(es)
An old reference to 'strikes' that will still be alight when disposable lighters are disposed of.

Cutty Sark   Nark
The world-famous tea clipper sets sail again as a police informer.

Cyril Lord   Bald
Suitably based on a British carpet and rug manufacturer (1911–84) as a 'rug' is a slang term for a wig, as worn by the 'deelab' – the backslang bald.

D for Dunce   Bunce

Reduced to 'deefer' in reference to money the taxman will never know about and goods received from the backs of hands – anything extra on top of wages. In old comics the class mooncalf was seen sitting in a corner wearing a large pointed hat with a D on it.

Dad & Mum   Rum

Old sailors with 'Dad & Mum' tattoos weren't necessarily sentimental old salts, they may just have been partial to a drop of what, in backslang, is 'mur'.

Dad's Army   Barmy

Based on the well-known TV sitcom in reference to anyone thought to be a penny short of a shilling.

Daffadown Dilly   Silly

An old term for a 'nut-nut' based on an even older piece of slang for a dandy.

Daft & Barmy   Army

A soldier may say he was daft to join and barmy to stay in the army – or he might say it about the government who sent him to Iraq.

Daffy Duck   Fuck

Late 20th-century example for the sex act used by the young and promiscuous for whom a holiday romance is a gallon of lager and a quick 'daffy duck'. Also, anything broken or worn out is said to be 'daffied'. Based on the Loony Tunes cartoon character.

Dagenham Girl Piper   **Wiper (Windscreen)**

A dopey statement heard in a car spares shop: 'The funny thing is there's nothing wrong with me dagenham girls when it's not raining'. Based on a musical Essex girl, a member of the long-running band of bagpipe players.

Daily Bread   **Head**

A 19th-century term for the head of the family, when father put the food on the table and His will be done.

Daily Distress   *Daily Express*

A 1930s reference to the newspaper known in the trade as 'the Distress'.

Daily (Tote) Double   **Trouble**

An old term based on a defunct bet. The DTD was the dividend paid on the winners of the third and fifth races of a meeting. Those in bother are in a bit of 'daily' or 'daily tote'.

Daily Express   **Dress**

Refers to the garment and the act of putting it on, but men also get 'dailied'.

Daily Growl/Wail   *Daily Mail*

A couple of terms from the early 20th century used by printworkers of the period.

Daily Mail   **a) Ale**

A regular drinker likes his regular pint of 'daily' – often a quiet drink in the local with his favourite newspaper.

b) Bail

An example from the underworld for the accused's temporary release money.

c) Nail

A piece from the carpentry trade to describe what hammers were made to whack.

d) Tail 1

The backside; busy people may work their 'dailys' off.

Tail 2

To follow someone; once PCs would 'daily' a villain. Now they spend more time sitting on their 'dailys' (1) writing reports.

Tail 3

The waggable part of a dog.

e) Tale

A deception or hard-luck story, as told by a conman or beggar.

Dairy Box   **Pox**

Venereal disease. Reduced to the 'dairy', an unwelcome complaint based on a box of chocolates, often a gift from man to wife – the chocs, that is. Double unfortunate if not!

Daisy Beat   **Cheat**

A piece from the 19th century when to 'daisy' someone was to swindle them.

Daisy Bell   **Hell**

Expressions of anger, disappointment or frustration are 'bloody' or 'fuckin' daisy'. Based on a well-known music-hall song.

Daisy Dormer   **Warmer**

The predecessor to the hot-water bottle was a long-handled bedpan in which hot coals were placed. This was a 'daisy'. A defunct term for an obsolete piece of equipment and based on a long-departed music-hall artiste (1883–1947).

Daisy Root   **Boot 1**

An old, but still wearing well term for a 'trottercase'. A backslang pair of boots becomes a 'ryap of toobs'.

Boot 2

A late 20th-century example for a car boot, hence a 'daisy sale'.

Damn & Blast   **Last**

Heard on a racecourse: 'Damn and blast, my horse came in damn and blast!'

Damon Hill   **Pill**

The link with Britain's former world motor-racing driver is speed and therefore this refers to amphetamines.

Damon Runyon   **Onion**

A piece from the theatre, a 'damon' is possibly the onion required for false teardrops, Based on the US writer (1884–1946), creator of *Guys N' Dolls*.

Damp & Soggy   **Foggy**

Obvious and appropriate allusion to 'pea-soup' weather, as opposed to 'fanny' weather – wet and warm.

Dan Dares   **Flares**

The comic-book hero from the future sees action as an item of legwear from the past.

Dan Leno   **Beano**

A drunken day-trip to the seaside taken by a bunch of boozers in a 'chara'. Formed on the name of the first superstar of British comedy (1860–1904).

Danny La Rue   **(a) Blue**

Based on a well-known Irish-born entertainer, this applies to anything blue, including a snooker ball, a dirty joke or a porn film.

(b) Clue

A condescending remark to an idiot: 'You ain't got a danny la rue, mate.'

Darby & Joan   **(a) Alone**

A loner spends most of his time on his 'darby'.

(b) Moan

Based on an elderly married couple from an 18th-century ballad, this would appear to be an apt example as old people and moaning tend to go hand in hand.

(c) Phone

A term from a simpler time, when a telephone didn't come with a thousand-page instruction book and there was no such word as 'texting'.

Darby Kelly   **Belly**

An infamous piece from the 19th century when the well fed had a full 'darby' or 'darby kell'. Inspired by a song from the Napoleonic Wars.

Darby Bands   Hands

Derived from an ancient phrase 'Father Darby's bands'. This was a binding agreement between a moneylender and a debtor which was, naturally, heavily stacked in the lender's favour.

Darky Cox   Box

Seating area in a theatre as described by your theatrical type; also a coffin. An early 20th-century term formed on the name of an Islington based boxer of the 1910s, who is presumably now in his 'darky'. Given the man's occupation, the term may also have alluded to the art of the pugilist.

Darling Buds of May   Gay

This had an instant currency in 1991 when a hugely popular TV series based on H.E. Bates' novel about the Larkin family was shown. Almost overnight homosexual men became 'darling buds'.

Darling Daughter   Water

An uncommon term for 'tap juice'.

Darling Wife   Knife

A World War I term based on 'her at home'. One can only wonder how many letters left the Front addressed to a 'darling wife' only to be delivered to a widow.

Darren Gough   Cough

An England fast bowler will be as one with ill health for evermore, courtesy of RS.

Date & Plum   Bum

An old term that's always pruned to the first element:
Wife: The dog's full of mischief today.
Husband: Yeah? Well, his date'll be full of my boot if he keeps on!

David Beckham   Peckham

How the ubiquitous England footballer became a slang-for-slang example of neckwear. See also 'Peckham Rye'.

David Bowie   Blowy (Windy)

A piece that followed in the storm-damaged wake of the

hurricane that struck southern England in 1987. Based on a British rock singer, it is often used as a massive understatement: 'It's a bit david bowie' may mean there's a gale blowing.

David Gower   **Shower**
A 1980s term demonstrating how an ex-England cricketer has evolved into B.O. bashing in the bathroom.

Davy Crockett   **Pocket**
Formed on the name of the early American frontiersman and senator (1786–1836), the term dates from the 1950s when a popular Disney film of the man's exploits had fathers all over Britain dipping into their 'davy's' to buy their sons a Davy Crockett hat.

Davy Dee   **DVD**
A modern piece for a modern piece of equipment, although probably also a pun.

Davy Jones' Locker   **Knocker**
Many a rentman, tallyman or any other unwanted caller has had to 'take it out of the davy jones till pay day'. Also, a name given to a 'welsher', a 'davy jones' never pays his debts.

Davy Large   **Barge**
An old riverman's term based on an old riverman: Mr Large was a 19th-century dockworker who became a union official.

Day & Night   **Light**
Applies to most forms of the word. It's what wasteful offices leave on day and night, what someone without matches may ask for and, best of all, a light ale.

Day's-a-Dawning   **Morning**
An old and obvious piece said as: 'See you in the day's-a'.

Dead Loss   **Boss**
An oft-relevant piece used by workers about the one who couldn't organise the proverbial drinking session in a beer factory.

Deaf & Dumb   **(a) Bum**
Applies to both the buttocks and the anus, therefore you

compliment a woman on her shapely 'deaf & dumb' and she may well tell you to poke your compliment up the same term.

(b) Plum
An example from the fruit and veg market.

Dean Martin   **Parting**
A forgotten piece from around 1960 regarding a hair parting, or 'flea's footpath'. Based on a US actor and singer and to resurrect an old joke: Why is a bald man like a depleted Rat Pack? No Dean Martin.

Dearie Me   **Three**
Old hands at bingo will know this. 'Erth' – a backslang tray.

Deep-Sea Diver   **Fiver (£5)**
A piece that's been floating around as a 'deep sea' since the 1970s. 'Reevif' – a backslang reference to the same thing, also known as a 'ching'.

Denis Law   **Saw**
A carpenter's term for his tool based on the name of a Scottish international footballer known for his sharpness in front of the goal.

Dennis Wise   **Rise**
Modern term amongst young working men seeking a pay rise. Based on an England international footballer, asking for a 'dennis' in today's climate could result in the sack and the job filled with cheap foreign labour.

Derby Brights   **Lights**
Illuminations, probably theatrical ones; starstruck actors always want to see their names in 'derbys'.

Derby Kelly   **Belly**
See Darby Kelly.

Derry & Toms   **Bombs**
Formed during the Blitz when 'derrys' were flattening the East End of London. Derry & Toms was a department store that closed in 1973 after 111 years of trading in London's Kensington High Street.

Derry-Down-Derry   Sherry

Aged theatrical piece known as 'ddd', 'Three ds' or 'derry-down'. It is based on a character of verse believed to be the creation of the poet Edward Lear (1812–88).

Des O'Connor   Goner

Anyone or anything that falls victim to the Grim Reaper is said to be 'dezzo'. In racing terms it is a fallen horse. Sometimes, sadly, it's both. Based on a London-born entertainer.

Desmond Hackett   Jacket

Based on a British newspaper sports journalist who may or may not have sported a 'sports desmond'.

Desperate Dan   Tan

The desired colour of a sun-worshipper courtesy of the tough-guy cowboy of a children's comic, who gets his suntan with a blowtorch. Or used to, until the politically-correct prannys got to him.

Deuce & Ace   Face

In the words of the man who won't back down, it's better to have your deuce punched in than to lose it.

Diana Dors   Drawers

Jokingly dropped to 'dianas' when mentioning women's unmentionables. Named after a British actress (1931–84).

Dick Dunn   Sun

A 19th-century term for the 'dazzler' based on a bookmaker who was apparently well-known in his day.

Dick Emery   Memory

A man with a bad 'dick' needn't have a social problem, just as a chap charged with having a short one doesn't necessarily need to feel ashamed. Based on a British comedian (1917–83).

Dick 'n' Arry   Dictionary

An old schoolboy's term that necessitates inclusion, albeit more of a pun than RS.

Dick Turpin   **(a) Gherkin**
An imperfect term for a pickle, from the tag to the joke: What's green and robs stagecoaches? Dick Gherkin.

(b) 13
A piece of RS that doesn't quite hold up but old-time bingo callers would stand and deliver it anyway. Based on the infamous English highwayman (1705–39).

Dick van Dyke   **Bike**
A piece of East-End slang based on the American actor who is generally accepted as having the worst cockney accent in film history after his performance in the 1964 film, *Mary Poppins*.

Dickory Dock   **(a) Clock**
'Dickorys' have been telling the time for over a century.

(b) Cock (Penis)
Sometimes extended to 'hickory dickory dock' but then, being too much of a mouthful, it gets reduced to 'hickory dickory'. Funny thing, rhyming slang!

Dicky-Bird   **Word**
Applies to the spoken rather than the written word, or rather the non-spoken word. The silent, like a mute parrot, never say a 'dicky-bird'.

Dicky Diddle   **Piddle**
Rarely-used alternative to the ubiquitous 'jimmy riddle' (qv), which smacks of too many shakes.

Dicky Dirt   **Shirt**
An old, but long-enduring piece. Fashions change but 'dicky dirts' go on forever.

Dicky Mint   **Skint**
Having no money, courtesy of the name of one of English comedian Ken Dodd's Diddy Men.

Didgeridoo   **Clue**
Used in a sense of cluelessness whereby those with no idea of what's going on, or the terminally thick, are said not to have a 'didgeri'. Based on an Australian musical instrument of sorts.

Didn't Ought   **Port**
What good girls supposedly said, when offered another drink. Didn't stop them having one, though!

Didn't Oughta   **Water**
Very old example that could find a new currency as a warning against swimming in the seas around Britain.

Diesel Fitter   **Bitter (Ale)**
Always halved to a pint of 'diesel'.

Dig a Grave   **Shave**
See next example.

Dig in the Grave   **Shave**
A World War I term, when soldiers regularly did both. Known as a 'dig' and sometimes said as 'dig a grave' or 'dig my grave'.

Dig My Grave   **Shave**
See previous example.

Ding-Dong   **Sing-Song**
When this was coined it applied to a bunch of people gathered round a piano and giving it a lot of vocal. It later evolved into a general party or a 'knees-up'.

Ding-Dong Bell   **Hell**
Most commonly heard in the phrase 'fucking ding-dong', an expression of surprise which dates from the 1940s.

Dingley Dell   **Bell**
Used in connection with telephone calls, i.e., 'gimme a dingley tomorrow'. The phone was a futuristic fantasy when Charles Dickens thought up the place for *The Pickwick Papers*.

Dip & Dive   **Drive**
Sounds more relevant to flying than driving.

Dipstick   **Prick (Penis)**
An appropriate piece when used for the 'hornpipe' but more commonly heard in relation to a fool.

Dirty & Rude   **Nude**
What all nakedness was in pre-permissive times and still is with people of a prudish disposition.

Dirty Daughter   **Water**
What grubby little girls should be dipped in.

Dirty Den   **Pen**
A term that came and went with the character who acquired this nickname in TV soap *EastEnders*. Occasionally heard in betting shops.

Dirty Dick   **Nick**
The 'dirty' is a rare term for a police station. The original Dirty Dick was one Nathaniel Bentley, an 18th-century dandy whose fiancée died on the eve of their wedding. He spent the rest of his life in squalor and when he died in 1809 his house was a tip, although he was filthy rich. A pub, Dirty Dicks, was built on the property in 1870, in London's Bishopsgate, and still survives.

Dirty Faces   **Laces**
A 1940s example that may arise from the dishevelled state of the old street-sellers of boot- and shoelaces. Many were wounded ex-servicemen who could find no other employment during peacetime.

Dirty Leper   **Pepper**
Not really what you want to hear at the dinner table: 'Pass the dirty leper'. 'Repep and teelas' – backslang pepper and salt.

Dirty Old Jew   **Two**
A bingo caller's term from pre-PC days, when the game was called Housey-Housey. Thankfully obsolete.

Dirty Rotter   **Squatter**
An early 21st-century term for an unauthorised resident.

Dirty Tyke   **Bike**
The dictionary gives three definitions of a tyke, so this is based on a dirty dog, a dirty child or a dirty Yorkshireman. Old Grid – an old-fashioned bike, a 'boneshaker'.

Dirty Whore   **Four**
Example from a barrack-room game of bingo. 'Rofe to eno' – backslang odds of 4/1.

Dish of the Day   **Gay**
An appropriate example given that 'dish' is a piece of homosexual slang for buttocks.

Divine Brown   **Go Down (Fellate)**
So apt it's divine providence for the slangman. Ms Brown was the prostitute caught by Los Angeles police in 1995 with her face down British actor Hugh Grant's trousers.

Dixie Dean(s)   **Bean(s)**
Most commonly baked beans, whereby beans on toast becomes 'dixies on holy ghost' (qv). Based on the legendary William (Dixie) Dean (1907–80), freescoring Everton and England footballer of the 1920s–30s.

Dixie Lid   **Kid (Child)**
A term from the army, where a 'dixie' is an iron cooking pot used to make military custard, soup, porridge, etc. It can also be used to boil eggs en masse for the dipping in of soldiers. 'Clever Dick' – a bright child of backslang.

Do As You Like   **Bike**
From a time when cyclists kept to the road, knew what red lights meant and could get nicked for riding without lights. Now, they do as they like.

Do Me a Favour   **Neighbour**
An imperfect rhyme but may be a perfectly fitting example if liberty-takers live next door. For many, the perfect 'do me' is one who's not there when he's not wanted.

Do Me Good   **Wood**
A piece commonly heard when coal fires were frequently lit and 'do me' came in penny bundles.

Do Me Goods   **Woods**
Applied to Woodbines, the much-loved cigarette of World War I soldiers. The term flies in the face of health warnings and

was used defiantly by smokers when cigarettes were first linked to cancer.

Do My Dags   **Fags**

An old and extinguished term based on a children's game of the dim and distant past, which meant 'follow my lead' or 'do as I do'. A fag was known as a 'do me' and was apt in that kids often followed their parents into a cigarette packet.

Docker's Hook   **Look**

Oldish, but never grabbed the attention away from 'butcher's hook' (qv) in the 'decko' stakes. In Australia it's a book, one made by a bookmaker. 'Eevach a kool' – Have a look (backslang).

Doctor & Nurse   **Purse**

A mugger will snatch a 'doctor' and leg-it.

Doctor Cotton   **Rotten**

An early 20th-century example, one of several making the 'cotton'/'rotten' connection. The identity of the old medic is not known.

Doctor Crippen   **Dripping**

The infamous wife murderer (1862–1910) gives his name to the infamous toast topping that is to healthy eating what the man was to marriage guidance.

Doctor Jekyll   **Freckle (Anus)**

Freckle is an Australian term brought to Britain in the 1980s. Mr Hyde's alter ego became attached to it soon after.

Doctor Legg   **Egg**

A 1980s term that was heard in a caff when a building worker in North London ordered a fry-up with two 'doctor leggs'. Based on an early character in TV soap *EastEnders*.

Doctor Who   **a) Screw 1**

A prison officer, a piece from his place of work, where he could, I suppose, be regarded as a 'time lord'.

b) Screw 2

A piece of hardware. Carpenters and joiners now use 'doctors'.

c) Two

This term from a 1960s bingo hall has recently seen service as £2.

Dog & Bone   **Phone**

A term first engaged in connection with the old bakelite jobs, when a phone was a phone, a camera was a camera and a combination of both was science fiction.

Dog & Boned   **Stoned**

Known as 'doggo' when people are out of their skulls on drink or drugs.

Dog & Cat   **Mat**

An apposite term as either of these pets will make the mat in front of the fire their own.

Dog & Duck   **Ruck (Fight)**

Probably formed on the name of a roughhouse of a pub somewhere.

Dog & Pup   **Cup**

Originally an Australian term for a sporting trophy or the receptacle your average sheep shearer wouldn't be seen dead drinking from.

Dog's Meat   **Feet**

Commonly said of aching feet: 'My dogs are barking like mad'.

Dog's Tooth   **Truth**

Apart from the obvious: 'You wouldn't recognise the dog's tooth if it bit you on the arse', this is used as an oath, something akin to God's truth.

Dolly Cotton   **Rotten**

When early 20th-century food or drink went on the turn, it became 'dolly cotton'.

Dolly Mixtures   **Pictures**

Sweets are synonymous with going to the cinema. They usually come in wrappers that rustle – which are synonymous with my *leaving* the cinema.

Dolly Varden   **Garden**

Formed on the name of a character from Dickens' *Barnaby Rudge*. Apart from your own small part of the world, it also applies to 'the Garden', i.e. Covent Garden, London's fruit and vegetable market. Fresh fruit and veg comes from 'the dolly'.

Don Lang   **Slang**

A 1950s term that has been stashed away and long forgotten in the dusty memory box of an old teddy boy who was fluent in the 'old don lang'. Based on a hit-making British musician of the period (1925–92). 'Kaycab genalus' – backslang in backslang.

Don Revie   **Bevvy (Drink)**

A term coined by boozers in the 1970s after the then England football manager (1927–89), previously successful with Leeds United.

Donald Duck   **(a) Fuck**

The number one bird of Disneyland lends his name to the sex act and if it doesn't bother him, then he 'don't give a donald'.

(b) Luck

Those born under a bad sign don't get the best of 'donald'.

Donald Peers   **Ears**

A nagging wife will give you GBH of the 'donalds' and it's all down to a British singer (1910–73), who had some chart success in the 1960s.

Donald Trump   **Dump**

Defecation in the name of the millionaire property developer from the USA, whose surname is already a slang term for a fart.

Doner Kebab   **Stab**

A noughties term likely to be heard in the past tense when victims have been 'donered'.

Donkey's Ear   **Year**

A suggested origin of the well-known 'donkey's years' meaning a long time, a possible connection with the length of the beast's ears. The donkey does, however, live a long time so maybe that's the link.

Don't Be Rude **Food**

Bitten off at the first two elements, old transport caff society would drop in for a spot of 'don't be'. 'Doof and kaynird' – backslang for 'nibble and guzzle' (food and drink).

Don't Make a Fuss **Bus**

Ancient term that's as apt today as it ever was. To make a fuss about the foul-mouthed, loutish behaviour of your fellow passengers, especially schoolkids, is likely to get you a mouthful of abuse – or worse.

Door to Door **Four**

A housey-housey (or bingo) term.

Doorknob **(a) Bob**

A pre-decimalisation term for a shilling (5p).

(b) Job

When people get to a certain age, the only 'doorknob' open to many of them is driving a minicab, the last refuge of the unemployed (and sometimes the unemployable).

Doppelganger **Banger (Sausage)**

A term created by a TV scriptwriter that makes it double-unlikely to be heard off-screen.

Doris Day **a) Gay (Homosexual)**

An American singer and film star of the 1950s–60s is the reason why gay men are called 'doris'.

(b) Way

To be 'on your doris' means you're in transit or being moved on by the police.

Dorothy Squires **Tyres**

How a set of tyres became a set of 'dorothys'. A 1950s term based on a British singer (1915–98).

Dot & Carried **Married**

To 'dot and carry one' is an old description of walking with a limp, so this ancient term brings into play the time-honoured view of marriage being a handicap. Also used are 'Dot & Carry' and 'Dot & Carriage'.

Dot & Dash   **(a) Cash**
Seldom-heard piece based on Morse Code, whereby those holding the folding are expected to 'stump up the dot'.

                           (b) Tash
A moustache – an example from early 20th-century soldiers, possibly the Signal Corps?

Dot Cotton   **Rotten**
Based on a character from TV's *EastEnders*, this applies to anything that has gone bad or mouldy: be it food, drink or a TV programme.

Double-Yolker   **Joker**
A term used ironically against someone trying to be funny, but isn't.

Doublet & Hose   **Nose**
Since actors are the only folk likely to wear this attire, it's quite possible this was conk-octed in the theatre.

Douglas Hurd   **(a) Third**
Student slang from the 1980s regarding a third-class honours degree.

                           (b) Turd
A piece of excrement, courtesy of a former Tory cabinet minister whereby a 'sit-down job' on the toilet is known 'dumping a douglas'.

Dover Boat   **Coat**
One to keep you warm on the cross-channel ferry, possibly with deep pockets to hide the duty-frees.

Dover Harbour   **Barber**
Men used to go to the 'dover' for a fourpenny all-off. Now they go to a hairdresser and get charged a fortune for the same haircut.

Down the Drains   **Brains**
Possibly a barbed comment on a wasted education, there are none so thick as those who don't want to learn.

D'Oyle Carte   **Fart**

A serious piece of 'arse music', a 'doyley' could stop an opera from 30 rows back! Based on the operatic impresario Richard D'Oyle Carte (1844–1901).

Dribs & Drabs   **Crabs**

Refers to crab lice, nasty little nippers of the pubic area. Itchy Aussies have 'dibs & dabs'.

Drip Dry   **Cry**

Apt when dropped to the first element: 'Don't drip, tell me what's wrong'.

Dripping & Toast   **Host**

A publican may change from mine host to mine 'dripping'.

Drum & Bass   **Face**

An early 20th-century term for the physog based on a noise masquerading as music. 'Eesaf' – a backslang 'mooey'.

Drum & Fife   **(a) Knife**

An old term from the army that was known as a 'drum and' (pronoun 'drummond'). Often paired as cutlery with 'roast pork' (qv). A knife and fork was known as a 'drummond and roce'.

(b) Wife

Comes from a time when wife beating was sadly perhaps more common than it is today, so it is easy to imagine a bullying husband referring to his wife as the 'drum'.

Duane Eddys   **Readys**

Cash money, provided by an American guitarist who had hit records over four decades.

Dublin Trick   **Brick**

Well-known on yesterday's building sites but has now probably been laid to rest.

Duchess of Fife   **Wife**

A famous piece long believed to be responsible for the term for 'dutch', as in the well-known music-hall song, 'My Old Dutch'.

Duchess of Teck   Cheque

Known as a 'duchess', she went arm in arm with her old man (see Duke of Teck), but both were cashed in years ago.

Duchess of York   Pork

Pig meat from the RS menu of the 1980s. 'Wyleb of kayrop' – a backslang belly of pork.

Duck & Dive   (a) Skive

To avoid work by keeping your head down, i.e. ducking and diving out of sight of the guvnor.

                            (b) Survive

Ask anyone of no obvious income how they are getting on and they'll invariably reply: 'Oh you know, ducking & diving'.

Duck's Arse   Grass

Sometimes shortened to DA, this is secondary slang for an informer. See also Grasshopper.

Dudley Moore   Sore

The Dagenham-born comedian and jazz pianist (1935–2002) lends his name to any unpleasant condition involving skin eruptions. Most commonly a 'dudley' is a cold sore, which in backslang is a 'deloc eros'.

Duke of Argyll   File

The underworld term for the cartoon prisoner's favourite cake ingredient. 'Lyon eelif' – a backslang nail file.

Duke of Argyll's   Piles (Haemorrhoids)

Sounds like the Scottish nobleman has a painful hereditary seat.

Duke of Fife   Knife

A term that's been on the table for over a century.

Duke of Kent   (a) Bent 1

Applies to anything misshapen, from a car bumper after an accident to Quasimodo.

                            Bent 2

Anything or anyone crooked or corrupt, like pirate videos, smuggled tobacco, coppers, politicians, sportsmen, etc.

Bent 3
A title bestowed on a homosexual.
b) Rent
From the days when home ownership was beyond the reach of the working-man and the landlord used to knock for the 'duke of kent'. Whether he got it or not was often another story.

Duke of Teck   **Cheque**
Beware 'rubber dukes' – they bounce. An old term that may be responsible for a 'duke' being a term for a restaurant bill.

Duke of York   **(a) Chalk**
Has been scribbling on the blackboard of RS since the 19th century and may still be heard at a pub darts match.

(b) Cork
The bung that seals a bottle; a vintage piece.

(c) Fork
Accompanied by the 'duke of fife' (qv), you're in noble company at meal times. Also applies to the fingers, for which 'forks' is an old term and by extension the hands, hence to 'put up one's dukes' is to engage in a fistfight.

(d) Pork
Still cooking after scratching around for many years. 'Kayrop poches' – backslang pork chops.

(e) Talk
Less common than 'rabbit & pork' (qv) but it wasn't always so, this being the older of the two.

(f) Walk
A piece that's been strolling off cockney tongues since the 19th century.

Dull & Dowdy   **Cloudy**
An obvious piece in relation to the weather but beer can be 'dull & dowdy' too.

Dumper Truck   **Fuck**
A piece from a building site, where unconcerned navvies 'couldn't give a dumper'.

Duncey Deedle   **Needle**

A 1950s term for that which sows, based on a rhyming slur used by children to ridicule a child of questionable education: 'Duncey, duncey deedle, can't threadle a needle'.

Dunkirk   **Work**

The scene of a lot of hard work in 1940 is a 1950s term for the place frequented by the employed on a daily basis.

Dunlop Tyre   **Liar**

Tread carefully around the bald-faced teller of untruths known as a 'dunlop'.

Dustbin Lid   **Kid (Child)**

East End nippers have long been known as 'dustbins' and had William Bonney hailed from the area, no doubt he would have been known as Billy the Dustbin.

Dustin Hoffmans   **Rothmans**

An American actor comes in as a brand of cigarettes, tobacconnists report of young men asking for '20 dustins'.

Dustpan & Broom   **Groom**

The household implements, the existence of which most bachelors are ignorant, are symbolic of a new way of life, of which all bachelors are ignorant.

Dustpan & Brush   **Thrush**

To have a 'touch of dustpan' is to suffer a fungal infection of the genitalia, forcing female sufferers into furtive bouts of 'snatch-scratching'.

Dutch Peg(s)   **Leg(s)**

So I said to this bloke with no 'dutches' at the bus-stop: 'How you getting on?'

Dutch Plate   **Mate**

An antiquated piece but far less common than 'china plate' (qv).

Dynamite   **Fight**

Known as a 'dyna', be it a fair fist-fight or a 'kick-bollock and bite' tear-up.

Earl's Court   **Salt**

Based on the part of West London that is famous for its exhibition centre and bedsits full of Australians. 'Teelas' – backslang seasoning.

Early Bird   **Word**

A fairly old term, 'an early in your ear'ole' is often a piece of good advice.

Early Door   **Whore**

An ancient piece for she who is willing to get her 'early doors' (qv) off.

Early Doors   **Drawers**

An old, jocular term for women's underwear based on an old music-hall custom of paying a few coppers extra to get in early, thus beating the crush when the hoi-polloi turn up.

Early Hours   **Flowers**

A piece from the old flower market and aptly based on the time that vendors have to arrive there to pick up the best blooms.

Early Morn   **Horn (Erection)**

Apposite piece as men often wake up with one. A visit to the lavatory usually takes it down a peg.

Eartha Kitt(s)   **(a) Shit(s)**

Based on an American songstress, this is either to defecate or to have diarrhoea, or a 'touch of the earthas'.

(b) Tit(s)

Largely secondary to (a), but a mention in a *Sunday Times* article in 2001 warrants an appearance here.

Earwig   **Twig**

To understand or catch on; to 'earwig' the meaning.

East & South   **Mouth**

Was in use before the 'trap' made a directional change to the now-common 'north & south' (qv).

East & West   **(a) Chest**

Anatomically applied to male or female, either can have a sore 'east & west'.

(b) Vest

Underwear; what's needed to enhance the effect of the sofa-loafing slonch.

East India Docks   **(a) Pox**

Based on one of the old docks of East London, where foreign seamen arrived, met dodgy women, caught the 'east indias' and left, taking their 'souvenirs of London' home with them.

(b) Socks

A pair of 'east indias' – an unwanted Christmas present from years ago.

Easter Bunny   **Money**

The ball-churning dream machine that has made 'If I win the Lottery' a national catchphrase provides us with a multi-million to one chance of having enough 'easter' to never have to waste it on necessities again; a wish called squander, so to speak.

Easter Egg   **Leg**

The seasonal confection, usually in the shops on Boxing Day, is one of several terms making the egg/leg connection.

Easy Rider   **Cider**

Rough or smooth, bottled or draught, it's all been 'easy' since the 1969 film of this name.

Eau de Cologne   **(a) Phone**

A term from the racecourse long known as an 'odour' or 'odie'.

(b) Polone

A gay theatrical's term for a young woman or effeminate man, itself an example of polari, slang based on Italian. In Italy, a polone is a chick.

Eddie Grundies　　　　　**Undies**

A late 20th-century example of underwear based on a character from the long-running BBC Radio 4 programme, *The Archers*.

Edgar Allan Poe　　　　　**Dough (Money)**

A racecourse term based on the American writer (1809–49), whose stories have made a wealth of 'edgar allan' for film-makers since the birth of motion pictures.

Edgar Britt(s)　　　　　**Shit(s)**

A piece from the 1950s based on a flat race jockey of the period that applies to a lavatorial deposit or, in plural form, i.e. 'the edgars' – several.

Edinburgh Fringe　　　　　**Minge**

A 1990s term for the vagina, possibly coined by a participant of the Edinburgh Festival.

Edmundo Ros　　　　　**Boss**

Based on a Trinidad-born bandleader whose Latin American orchestra was seldom off the box in the 1950s and 60s. 'Edmundo' shares a podium with 'joe loss' (qv) in the gaffer stakes.

Edna May　　　　　**Way**

An early 20th-century term based on an American actress and singer of the period (1878–1948), used solely in the context of moving someone on: 'Come on, on your edna'.

Edward Heath　　　　　**(a) Beef**

Jointly known as 'edward' and 'ted heath' (qv). Based on a knighted former Prime Minister (1916–2005), whereby you may snack on a 'corned edward' sandwich or dine on a sirloin of 'sir edward'.

(b) Teeth

This ex-PM was a renowned 'gnasher-flasher' when he laughed as he took us into Europe. The nation has been gnashing its collective teeth ever since.

(c) Thief

An extension of 'ted heath' (qv) for a blagger, shoplifter or petty sneak-thief.

Edwin Drood   **Food**

One of many Dickens' characters to make the list, this from the novel he was writing when he died. Probably a theatrical term coined by a starving actor in need of some edwin'.

Eels & Liquor   **Nicker (£1)**

The liquor involved here is not alcohol but the gravy accompanying stewed eels and sold only in pie-and-eel restaurants. A pound is an 'eels'.

Egg & Spoon   **Coon**

A derogatory term for a black person.

Eggs & Ham   **Exam**

A late 20th-century piece from late 20th-century students.

Eggs & Kippers   **Slippers**

How rivals of the breakfast table became comfortable footwear.

Egon Ronay   **Pony**

An example of secondary slang: a 'pony' is a well-known term for defecation (see also Pony & Trap), so to go for an 'egon' is to visit the lavatory. Based on a famed gastronome who knows all the best places to fill up with 'scran' – and now, it seems, where to dump it.

Egyptian Hall   **Ball (Dance)**

The party's well and truly over for this piece formed on the name of an exhibition hall that stood in London's Piccadilly from 1812 until it was demolished in 1905.

Eiffel Tower   **Shower**

The Parisian landmark becomes a peeping tom's delight, an 'eyeful in the eiffel'.

Eighteen Carat   **Claret**
Although this could apply to fine wine, its main use is to do with blood.

Eighteen Pence   **Sense**
Formed in the days when this was a shilling and six old pence and it bought a couple of pints of beer. A halfwit is said to have 'no eighteen pence'.

Eighty-Six   **(a) Fix**
Underworld term for a murder, often a revenge hit whereby a rival is 'eighty-sixed'.

        (b) Nix (None/Nothing)
A piece from the restaurant trade that was used of a commodity that had run out, i.e., there was none left. Also, if a customer was not to be served he got 'eighty-six'.

Eisenhower   **Shower**
A World War II term based on the US general and later President, Dwight D. Eisenhower (1890–1969). Sometimes watered down to an 'eisen', it applies to ablution and secondarily a rain shower.

Electric Light   **Tight**
Applies to meanness and said of a tightwad: 'He's so electric light, if he found an eye-patch he'd put a bit of dirt in his eye.'

Elephant & Castle   **(a) Arsehole**
The things people have told their fellow human beings to shove up their 'elephants' are enough to make even Jumbo's eyes water! Based on an area of South-East London.

        (b) Parcel
A term from the post office regarding that which should be dropped, if marked 'fragile'.

Elephant's Trunk   **Drunk**
To get 'kaylied' is famously to 'cop an elephant' and has been since the early 20th century. 'Kaynurd' – lagged in backslang.

Eli Wallach(s)   **Bollock(s)**
A testicle or two from the 1960s, based on the American actor

whose character dropped a major 'eli' when he took on the original Magnificent Seven.

Elizabeth Regina   **Vagina**
A piece culled from the theatre, possibly Her Majesty's.

Elky Clark   **Mark**
Applies to a starting point or meeting place: 'Be on the elky at nine'. Based on a Scottish boxer (1898–1956), a British and European flyweight champion of the 1930s.

Ellen Terry   **Jerry**
An archaic piece formed on the name of a Shakespearean actress (1847–1928), who probably deserved better than to be remembered as a chamber pot.

Elsie Tanner   **Spanner**
A 1960s term for a nut-turner formed on the name of a popular character from TV's *Coronation Street*.

Elton John   **Con**
The knighted musician goes on record as any kind of stitch-up, tuck-up or take-on; if you stand for the 'three-card trick', you've been 'eltoned'.

Emma Freuds   **Haemorrhoids**
Known as 'emmas' and as much a pun as RS. Probably something this British TV and radio presenter has had to put up with all her life – I blame the parents.

Emmerdale Farm(s)   **Arm(s)**
Based on the name of a long-running TV soap, and like the programme RS loses the 'farm': 'Alright, if you're twisting my emmerdale I'll have a scotch'.

Engelbert Humperdinck   **Drink**
A mouthful from the 1960s that's reduced to an 'engelbert' or an 'humperdinck', never both. Based on a British chart-topper of the period, who only found fame after switching his name from Gerry Dorsey to that of a 19th-century German composer.

Engineer's Spanner   **Tanner**
Time's up for this old term for sixpence in old money.

Engineers & Stokers   **Brokers**

A 19th-century term for those who come and snatch back goods for which payment has not been kept up.

English Channel   **Panel**

Refers to an old state sickness benefit regulation. People drawing sick pay for more than 13 weeks had to go before a panel of doctors who would decide whether payment could be continued or not.

Enoch Powell   **(a) Towel**

Heard round a Spanish hotel swimming pool: 'This is bloody ridiculous, every sunbed's got an enoch on it.'

(b) Trowel

A 1960s reference to the tool of the bricklaying trade based on the controversial British MP (1912–98).

Epsom Races   **(a) Braces**

A 19th-century term that may be used for as long as men need to hold up their trousers.

(b) Faces

An ancient term for an ancient in-crowd, it would seem.

Ernie Marsh   **Grass**

No narcs or narks involved here, just an old term for nature's carpet. Don't know who old Ernie was, maybe a park's gardener of yore.

Eros & Cupid   **Stupid**

An early 21st-century term from the suburbs, whereby the Greek and Roman love-archers get together to produce a 'wally' or a nonsensical situation.

Errol Flynn   **(a) Bin**

A waste bin, hence to dispose of something is to 'errol it'.

(b) Chin

To 'take it on the errol' is to accept what's coming to you, to take it like a man. Based on the Australian-born film star with a big reputation (1909–59).

Errol Flynns   **Bins**

Originally a racecourse term for binoculars, 'errols' later became spectacles.

Eskimo Nell   **Bell**

Even though telephones no longer ring, people are still inclined to give each other an 'eskimo'. Based on the whore who cut Dead-Eye Dick down to size in 'The Ballad of Eskimo Nell'.

Evening Breeze   **Cheese**

Sometimes carries the prefix 'sweet', which may be a bit ironic if the wind brings forth cheesy aromas.

Evening News   **Bruise**

Often refers to a love-bite, which is usually news from the previous evening. Based on a defunct London newspaper.

Everton Toffee   **Coffee**

People have been percolating pots of 'everton' for well over a century. 'Gum of eefock' – a backslang mug of coffee.

Exchange & Mart   **Tart**

Based on the weekly publication for those wishing to buy or sell anything, this aptly applies to a woman who sells herself and often buys trouble.

Eyeballs In The Sky   **Spy**

Humorous term for someone with a watching brief, such as a security person who watches CCTV. A piece that would work if it wasn't RS and is based on a once-annual feature of the defunct *Daily Mirror* strip cartoon 'The Perishers'.

Eyelash   **Slash (Urinate)**

A threat heard in a nightclub: 'I'm going for an eyelash, don't be here when I get back'.

Eyes Front   **Cunt**

Said at the approach of a despicable shit-cake 'Look out, eyes front!'

Eyes of Blue   **True**

Often said as 'two eyes of blue', signifying complete agreement.

Fag Packet   **(a) Jacket**
Entry into the best places is forbidden without a 'fag' on.
         (b) Racket
Applies in all senses of the word, all of which can be used at Wimbledon. Firstly it's the tennis bat, secondly, it's the exorbitant prices they charge for the traditional strawberries and thirdly, it's the noise people should make about having to pay them.

Fainting Fit(s)   **Tit(s)**
Sounds like those that make men swoon.

Fair Enough   **Puff**
Said as 'fairy nuff' in relation to an homosexual male, but not often these days.

Fairy Story   **Tory**
Always employed in the first element, giving access to many humorous possibilities. 'Vote fairy', for instance, or the leader of a party may be 'King (or Queen) of the Fairies'.

False Alarm   **Arm**
Always used in full, as asking a woman to hold something in her 'falsies' is likely to lead to violence.

Family Tree   **Lavatory**

An old example that's used as: 'I'm just going to water the family tree'.

Fanny Blair   **Hair**

A 19th-century term that may incorporate the pubic variety, it's based on a song from 1890, recounting the true story of Fanny Blair, an 11-year-old girl from Northern Ireland who, in 1785, was the victim of rape. A man called Egan or Hegan was hung for the crime and the song protests his innocence.

Fanny Craddock   **Haddock**

Applies to the fish on a dish and served up by one of the first TV cooks (1909–94).

Fanny Hill   **Pill**

Based on the promiscuous heroine of John Cleland's book, *Memoirs of a Woman of Pleasure*, this chiefly applies to the contraceptive pill.

Far & Near   **Beer**

As ordered at the 'near & far' (qv).

Faraway Place   **Case**

Generally a suitcase and probably coined by a holidaymaker who, on his return to London, found that his luggage was en route to Melbourne or Mexico City, or some other faraway place.

Farmer Giles   **Piles**

This old man of the soil is by far the most common of the many terms that have sprung up for the anal horrors of haemorrhoids. Well-known as 'farmers'.

Farmer's Daughter   **Quarter**

A drug-user's term for a quarter of an ounce of their chosen poison.

Fashoda   **Soda**

Whisky's favourite accompaniment: after an incident at Fashoda, Sudan, in 1898, when a force of Senegalese troops under French command occupied the fort to secure a French presence on the upper Nile. A strong British show of force under General Kitchener, however, caused them to back down.

Fat & Wide Bride

As she may appear on a seaside postcard or can allude to the belle of a shotgun wedding, from the comic version of 'The Wedding March': 'Here comes the Bride, all fat and wide: See how she waddles from side to side'.

Fat Guts Nuts

Refers to the edible kind – especially peanuts when eaten at the bar – and smacks of overindulgence.

Fatboy Slim Gym

Aptish piece from the early 2000s based on the working name of British DJ Norman Cook.

Father O'Flynn Gin

A late 19th-century term based on the title of a popular song of the period. Downed as a 'drop o' father'.

Father Ted Dead

A late 1990s piece based on a TV sitcom: the eponymous hero was played by Dermot Morgan, who sadly died in 1998, aged 45.

Feargal Sharkey Darkie

How a white Irish singer became a derogatory term for a black person.

Feather & Flip Kip

Pertaining to sleep and, by extension, to bed, this has been part of the tramp's lexicon since a couple of pence bought a night's 'feather'.

Feather Plucker Fucker

Only used in a jocular vein, if someone deserved to be called a fucker, words would not be minced.

Feel Fine Nine

A 'feel' is a rare expression for £9. 'Eenin ecnep' – nine pence worth of backslang.

Feet & Yards   **Cards**
Refers to playing cards, whereby 'feet' are cut, shuffled and turned into hands.

Feminist   **Pissed**
Said as 'fem-n-ist' and used solely of a drunken woman; a ladette.

Fiddle-de-Dee   **Pee/Wee**
Normally slashed to a 'fiddly', especially when a button fly is involved.

Fiddlers Three   **Pee/Wee**
Old King Cole's string combo are reduced to playing in the toilet – or occasionally a shop doorway in the middle of the night; always a 'fiddlers'.

Field of Wheat   **Street**
Nice sarcasm here. A dirty, littered, traffic-choked street may be pointed out as a 'nice field o' wheat'.

Fife & Drum   **Bum**
The buttocks. Naughty kids often got a smack on the 'fife' before it became possible to sue the smacker for assault.

Fifteen Two   **Jew**
An example borrowed from the game of cribbage for the 'red sea pedestrian'.

Fighting Fifth   **Syph(ilis)**
An old soldier's term for what was commonly an old sailor's disease.

Figure of Eight   **Plate**
A twice-removed example for oral sex. See also 'Plate of Ham'.

Fillet of Cod   **Sod**
Reduced to the first element as a form of mild admonishment: 'Come 'ere, you little fillet'.

Fillet of Plaice   **Face**
A man in a department store discussing Christmas presents

with his wife was heard to say: 'Why don't we get your mother some wrinkle cream? She's got a fillet like a chewed toffee these days!'

Fillet of Veal   **Steel**
'Steel' is an archaic term for prison and this is an ancient piece of RS.

Filthy Beast   **Priest**
Formed in the late 20th century in light of many reports of child abuse by Catholic clergymen.

Filter Tip(s)   **Lip(s)**
Based on the end of a fag that smokers put between their 'filters'.

Fine & Dandy   **Brandy**
How a medicinal tot is meant to make you feel.

Fingal's Cave   **Grave**
A 'dugout' based on a sea cave on the Scottish island of Staffa, which inspired German composer Felix Mendelsohn (1809–47) to write 'The Hebrides Overture' in 1830. Rumour has it that a church in a small village in Ireland has a sign, which reads: 'Only deceased people living in the village will be buried in this churchyard'.

Finger & Thumb   **(a) Chum**
A person with no 'fingers' has none to count on.

       (b) Drum
Tramp's term for the road, for which 'drum' is an old Romany word.

       (c) Mum
Only used in the third party, you might talk about your 'finger' but you wouldn't call her it.

       (d) Rum
An old, but still current example amongst drinkers of 'nelson's blood'.

Finsbury Park   **Arc (Light)**
An example from the technical side of film-making.

Fire Alarm(s)   **Arm(s)**
A military piece for weapons and a civilian anatomical term.

Fireman's Hose   **Nose**
Always reduced to the first element: 'Don't pick your fireman's, you'll go bandy'.

First Aid   **Blade**
Refers to a knife as wielded by a thug and inspired by what his handiwork will bring about. Less menacingly, can also apply to a razor blade.

First Aid Kit(s)   **Tit(s)**
'First aids' are nature's comforters.

First of May   **Say**
An old term regarding speaking up for oneself, having your 'first o' may'.

Fish & Chip   **Tip**
A 'fish' is a gratuity or piece of information regarding a horse or greyhound.

Fish & Chip(s)   **Lips**
In many cases, when shortened to 'fishes', this is a descriptive example – especially a 'trout pout'.

Fish & Shrimp   **Pimp**
An American piece, 'fish' is now heard here but on a small scale.

Fish & Tank   **Bank**
Underworld term for a likely target.

Fisherman's Daughter   **Water**
Shortened to 'fishermans', this is a 19th-century accompaniment to scotch and may be inspired by the title of a popular song of the period.

Five Acre Farm(s)   **Arm(s)**
Archaic piece long ploughed over.

Five-Star Nap   **Jap**
A World War II term for an enemy of the day based on a newspaper of the day and its top racing tip of the day.

Five To Four   **Sure**
Based on odds short enough to represent a reasonably sure thing. Usually said in disbelief or astonishment: 'Are you five to four about that?'

Five To Two   **Jew**
An odds against term from the racecourse where Jews have long been an integral part of the scene, either as layers or backers.

Five To Twos   **Shoes**
An old example rarely quoted these days.

Flag Unfurled   **World**
Originally applied to a 'man of the world', but now our planet is aptly known as 'the flag'.

Flake of Corn   **Horn (Erection)**
Waking with a 'flake on' could signify breakfast in bed. Or a man may just be 'piss-proud'.

Flanagan & Allen   **Gallon**
Used solely in connection with the measurement in which petrol used to be sold. Now we have to know there are four and a half litres in a 'flanagan' before we can work out how much we are being fleeced. Bud Flanagan (1896–1968) and Chesney Allen (1894–1982) were a British comedy duo, part of The Crazy Gang.

Flash of Light   **Sight**
Anyone who dresses loudly, gaudily or over-the-top has, for a century or so, been seen as a 'right flash o' light'. Now, in reduced form, 'flash' has entered the language as a word in its own right and 'flash gits' are commonplace.

Flea & Louse   **House**
Descriptive of a run-down hovel that makes you feel itchy just to look at it. Such homes were all too common when the term was coined, pre-World War I.

Fleabag   **Nag**
A scruffy old horse once employed by the coalman or rag and bone man.

Fleas & Lice   **Ice**
Worth knowing just to see a barmaid's face when you ask if she has any 'fleas'.

Fleetwood Mac   **Back**
A 1980s term based on an enduring British/US rock band. Main usage is anatomical but you'll always find the tradesman's entrance round the 'fleetwood'.

Florence & Dougal   **Bugle (Nose)**
That which may need blowing, hence 'bugle', which acquired this piece of RS in the 1970s and is based on a couple of characters from the cult children's TV programme *The Magic Roundabout*. So, a lesson for a nipper with a runny nose: 'Don't cuff it, blow your florence'.

Flounder & Dab   **Cab**
Originally applied to a horse-drawn taxi but survived mechanisation so that people still hail a 'flounder'.

Flour Mixer   **Shixa/Shikse**
Example from Jewish cockneys regarding a girl who is not of their religion. 'Goydish' – a gentile who mixes closely with Jews and effects their mannerisms. A hybrid of 'goy', a gentile, and 'yiddish'.

Flower Pot   **(a) Cot**
Where all little seedlings get their heads down.

(b) Hot
Used almost exclusively in terms of a scolding, to 'cop a flower pot' is to 'cop it hot', i.e., to be severely reprimanded.

Flowers & Frolics   **Bollocks**
Irish term for the testicles and also rubbish talk, whereby 'You're talking a load of bollocks' becomes: 'You're talking a bunch of flowers'. 'Scollobs' – backslang tablets.

Flowery Dell   **Cell**
An early 20th-century term for where the prisoner does his time: in a 'flowery'.

Flunkey & Lackey   **Paki**
A 'flunkey' is a derogatory term for a Pakistani.

Fly By Night   **Tight (Drunk)**
A century-old reference to someone who has had a skinful.

Fly By Nights   **Tights**
Known as 'fly bys', an example that flew in when stockings went out as primary legwear, causing dopey bank-robbers to go round in pairs.

Fly My Kite   **Light**
Ancient and lost to the wind: 'got a fly me?' was an old request for a match.

Fly Tipper   **Nipper (Child)**
A term to be used in the first element, whereby: 'How are the flys?' puts kids on the same plane of peskiness as flying insects.

Flying Duck   **Fuck**
Only used in terms of not caring, i.e. when you don't give 'flying duck'.

Flying Trapeze   **Cheese**
Early 20th-century example usually grated down to 'flying' and occasionally, rather off-puttingly, to 'fly-trap'.

Fog & Mist   **Pissed**
The 'well fog & mist' are a step up from being 'as drunk as a lord': they are 'as drunk as the House of Lords'.

Food & Drink   **Stink**
Most commonly used when the stench of someone's dinner has passed through their waste disposal system and escaped noisily from their back-end.

Football Kit(s)   **Tit(s)**

As this is always reduced to 'footballs', it just has to apply to big ones that are fun to play with. 'Football supporters' – brassières.

Foreign Language   **Sandwich**

A 1990s term, which is apt when mortadella and ciabatta or the like are involved.

Fork & Knife   **(a) Life**

Said in full, as in, 'not on your fork'n knife' to sound like something stronger.

(b) Wife

A late 19th-century piece that may be used in the same way as when you 'hope the fork'n knife don't find out', for example. Or she may just be your 'fork'.

Forrest Gump   **Dump**

Defecation 1990s style, when people would 'go for a "forrest"'. Also an unsavoury place or a dive. Based on the title of the Oscar-winning film of 1994.

Forsyte Saga   **Lager**

A 1970s term based on a popular TV serial, a dramatisation of John Galsworthy's novel. Down-in-the-mouth people may be asked: 'What's up? You look like you've lost a 12-year-old malt and found a forsyte'.

Fortnum & Mason   **Basin**

The Piccadilly store lends its name to a receptacle and, more mockingly, to a type of haircut, whereby a 'fortnum' is placed on the head and the protruding 'barnet' lopped off.

Fortune & Fame   **Game**

Applies to prostitution so should be 'on the game' or 'on the fortune'. Some girls may find this fitting, but for the vast majority of working girls it's a hugely ironic piece.

Forty-Four   **Whore**

A prostitute, and probably a successful one if this is her chest size.

Fosdyke Saga   **Lager**

A 1970s alternative to 'forsyte saga' (qv) based on the name of a *Daily Mirror* cartoon series by British writer Bill Tidy. 'Flatch a teenip o' regal' – half a pint of backslang lager.

Four By Two   **Jew**

Generally reduced to 'fourbee' and based on a piece of rag issued to soldiers to clean their rifles.

Four-Poster   **Toaster**

The traditional bed of the honeymoon suite comes in for the ever-popular wedding present.

Four-Wheel Skid   **Yid (Jew)**

A 'four-wheeler' is a less common alternative to 'front-wheeler'. See also Front-Wheel Skid.

Fourpenny Bit   **Hit**

An ancient piece based on an archaic coin that is still heard as a 'fourpenny one'.

Fourth of July   **Tie**

An example brought over here by American soldiers in the 1940s and largely ignored by the British ever since.

Fox & Badger   **Tadger (Penis)**

A piece from the 1990s for a 19th-century slang term for the 'rogering stick', as it was also known.

Fox & Hound   **Round**

A round of drinks, that is: 'Who's up the jump?' (bar) – who's 'fox' is it? Probably based on a pub of this name as riding to hounds never really caught on in the East End.

France & Spain   **Rain**

A late 19th-century term apparently coined by cab drivers of the day. Reduced to 'frarney', it was probably used ironically by dripping drivers as their horse-drawn carriages trundled through the rain-soaked streets of London.

Francis Drakes   **Brakes**

Inspired by the English admiral and navigator (1540–96), who in 1588 put the brakes on the Spanish Armada, ensuring no

Englishman would have to eat paella, fight bulls or wear moustaches like their mother's.

Frank Bough   **Off**

Refers to food, especially milk that's on the turn, whereby rank scoff becomes 'frank bough'. Also used in relation to leaving: when it's time to go, it's time you were 'frank bough'. Based on an English TV and radio presenter of the mid to late 20th century.

Frank Skinner   **Dinner**

An early 21st-century meal gets on the menu as an alternative to the older 'lilley & skinner' (qv) and is served up by an English comedian.

Frank Swift   **Lift**

A 1950s term for an elevator that was heard when the bomb-ravaged streets were cleared to make way for high-rise flats. Based on an England goalkeeper of the period (1914–58).

Frank Zappa   **Crapper (Lavatory)**

The founder member of US rock band Mothers of Invention (1940–93) comes in as the seat of necessity.

Frankie Dettori   **Story**

An early 21st-century lie or excuse based on an Italian jockey riding in Britain since 1984. If you can't think up a believable 'frankie' you might as well tell the truth.

Frankie Durr   **Stir (Prison)**

A 1960s term based on a classic winning British jockey of the period (1925–2000).

Frankie Fraser   **Razor**

Fittingly based on the name of a well-known British villain turned film and TV celebrity noted for his use of the barber's tool as a weapon.

Frankie Howerd   **Coward**

A British comedian (1917–92) lends his name to the type of character he often portrayed on stage, screen and television.

Frankie Laine   Chain

A 1950s term based on the multi-hit-making US singer (1913–2007), it refers to the old-fashioned toilet flusher. Although it has all but disappeared in the modern lavatory, people still tend to 'pull the frankie' as a means of consigning yesterday's dinner to the sewer.

Frankie Vaughan   Prawn

The popular shellfish takes on the name of a favourite British entertainer (1928–99).

Frazer Nash   Slash (Urinate)

A 1930s term based on the name of British car manufacturers of the period, when the nobs had the cars and the working-man didn't have a pot to 'frazer' in.

Fred Astaire   Hair

This differs from the ultra-familiar 'barnet fair' (qv) in that it applies to individual hairs. You wouldn't find a 'barnet' in your dinner but a 'fred'. Based on an American entertainer (1899–1987).

Fred Astaires   Stairs

A 1940s example for what the man famously danced up and down in films. 'Ryats' – backslang climbers.

Fred Perry   Jerry

An old term for a chamber pot and a bit out of order really that the finest male tennis player to come from these shores (1909–95) should end up under the beds of yore. Game, set and match on this one now, methinks.

French Kiss   Piss

Always said in full, going for a 'french kiss' is one of the many ways in RS to go for a 'oui, oui'. Sorry!

French Loaf   Rofe (Four)

A piece of secondary slang from the racecourse, 'Rofe' is an example of backslang.

Friar Tuck   (a) Fuck

Can be used in most senses of the word; those who don't care 'couldn't give a friar' and the bemused may wonder 'What the friar tuck is going on' but most commonly it is used in connection with the sex act. Prostitutes in the old East End of London would proposition potential clients with: 'D'you wanna friar tuck?' To which the stock answer was: 'I'd sooner fry a sausage'.

(b) Luck

In the 1950s TV series *Robin Hood*, the Sheriff of Nottingham was often left cursing his 'friar tuck' when the merry men of Sherwood escaped his clutches once again. Hurrah!

Fridge Freezer   **Geezer**

An early 21st-century piece of youthspeak heard when spoken of a Chelsea supporter: 'A fridge from the bridge'. Stamford Bridge being the home of Chelsea FC.

Fried Bread   **Dead**

One of several terms linking the staff of life with death.

Fried Egg   **Leg**

Eggs and legs get linked a lot in RS; this one was heard recently at the Homerton hospital, East London, when a young man on a mobile was reporting that his mate had broken his 'fried egg' in a car crash.

Frock & Frill   **(a) Chill**

A late 19th-century term for a cold, now well out of fashion. Was once also used in the form of illness in general: Victorians weren't very well when they were 'frock & frill' – ill.

(b) Ill. See (a).

Frog & Feather   **Leather**

A pickpocket's term for a wallet. Known as a 'frog', this is one form of pond life being the jargon of another.

Frog & Toad   **Road**

One of the best-known terms of RS, cockneys have been crossing the 'frog' since the days of horse-drawn traffic jams.

Frog in the Throat   **Boat**

A World War I example coughed up and spat into obscurity before World War II.

Frog Spawn   **Horn**
An erection, of course: a case of 'frog spawn' resulting in sprogs born. A 'frog on' for short, or not so short, as the case may be.

Fruit & Nut   **Cut**
Applies to an injury, a knife will inflict a nasty 'fruit & nut'.

Front-Wheel Skid   **Yid**
Whereby a child of Israel is known as a 'front-wheeler' and has been since the early days of motoring.

Frying Pan   **(a) Fan**
Most artistes have their admirers or 'frying pans'. Apparently there's a young lady in America who is a fan of *Cockney Rabbit*. Hi Gillian. You're a million, Gillian. Maybe even a billion. Oh what the heck! You're a trillion, Gillian.
(b) Hand
An old reference to the 'grabs' and it matters not about the 'd' – it isn't sounded anyway.
(c) Man
Usually the 'old frying pan', meaning a husband or father. 'The delo nam' – the old man – a backslang husband or father.

Full Moon   **Loon**
Appropriate term for anyone given to acting crazily. The connection between lunacy and the moon is plain to see.

Fun & Frolics   **Bollocks**
Originally an Irish term for the testicles and since many people speak fluent bollocks, one of their more outrageous statements may necessitate the reply: 'What a load of fun you do talk'. 'Kaycolobs' – backslang for tabs.

Funny Face(s)   **Lace(s)**
A juvenile piece applying to boot or shoelaces especially when undone: kids are told to 'be careful you don't trip on your funny face'.

Funny Feeling   **Ceiling**
Fitting when you've had a few and the 'lid' won't stop spinning.

Fusilier   **Beer**

An old piece regarding 'sloshery' that's based on an old soldier who still appears to be on parade.

Fusilier(s)   **Ear(s)**

One of several terms for the 'spectacle hangers'.

Gadaffi NAAFI

An example of military slang from the early 21st century when British troops were active in Iraq. The NAAFI (Navy, Army and Air Force Institutes) is a shop or canteen used by military personnel. The term is formed from the name of Libyan leader Colonel Muammar Gaddafi.

Gamble & Proctor Doctor

Loosely based on the pharmaceutical company Proctor & Gamble, which is loosely connected with healthcare. 'Rotcod On' – a backslang Bond villain.

Game of Nap (a) Cap

Based on a card game and refers to the old type of cap rather than the ubiquitous baseball variety which seems to be taking over the world.

(b) Crap

Alternative to the much more common 'pony & trap' (qv), but only in a sense of defecation and unlike 'pony', this is always used in full. When there's 'a dog in trap one and the hare's running', you badly need a 'game o' nap'.

Gammon Rasher Smasher

Anything marvellous or smashing: be careful when using it in connection with a woman, though – she may think you're calling her a pig.

Garden Gate   **(a) Eight**

As well as a bingo term a 'garden' is a reference to £8. 'Theg eelims' – eight miles backslang.

                  (b) Magistrate

An old piece, but lawbreakers still go before the 'garden'.

                  (c) Mate

This rare alternative to 'china plate' (qv) was more common in the Merchant Navy as a reference to the first officer.

Garden Gate   **Plate**

An example of secondary slang for fellatio – see also 'plate of ham' for explanation.

Garden Gates   **Rates**

An old term for the local taxes in place before firstly, the Poll Tax of 1990 and later, the Council Tax became the local government charges.

Garden Gnome   **Comb**

There are many connections in slang between a head of hair and a garden. Hair is 'grass', scissors are 'shears' and a comb is a 'rake' as well as a 'garden'.

Garden Hop   **Shop (Inform On)**

An early 20th-century term from the underworld relating to betrayal.

Garden Hose   **Nose**

Apt if the said honker is long or dripping.

Garden Path   **Bath**

Only too common to be in the 'garden' when the phone or doorbell rings.

Garden Plant   **Aunt**

Generally used in the third person when speaking of a 'garden and carbuncle' (qv).

Garden Shed   **Red**

The red ball in a game of pool: if you are 'gardens', your opponent is 'cinderellas' (qv).

Gareth Hunt   **Cunt**

Another branch of the Hunt family tree gets to make a rhyme for a fool or a wrong'un. Based on a British actor (1943–2007).

Garibaldi Biscuit   **Risk It**

To 'do a garibaldi' is to take a chance.

Gary Ablett   **Tablet**

A 1990s term from the world of young drug-takers. Based on a footballer of the period, who made his name kicking a 'pill' about for Liverpool FC, or an Australian Rules Footballer of the same name, as suggested by the 2006 Partridge dictionary of slang.

Gary Glitter   **(a) Bitter**

Beer: a piece that went down the drain along with this British pop singer's career after being convicted of paedophilia.

(b) Shitter

The anus, that is – and apt in that his first hit was a song called 'rock and roll'. See also Rock'n'Roll (b).

Gary Lineker   **Vinegar**

People were actually sprinkling 'gary' on their chips long before the former England footballer's 'Salt & Lineker' crisp adverts appeared on TV in the late 1990s.

Gasp & Grunt   **Cunt**

An uncommon variant of 'grumble & grunt' (qv) and also a low, despicable person; a 'spunkdrinker' or someone equally base.

Gates of Heaven   **Seven**

A 1950s term from the bingo hall. 'Nevis to rofe' – backslang odds of 7/4

Gates of Rome   **Home**

Be it ever so humble, there's no place like your 'gates'.

Gavel & Wig   **Twig**

To 'twig' is to scratch an itchy anus and is crudely based on a Twiglet, a savoury snack, the inference being that it resembles a faecal-stained finger after a 'good old scratch' or 'gavel'.

Gay & Frisky   **Whisky**

An old term for a long-serving member of the top-shelf fraternity.

Gay & Hearty   **Party**

An old-fashioned piece from the time when 'gay' meant happy and aptly described a 'knees-up'.

Gay Gordon   **Traffic Warden**

Based on the name of the dance that you would like to do on the grave of the one who gave you that ticket.

General Booth   **Tooth**

Based on William Booth (1829–1912), the founder of the Salvation Army, the term is a bit long in the 'general' and from common use has probably suffered an extraction.

General Election   **Erection**

Polite allusion to a standing member. 'Drach-no' – a backslang hard-on.

General Smuts   **Nuts (Testicles)**

Reduced to 'generals', probably to signify their importance. Formed on the name and rank of a Boer War officer and later Prime Minister of South Africa, Jan Smuts (1870–1950).

Geoff Hoon   **Buffoon**

A Labour politician, former Secretary of State for Defence and Minister for Europe gets the RS treatment as a fool, someone thought to be as useful as a second-hand stamp. Largely seen as inadequate by the popular press, one newspaper labelled him 'Buff-Hoon' and it stuck. Hence the inclusion here.

Geoff Hurst   **(a) First**

England's World Cup hero of 1966 becomes a first-class honours degree at university.

      (b) Thirst

Those gagging for a drink may claim to have a raging 'geoff hurst'. The ex-Hammer was knighted in 1998.

Geoffrey Chaucer   **Saucer**

No UFOs involved here, never heard of a 'flying geoffrey' so its use is solely restricted to what the unrefined drink their over-hot tea from. Wonder what the father of English poetry (1342–1400) would make of his inclusion?

George & Ringo **Bingo**
Occasionally heard during the heydays of the game and The Beatles. George Harrison (1943–2001) and Ringo Starr are the group members involved.

George & Zippy **Nippy**
Based on a pair of TV puppets from the 1970s, this relates to cold weather and is not descriptive of Japan. Shortened in perishing conditions to 'georgian' (george 'n').

George Bernard Shaw **Door**
Putting the wood in the hole is reduced to closing the 'george bernard' and is based on the Irish writer (1856–1950). 'Texan rood' – next door (backslang).

George Blake **Snake**
Not so much the reptile as a slippery, untrustworthy dodgepot such as this British traitor, a Soviet spy during the Cold War of the 1950s.

George Bohee **Tea**
A late 19th-century term for the cup that cheers based on a Canadian-born minstrel who, with his brother James, played the British music halls as the Bohee Brothers. They sang, danced and played the banjo.

George Bush **Moosh (Face)**
A 2000s example, so probably based on American president George Dubya rather than Bush senior. Defeat or rejection is a slap in the 'george'. And: 'Look at the george bush on that poor sod!' means an ugly person is under scrutiny.

George Melly **Belly**
A British jazz singer and art critic (1926–2007) comes in as a paunch or beer-gut.

George Michael **Cycle**
An example of popney from the 1990s based on a British singer-songwriter; a piece which may have become apt in 2007 when he was banned for driving for two years and had to have it on his bike.

George Raft (a) **Draft**
A piece from the used car trade to describe a banker's draft. Based on an American film actor (1895–1980).

(b) **Draught 1**
A waft of cold air; gaps under doors call for 'george' excluders.

Draught 2
Draught beer whereby Guinness may come in bottles, cans or on 'george raft'.

(c) **Graft**
A reference to hard work, but given the man's well-known underworld connections it could also apply to corruption.

George Robey **Toby**
Based on the English comedian billed as the 'Prime Minister of Mirth' (1869–1954), this originally applied to a road, for which 'toby' is an old slang term. Later it was more commonly used when ordering this brand of beer.

George the Third **Turd**
Applies to that reeking piece of gunge on the pavement that you didn't see, otherwise you wouldn't have stepped in it. King George III (1738–1820) reigned from 1760. 'Aero' – a floating turd, one that won't flush away.

Georgie Best (a) **Guest**
A piece from the suburbs used in an invitational sense: 'D'you mind if I sit here?' 'Be my georgie best'.

(b) **Pest**
Based on the legendary Irish footballer and drinker (1946–2005), this applies to the drunken pest who won't leave you alone when your one desire is to be on your tod.

(c) **Vest**
How an undergarment became a 'georgie'.

Germaine Greer **Beer**
One of many terms that have emanated from the suburbs in recent years, this one based on an Australian feminist and journalist. Can't say I've ever heard it used, though.

German Band(s) **Hand(s)**
An early 20th-century piece that is always reduced to

'germans' and inspired by the fact that such musicians were a common feature in London parks at the time. 'German job' – masturbation.

German Flute(s)   Boot(s)

A 19th-century example from the woodwind section that's been 'given the air' (i.e. blown out).

Gerry Cottle   Bottle

A container but mostly a reference to courage; based on the name of a circus owner, which is apt considering the 'gerry' needed to perform most circus stunts. See also 'Bottle & Glass'. 'Eltob o' rageniv' – a backslang bottle of vinegar.

Gert & Daisy   Lazy

Based on the comic stage personas of music-hall and variety artistes Elsie (1894–1990) and Doris (1904–78) Waters, this is used as a direct attack on a layabout, a sofa-loafer who would know what sloth meant if he wasn't too 'gert & daisy' to look it up.

Gertie Gitana   Banana

An early 20th-century example based on the British music-hall turn (1888–1957), who gave the song 'Nellie Dean' to the world and in turn to the drunk's repertoire. 'Ananab' – a backslang nana.

Gianfranco Zola   Cola

Pepsi, Coke or whatever passes for cola in a pub takes the name of an Italian footballer, a star player at Chelsea FC, c.2000, and manager of West Ham in 2008.

Gianluca Vialli   Charlie (Cocaine)

A late 1990s term based on an Italian footballer who played for, and later managed Chelsea FC. As a player he spent most of his career getting up the noses of opposing defenders.

Giggle & Titter   Bitter (Ale)

Once commonly known as 'giggle' and apt because it gets you merry.

Gilbey's Gin   **Chin**
This brand of gin is an example from boxing circles – you don't
get anywhere if you can't take one on the 'gilbeys'.

Gillie Potter   **Trotter**
A British comedian (1887–1975) lends his name to a term for
a foot that steps back about 400 years. A 'gillie' was also a
pig's trotter sold as food.

Ginger Ale   **Gaol**
A piece originally from the US, therefore an American 'ginger ale'.

Ginger Beer   **(a) Queer**
In the cut-down form of 'ginger', this has had a wide usage
since the days when homosexuality was illegal, and was mainly
derogatory.

                                             (b) Engineer
A piece from the navy used to describe the seaman who makes
the boat go.

Ginger Pop   **Cop**
A police officer – and generally arrested at the first element. In
the late 19th century the term made a rhyme with the
backslang version of a rozzer: 'slop' or 'eslop' – police. It helps
to get this one if you read the 'ice' in 'police' as an 's'.

Giorgio Armani   **Sarnie (Sandwich)**
A piece in vogue in the 1990s and based on the name of an
Italian fashion designer who strives to be in fashion all the time.

Giraffe   **Laugh**
What to do in response to a tall story? 'Giraffe' it off.

Girl & Boy   **(a) Saveloy**
An early piece for an early take-away that seems to have
disappeared with the once-common 'sav and peace pudding'
stalls.

                                             (b) Toy
A fitting piece if the girl and boy are under seven – after that
toys give way to mobile phones, computers and designer
wear. Past twelve it's condoms and pregnancy-testing kits.

Girls & Boys   **Noise**

An appropriate example given the synonymity of the word and the term.

Give & Get   **Bet**

The origin of this speaks for itself. You give the bookie your money and if you're lucky, you get your winnings. A more common scenario, however, is you give him your money and he gets to keep it.

Give & Take   **Cake**

A stale piece from the 19th century.

Gladiator   **Potato**

A rhyme from around the turn of the millennium when an Oscar-winning film of this title hit the screens and 'double pie and gladiators' was an overheard order in a Poplar pie and mash shop.'Ottatop' – a backslang potato, or more commonly 'rutat'/'reetat' – tater.

Gladys Knight   **Shite**

An American soul singer provides us with a term for both excrement and rubbish. To go for a 'gladys' is to defecate and tall storytellers may talk a load of it! Both at the same time if the bullshitter takes his mobile in the carsey with him.

Glasgow Boat   **Coat**

To be worn when the wind whistles round the Clydebank shipyards.

Glasgow Ranger   **Stranger**

Shortened to 'glasgow' by look-outs keeping an eye out for the police during illegal activities.

Glass Case   **Face**

Heard at the end of an over-40s or Grab a Granny do: 'I didn't realise how old she was till the lights came on. Her glass case was like a piece of second-hand chewing gum'.

Glass of Beer   **Ear**

Good advice often comes with 'a word in your glass o' beer'. 'Deerow in your ree' – a backslang word in your ear.

Glass of Plonk   **Conk (Nose)**
Generally a large vintage red and the result of an over-bending of the elbow.

Glenn Hoddle   **Doddle**
A simple task, courtesy of a former England footballer of whom sportswriters never seemed to tire of the headline: 'A Doddle for Hoddle'.

Glenn Roeder   **Soda**
Heard for a while when this ex-footballer became manager of West Ham United FC. Some whisky-drinkers took their tipple with a dash of 'glenn roeder'.

Gloria Gaynors   **Trainers**
Footwear, thanks to the American singer known as the Queen of Disco whose music went straight to the feet of drunken revellers in the 1970s.

Glorious Sinner   **Dinner**
A mid 19th-century piece that seems to have purported that only the decadent got to eat.

Glory Be   **Tea**
An example occasionally brewed as the drink that warms the cockles, but also doubles as the evening meal. Playing kids were called in off the street when their 'glory be' was on the table.

Glue Pot   **Twat (Vagina)**
The touching of which results in a sticky finger.

Gobstopper   **Chopper (Penis)**
Often used in connection with oral sex: 'Suck it and see if it changes colour'. Based on a sweet that does when you do.

God Almighty   **Nightie**
Probably one of those sexy, not-to-be-slept-in jobs that get men drooling and taking the Lord's name in vain.

God Damn   **Jam**
Has been spread on 'holy ghost' since the Lord knows when.

God Forbid   **(a) Kid**

Coined in the days when the method of birth control was often the prayer: 'God forbid we have another god forbid'. On the whole it wasn't a very successful method.

(b) Lid (Hat)

A seldom-worn piece although it has been used in connection with a crash helmet (skid-lid). The inference seems to be 'God forbid I ever need it'.

(c) Quid (£1)

Coined in the days when your 'god forbid' was made of paper.

(d) Yid (Jew)

An obvious piece since this expression is as much a part of Jewish tradition as matzos, salt beef and the Ten Commandments.

God in Heaven   **Seven**

An old example from the bingo hall, also said as: 'God's in Heaven'.

God Love Her   **Mother**

A piece used in the third person when talking about your 'gawd luvver'.

God Save the Queens   **Greens**

Jocular reference to green vegetables and used in full when trying to get the kids to eat them. 'Neergs' – backslang greens.

Goddess Diana   **Tanner**

If this old coin was still with us, no doubt it would have been renamed 'princess diana'. A tanner was six old pence and therefore the Roman Goddess of the Hunt has become a piece of redundant RS.

Godfrey Winn   **Gin**

A 1960s example based on a British actor, journalist and novelist (1906–71). A less than rugged character, he was often on TV, and whilst men had a pint at the pub, women would have a drop of 'godfrey'.

Gold Ring   **King**

At the moment this applies to the playing card, but a piece of RS patiently awaits our next male monarch.

Gold Watch   **Scotch**
Presently the most common term for whisky and one never said in short.

Golden Gate   **Eight**
A late 20th-century term from the City of London that chiefly relates to £800.

Golden Hind   **Blind**
Said sympathetically: 'Bad eyes? She's almost golden hind, poor cow'. Inspired by the name of the ship in which Francis Drake plundered the Spanish treasure ships whilst sailing round the world in 1579–80.

Goldie Hawn   **Prawn**
A 1990s update of the older 'frankie vaughan' (qv) and based on an American film actress. 'Goldies' still form part of the traditional bar snack laid on by publicans on Sunday lunchtimes, even if they are no longer 'frankies'.

Goldilocks   **Pox**
One of many references to VD, this is the type that may be caught through sharing a bed with a bear or three.

Golliwog   **Dog**
Applies to all mutts but mainly to greyhounds, whereby to go dog racing is to go to the 'gollies'.

Gollywog(gy)   **Fog(gy)**
When you can't see your hand in front of your face you've either got your eyes closed or it's 'bloody golly'.

Gone to Bed   **Dead**
Sadly stated: 'Old Steve's gone to bed and he ain't getting up'.

Gonzo the Great   **State**
To be in a bad way, a state of panic, agitation, drunkenness, etc., is to be in a right 'gonzo'. A 1990s term based on a character from TV's *The Muppet Show*.

Good & Bad   **Dad**
Old term for the old man.

Good Ship Venus   Penis

Based on the title of a well-known rugby song, it's a ship to go down on.

Goodie & Baddie   Paddy

Reduced to a 'goodie' in reference to an Irish person, even if they are a baddie.

Goodnight Kiss   Piss

Another of many terms rhyming kiss and piss, this will be the last one before retiring for the night, presumably.

Goose & Duck   Fuck

A brace of wildfowl come in for sexual intercourse but it's the first one that gets all the attention and it's always a 'goose'. Gossip columns are all about who's 'goosing' who and those in a hopeless situation may be 'goose & ducked'.

Gooseberry Pudden   Woman

Used as the 'old gooseberry' meaning the wife. Not a great rhyme but it's too old to care about. 'Delo namow' – a backslang old woman.

Gooseberry Tart   (a) Fart

Similar to the dropping of an apple tart: same pastry, different filling…and possibly a different aroma.

      (b) Heart

One of several desserts making the pump connection.

Goose's Neck   Cheque

Always reduced to the first element, a duff cheque is a 'rubber goose's' – it bounces.

Gordon & Gotch   Watch

Always stopped at a 'gordon', this is based on a small firm from East London which dealt in books and magazines before getting into computers and moving to a City address.

Gordon Brown   Clown

A piece of satire from 2008 based on the Prime Minister of the day. Many political pundits would consider it apt.

Gorillas in the Mist   **Pissed**
A late 20th-century piece based on a 1988 film of this title. You're well 'gorillas' when you see pink elephants in the Red Lion.

Gospel Oak   **Joke**
From an area of North-West London comes an example that's about as likely to be heard as a joke on *EastEnders*.

Got Out of Pawn   **Born**
A mid 20th-century term that can be used when refuting gullibility: 'What d'you think, I've just been got out of pawn?'

Graeme Hick   **Dick/Prick**
The penis. Man's middle stump, aptly provided by an England test cricketer of the 1990s.

Graham Gooch   **Hooch**
An Essex and England cricket captain of the 1970s–90s gets the treatment as a brand of alcoholic drink much-loved by the young, drink-from-the-bottle brigade, who coined the term in the 90s.

Grand Coulee Dam   **Ham**
Probably unheard for forty-odd years, but when this title formed a Top Ten hit for Lonnie Donegan in 1958, a 'grand coulee' sandwich was popular in some quarters. The Grand Coulee Dam crosses the Columbia River in America's Washington State.

Grandfather Clock   **Cock**
If a cleaner offers to polish your 'grandfather clock', let her!

Granite Boulder(s)   **Shoulder(s)**
Rock-solid, dependable 'granites' are just what's needed when burdens and troubles need bearing.

Grannie Grunt   **Cunt**
No anatomical usage here, it's someone who is annoyingly sensible or old womanish. The Sunday driver with the three-mile queue of traffic behind him, for instance, is a typical 'grannie'. Not sure who the old girl was, but she's been around a long time.

Grannie's Wrinkle **Winkle**
The seafood; part of the traditional cockney Sunday tea is known as a 'grannies'.

Grapevine **Line**
The major employment here is a clothesline – never heard of a drowning person being thrown a 'grape'.

Grass in the Park **Nark**
An informer; an extension of 'grasshopper' (qv) as the police are also called the 'narks'.

Grasshopper **Copper**
So familiar is the shortened version, 'grass', that it has passed into everyday English for an informant or anyone who 'turns copper'. Still applies to a police officer but very much secondarily. 'Grass stained' – a victim of an informant. 'Whispering grass' – someone who has a quiet word or speaks 'behind the hand' to land someone in trouble.

Grave-digger **Nigger**
Grave-diggers is an old term for the card suit spades and a spade is also a black person hence the connection. A derogatory piece.

Gravel & Grit **Shit**
Always reduced to the first element, whereby the constipated are in dire need of a 'gravel' – and the lumbered are landed in it.

Greengage **Stage**
A theatrical expression for the boards that are trodden: The Greengage – the showbusiness trade paper, *The Stage*.

Greengages **Wages**
A 19th-century term for a weekly pay packet, usually shortened to 'greens'.

Greens & Brussels **Muscles**
Apt since we are told from an early age that green vegetables make us big and strong. 'Beer Muscles' – courage in drink.

Gregory Peck **(a) Cheque**
An example well-known amongst the criminal fraternity, who want cash in hand and no 'gregorys'.
(b) Neck
Based on an American actor (1916–2003), this has acquired a wide usage. A nuisance is a 'pain in the gregory'.

Gregory Pecks **Kecks (Trousers)**
Scousers have been wearing kecks for years, but now they wear 'gregorys'.

Greville Starkey **Darkie**
This British ex-jockey is a derogatory reference to a black person.

Grey Mare **Fare**
An example from the days of the horse-drawn cab that's still on the road.

Grimsby Docks **Socks**
Given this town's connection with the fishing industry, this just has to apply to socks that cover kipper feet or ones that reek of dead haddock.

Groan & Grunt **Cunt**
A 'groan' is a despicable, low person; a 'wankstain of a nonce' – and you can't get any lower than that. Also, a rare alternative to 'grumble & grunt' (qv).

Grocer's Shop **Wop (Italian)**
A 'grocer's' is a 1970s term that now seems to be closed. A derogatory example that won't be missed.

Grosvenor Squares **Flares**
Often used condescendingly by the young when they see anybody wearing this wide-bottomed legwear, whether on a die-hard hippy or in their parents' wedding photos. Always 'grosvenors', after the London address of the US Embassy.

Groucho Marx **Sparks**
From the 1960s, a building site worker's reference to an electrician. Repeated showings on TV of Marx Brothers' films resulted in a cult status for Groucho (1890–1977) and his siblings.

Growl & Grunt   **Cunt**
Used anatomically of the vagina in the guise of a 'growler'.

Gruesome & Gory   **Cory (Penis)**
Always a 'gruesome' and inspired by the old 'Touch it again, it's gruesome more' joke. Cory comes from the Romany word 'kori' meaning a thorn, therefore a prick.

Grumble & Grunt   **Cunt**
In the reduced form of 'grumble' this applies to women as sex objects. Men go out to 'pull a bit of grumble'.

Grumble & Mutter   **Flutter (Bet)**
Inspired by what the losing punter does all the way home from the betting shop – or wherever else he's 'dropped his conkers' – done his money.

Guillemot   **Twat**
The seabird swoops in as an expression for a fool, often in the guise of a 'gilly'. This is the useless individual who is thought to be a waste of rations.

Guinea Pig   **Wig**
A mocking piece heard at the sight of the ghastly gagga that resembles a small furry animal: 'Cop the geezer with the guinea pig on his head'.

Gunga Din   **Chin**
Based on a character of Rudyard Kipling's creation, whereby the upper-class chinless wonder type is said to have 'got no gunga'.

Gunpowder Plot   **Hot**
Possibly from standing too close to a bonfire on 5 November, but not one of those virtual reality jobs.

Gus Dalrymple   **Pimple**
A long-forgotten piece from the 1960s based on a columnist from *The Sporting Life*, a defunct horse-racing journal. The term was peculiar to betting shops and spotty counter hands.

Guy Fawke   **Walk**
A 19th-century term and one most commonly connected with an easy victory, especially of a horse or greyhound: 'The

favourite guyed it'. Based on 16th-century terrorist and gunpowder plotter Guy Fawkes (1570–1606).

Guzunter   **Punter**
An old expression for the bookie's bread and butter. The term is a variation of 'guzunder', a chamber pot, that which 'guzunder' the bed. Fitting then, as bookmakers like nothing more than a losing punter, one whose bet goes under – loses.

Gypsy Rose Lee   **Tea**
A piece from the theatre formed on the stage name of Rose Louise Hovick (1911–70), an American striptease artiste. The term dates from the 1960s and seems to have followed in the wake of the film *Gypsy* (1962), which is based on her life. It seems some performers liked a drop of 'gypsy rose' in their whisky.

Gypsy's Kiss   **Piss**
A mid 20th-century example, since when it's been common for men to leave their beers for a 'gypsy's'.

Gypsy's Warning   **Morning**
Generally halved to the first element: 'See you in the gypsy's'. A gypsy's warning is an old slang term for no warning at all.

Hackney Marsh(es)   **Glass(es)**

A 19th-century term for a drinking vessel, but newer in relation to spectacles or binoculars, it's based on that part of East London where generations of footballers have turned out for their pub teams of a Sunday morning.

Hackney Wick   **Prick (Penis)**

Given Hackney's location in East London, it's a puzzle as to why this is of secondary usage to the widely-used 'hampton wick' (qv). 'Kaykirp'/'kirp' – backslang plonkers. The stadium has now been demolished as part of the Olympic site.

Haddock & Bloater   **Motor (Car)**

An example from the time before King Car ruled and only the nobs had 'haddocks'.

Haddock & Cod   **Sod**

Always reduced to the first of this finny duo and used as a mild expletive. A cheeky child may be a 'saucy little haddock'.

Hail & Rain   **Train**

An early 20th-century piece that seems to have run out of track. 'Nyart' – a backslang train.

Haircut & Shave   **Grave**

Heard in the moan of a harassed father whose wayward son was bent on sending him to an 'early haircut'. Also to paraphrase the saying: 'There will be two dates on your haircut, but all that matters is the little dash between them'.

Hairy Ape   **Rape**
Piece from the pen of a 1990s TV writer that demeans apes.

Hale & Hearty   **Party**
A post-war knees-up or backslang 'wytrap'.

Hale & Pace   **Face**
A 1990s term based on British comedy double act Gareth Hale and Norman Pace, whereby a miserable person may have a 'hale & pace like a squeezed orange'.

Half-a-Crown   **Brown**
Heard in a snooker hall regarding this colour ball. Half-a-crown was a pre-decimal coin worth twelve and a half pence.

Half-a-Dollar   **Collar**
Most likely to be heard these days in connection with a dog's collar, but not often. 'Half-a-dollar' was the same sum of money as the previous entry.

Half-a-Gross   **Dose (VD)**
How a dose of the clap became an 'arfa'.

Half-a-Nicker   **Vicar**
Shortened to 'arfa', this is an irreverent reference to His Reverence. Half a nicker is 50p.

Half-Inch   **Pinch**
This early 20th-century piece never gets shortened. Goods and money may get 'half-inched', as may the thief if the police get hold of him – but probably not these days.

Half of Marge   **Sarge**
Underworld reference to one who leaves a nasty taste in the mouth of the criminal: a police sergeant.

Half-Ounce   **(a) Bounce (Beat Up)**
May you never find out how many 'half-ounces' there are in a pounding.

         (b) Bounce (Cheat)
Anyone gullible enough to try to find the lady in a three-card-trick deserves to be 'half-ounced'.

Half-Ouncer **Bouncer**
A doorman; a professional chucker-outer. An overheard conversation: 'A cousin of mine has just taken over a club that was such a dump, they had a 'half-ouncer chucking people *in*'.

Half-Ounce of Baccy **Paki**
A variant of 'ounce of baccy' (qv) and reduced to 'half-ounce', often in relation to a Pakistani child. Used derogatorily.

Half Past Two **Jew**
One of many terms culminating in two for the chosen one.

Half-Stamp **Tramp**
An early 20th-century term possibly based on a slow walk, a stamp being slang for a walk. 'Peemart' – a backslang dosser.

Ha'penny Dip **(a) Kip (Sleep)**
Based on an old East End custom whereby shopkeepers would, in the 1930s–40s provide a ha'penny bran tub or lucky dip. Forty snoozewinks was known as a 'short ha'penny' or an 'ha'porth o' kip'. A 'ha'penny' was a halfpenny coin.
(b) Ship
A piece that was common amongst London's dockworkers when dockers were common in London.

Ha'penny Stamp **Tramp**
Short-changed to 'ha'penny' and symbolic of the down and out's financial state.

Ham & Beef **Chief**
A 19-century prisoner's reference to a chief warder.

Ham & Egg(s) **Leg(s)**
Usually employed in relation to shapely female pins. Women with thick, unshapely 'hams' may acquire the unfortunate nickname 'Annie Oaklegs', a pun on Annie Oakley (1859–1926), the American sharpshooter.

Ham Shank **(a) Wank**
A 1990s term for 'rubbing up the right way' – masturbation; also, anything of little value isn't worth a 'hamshank'.

(b) Yank

A World War II term for an American that's still quite common: 'Ham shanks? My favourite meat,' said a London taxi driver (whilst rubbing his hands together hard enough to start a small fire).

Hambone   **Phone**

Occasionally used, but by and large is gobbled up by the 'dog'. See 'Dog & Bone'.

Hammer & Discus   **Whiskers**

Facial hair – probaby as grown by Eastern Europeans of yore who swept the board in chucking-heavy-objects-great-distances events. The men were pretty good too.

Hammer & File   **Style**

An example from World War II, when a slick, smart or smooth operator was said to have 'had some hammer'.

Hammer & Nail   **Tail**

Normally reduced to the first element, it means to follow. Show me someone driving at 30mph and I'll show you someone who's being 'hammered' by the police. A dog may also wag its 'hammer'.

Hammer & Saw   **Law**

Everyone should respect the law…but the police have to earn it.

Hammer & Tack   **Back**

Once common on building sites, when a foreman wanted the navvies to put their 'hammers' into it.

Hampden Roar   **Score**

Based on the noise made by Scottish football fans at Hampden Park, a 'hampden' is generally £20, but it also applies to a result or state of play: 'What's the hampden at Chelsea?' An 'eerocs' is £20 of backslang.

Hampstead Heath   **Teeth**

A 19th-century example still going strong in the reduced forms of 'hampsteads' or 'hamps'. Based on an area of North London.

'Shampsteads' – false teeth. Topsy-turvy backslang turns teeth into 'theet' – said as 'feet' – and feet into 'teef'.

Hampton Court   Salt

It's not only the women in porn movies who pass the 'hampton'. See also 'Hampton Wick'. Based on the royal palace in Middlesex.

Hampton Wick   Prick (Penis)

A well-established piece and one that is unusual in that it can be reduced to both elements. The male member is commonly termed 'hampton' and many a comedy sketch has included a character named Hugh Jampton. The second part is equally familiar – when a man has sex, he 'dips his wick' and few people realise what 'you get on my wick' means.

Hamshanker   Wanker

A useless or valueless person. Over the years West Ham United have had many such players and the fans haven't been slow to point them out. They have also had some great players, but never 11 at the same time.

Hand & Fist   Pissed

A piece that's never shortened, if your 'back teeth are floating' you're 'hand & fist'.

Hand Over Fist   Pissed

An extension of the previous entry that sees the stupefied drunk as 'well hand over'. Probably from the way he crawls home.

Handicap   Clap (VD)

A pertinent example since a 'handicap' makes you a non-runner in the sex stakes and there'll be no 'testing the oil level' (inserting the dipstick) for the duration.

Handicap Chase   Face

Usually employed at the sight of a custard-curdling geseech, or face: 'Nice bloke? Well, he'd have to be with an handicap like that – he'd have to have something going for him.'

Handley Page   Stage

An old theatrical piece for the theatrical boards, based on Sir

Frederick Handley Page (1885–1962), the pioneering British aircraft designer.

Hands & Feet　　　　　**Meat**
A vegetarian's nightmare: a plate of 'hands'.

Hangar Lane　　　　　**Pain**
This is pain in the sense of being a nuisance or annoyance and is a diminutive of pain in the neck or arse. An appropriate example because Hangar Lane is a road junction in West London notorious for traffic jams.

Hangnail　　　　　**Snail**
Not so much the mollusc as a slow, dawdling person, especially the pain behind the wheel of a car with dead flies on the rear window.

Hank Marvin　　　　　**Starving**
The name of this British guitarist was possibly first uttered by a dieter who was a shadow of his former self.

Hannibal Lecter　　　　　**Inspector (Ticket)**
The scourge of the fare dodger and based on the character who's on a different train to everyone else as far as fare is concerned: the cannibalistic anti-hero of the film and novel *Silence of the Lambs* by Thomas Harris.

Hansel & Gretel　　　　　**Kettle**
In old cockney sculleries the 'hansel' was always on the go. Based on the fairy-tale siblings.

Hansom Cabs　　　　　**Crabs**
Crab-lice, known as 'hansoms'. Ironic really, because the parasitic critters that infest the pubic areas are anything but han'some. 'Barks' – backslang for knacker nippers.

Happy Hour(s)　　　　　**Flower(s)**
If you come home late and your dinner's ruined because you've been in the pub for happy hour, a bunch of 'happy hours' won't cover it.

Harbour Light   Right

Applies to correctness: if everything's alright then it's 'all harbour', and has been since the 19th century.

Hard Hit   Shit

To go for a 'hard hit' is to defecate – sounds like the long slog of constipation.

Hard Labour   Neighbour

Might be apt if getting along with 'them next door' is hard work.

Hare & Hound   Round

As a round of drinks this is an exact variation of 'fox & hound' (qv).

Haricot Bean   Queen

Theatrical example for an overt homosexual.

Harold Lloyd   Celluloid

Underworld term for a strip of plastic for picking locks, often known simply as a 'lloyd' and based on an early American film comedian (1893–71).

Harold Macmillan   Villain

Reduced to an 'arold', this is how a former British Prime Minister (1894–1986) became a baddie.

Harold Pinter   (a) Printer

A 21st-century piece concerning a peripheral part of a personal computer system.

(b) Splinter

An example that first caused pain in a 1960s timber yard – always cut to an ''Arold' after the British playwright and dramatist, later Sir 'Arold.

Harold Wilson   Stillson

A British Prime Minister (1916–95) takes his seat in the house of common slang as a plumber's term for what is also known as a monkey wrench. Sir Harold later became Baron Wilson of Rievaulx.

Harpoon　　　　　　**Spoon**

An early to middle 20th-century term often fired in the docks when the mobile canteen came around and dozens of men had to make do with a couple of 'harpoons'.

Harris Tweed　　　　　**Weed**

A term for a skinny little, ineffectual type, often the butt of a bully. He'd do well to remember that when the bullied stand up, the bully stands down. Sometimes.

Harry Bluff　　　　　　**Snuff**

Used to be quite common, but then so did snuff.

Harry Dash　　　　　　**Flash**

A lairy person may acquire this name or he may be seen as 'too 'arry dash for his own good'.

Harry Grout　　　　　**Snout (Cigarette)**

Inspired by a character from the TV sitcom *Porridge*. Set in prison, where the genial Harry Grout was the tobacco baron. Not to be confused with 'harry wragg' (qv).

Harry Hill　　　　　　**Pill**

A British comedian lends his name to any kind of pill, possibly one that makes you burp.

Harry Huggins　　　　**Muggings**

A name given to a dupe or mug, often the poor binhead left to carry the can or the sap who gets the worst job.

Harry Lauder(s)　　　　**(a) Border(s)**

A theatrical term for a stage hanging and also what the soldiers of the Border Regiment called themselves.

(b) Order(s)

What should be obeyed and also an old publican's alternative to those three terrible words: 'Last orders, please' – 'Last harry lauders'.

(c) Warder

An early 20th-century term for a prison officer based on a Scottish entertainer (1870–1950), knighted for his contribution to the war effort.

Harry Lime Time

Based on a well-known film character of the 1940s, this applies to the time of day. People still enquire as to 'What's the harry lime?' The stock answer amongst kids in the 1950s was 'Half past kiss me arse and tuppence back on the bottle'.

Harry Monk Spunk (Semen)

Always shot down to the Christian name, where to ejaculate is to 'heave one's harry'.

Harry Nash Cash

An old localised term from London's docks, appropriately based on a former wages clerk within the industry.

Harry Potter Squatter

The young wizard of J.K. Rowling's imagination comes in as a 21st-century trespasser.

Harry Randall (a) Candle

Coined by soldiers of World War I, who needed 'harrys' to light up their trenches.

(b) Handle

A 19th-century term based on a British music-hall comedian (1860–1932). Coming at the beginning of motorised transport, it may refer, amongst other handles, to a starting handle.

Harry Ronce Ponce

Along with Charlie, Joe and Johnny (see All), the Ronce boys seem to have turned living off immoral earnings into a family enterprise.

Harry Tagg(s) Bag(s)

Originally a theatrical term for luggage based on a British boat builder and hotelier (d. 1925). The piece transferred for a while to trousers, when great baggy legwear (bags) was in vogue for a spell in the 1920s–30s. Upper-class chappies christened them 'harolds'.

Harry Tate (a) Eight

A bingo-caller's term and a reference to £8. 'Taich sithnoms' – eight months in the backslang calendar (or 'radneylac', in backslang).

(b) Late

Based on a British comedian (1872–1940), who became a byword for bad timekeeping.

(c) Mate

A wartime example from the Merchant Navy regarding the first officer.

(d) Plate

It can be the best china or a tin one. If you can eat off it, it's an 'harry tate'.

(e) State

To be in a right old 'harry tate' is to be in a state of excitement or nervousness.

Harry Tate(s)   **Weight(s)**

Fat people may be carrying too much of it, but this mainly applied to a popular brand of cigarettes, Player's Weights.

Harry, Tom & Dick   **Sick**

When you feel a wee cough coming on, it may be time for a week off on the 'harry tom'.

Harry Wragg   **Fag (Cigarette)**

The name of this English jockey (1902–85) will live on for as long as people enjoy a puff.

Harvey Nichol   **Pickle**

The Knightsbridge store lends its name to a predicament. Those in a 'preserve' are in a 'bit of an 'arvey'

Harvest Moon   **Coon**

Abusive term for a black person.

Harvey Nichols   **Pickles**

Piccalilli, gherkins, pickled onions and wallys, they're all 'harveys'.

Has Beens   **Greens**

Originally a convict's term for green vegetables, which presumably have been boiled to a pulp.

Hat & Coat   **Boat**

An old term from the docks, often regarding a refrigerated

cargo ship, the unloading of which required the docker to wear his 'hat and coat'.

Hat & Feather — Weather

Generally used in full when complaining of 'this poxy hat & feather', but sometimes humorously as 'hatton':

1st man: What's the hatton like?

2nd man: Raining, you better put your hatton.

Hat & Scarf — Bath

Can't really see the relevance of this one. Who wears a scarf in the bath?

Hattie Jaques — Shakes

A British comedy actress (1924–80) gets on the RS casting list as drunken trembles or, a touch of the 'hatties'.

Haystack — Back

Applies anatomically, millions of days' work are lost through dodgy 'haystacks'. And deliveries are generally made to the rear of a building, or 'round the haystack'.

Heap of Coke — Bloke

A 'heap big heap' as Geronimo may have described his largest brave, had he come from East London's Bow. Or possibly Harrow.

Hearth Rug — (a) Bug

An ancient piece that may make a comeback (as the vermin has) in insanitary hotels and hostels.

(b) Mug

A dupe, simpleton or puttyhead; someone regularly stepped on, i.e., conned or put-upon.

Hearts of Oak — Broke

Refers to taking up financial residence in Shit Street with nuppence to pay the rent. Based on the piece of music that is the official march of the Royal Navy.

Heaven & Hell — (a) Shell

A wartime term from the army regarding a projectile, a

convenient example based on the two places an exploding one may send its victims to.

(b) Smell

Rotten smells 'don't half heaven'.

Heavenly Bliss   **Kiss**

An old term that's originally from America and apt, especially when not confined to a mouth-to-mouth arrangement.

Heavens Above   **Love**

A happy example when applied to a new romance: people are not quite earthbound when in 'heavens'.

Hedge & Ditch   **Pitch**

A playing area and also the spot where a stallholder may set up shop, or a bookmaker his 'joint'.

Hedgehog   **Wog**

An example from the xenophobe, who may maintain that all 'hedgehogs' start at Calais.

Helter-Skelter   **Shelter**

Originally an air-raid shelter from World War II, now obsolete except in reminiscences of people who survived the Blitz. Still applies to a bus shelter, though. Some backslangers continue calling it a 'retlesh'.

Henley Regatta   **Natter**

An old source of friction between man and wife is when he's waiting for his dinner and she's having an 'henley' with her next door.

Henrietta   **Letter**

A girl who gets addressed as a boy when going to post as an 'henry'. 'Rettle exob' – a backslang letterbox.

Henry Fonda   **Honda**

Based on an American film actor (1905–82) and limited to some would-be taxi drivers doing the knowledge. It refers to a Honda 90 motorcycle, the commonest 'knolly-bike'.

Henry Halls   **Balls**

A British bandleader (1898–1989) of the danceband era takes the floor in a testicular sense as 'henrys'.

Henry Meville   **Devil**

A piece from a line in an 1887 ballad 'Tottie' by George R. Sims (1847–1922). Used as 'What the henry meville's going on?'

Henry Moore   **Door**

Based on the English sculptor (1898–1986), this is a piece of student's slang, so 'close the henry' is most likely an order to shut a college door.

Henry Nash   **Cash**

An elderly piece regarding 'poshery' (the word for 'money' back when only posh people had it) that doesn't appear to be attracting much interest these days. 'Shack & wyrac' – backslang 'cash & carry'.

Henry the Third   **Turd**

The long-reigning English monarch (1207–72) rivals fellow kings George III and Richard III in the excrement stakes. If the present Prince of Wales ever becomes Charles III, well, I hope he knows what he's in for. Henry III reigned from 1216 until his death.

Herbie Hides   **Strides**

A 1990s piece of youthspeak, when young 'erberts of the day referred to their trousers or jeans as 'herbies'. Based on a British boxer, who twice held a version of the world heavyweight title in the 1990s.

Here & There   **Chair**

A piece that's never shortened, the ubiquitous piece of furniture is always a 'here & there'.

Herman Fink   **Ink**

A term drawn up in the theatre before the ballpoint took over. Most likely based on a London-born composer and conductor (1872-1939), a regular performer in early 20th century theatres.

Herring & Kipper　　**Stripper**

Always reduced to the first element and since 'peelers' began performing their act in pubs, suggestions to go and see them have been rebuffed with: 'I don't want to see some old herring getting her kit off. Let's go for a quiet pint'.

Herring Bone　　**Phone**

A 1990s term, a 'herring' is most likely to be a mobile job.

Hey Jude　　**Food**

Based on the title of a 1968 hit for The Beatles, which makes a food faddist, gourmet, celebrity chef or any other kind of 'foodie' a 'hey judy'.

Hi-Diddle-Diddle　　**(a) Fiddle**

Refers to gaining by dishonest means, which may take the form of petty larceny from the workplace or a much larger tax fraud. A working-man's maxim: If you see a fiddle, play it. No one ever got rich working for a living.

(b) Fiddle

A violin, as played by a 'hi-diddle-diddler'.

(c) Middle

Most commonly a reference to the bulls-eye on a dartboard, the nearest the 'hi-diddle' throws first.

(d) Piddle

From the nursery rhyme in which the little dog 'hi-diddled' himself o' laughing to see such fun.

Hi Jimmy Knacker　　**Tobacco**

Refers to pipe or rolling tobacco and is based on a street game of the dim and distant past. 'Occabot' – backslang bacca.

Hickory-Dickory-Dock　　**Clock**

The extended version of 'dickory-dock' (qv), which then gets reduced to a 'hickory-dickory'.

Hide & Seek　　**(a) Boutique**

A piece from the 1960s, the decade when young people ceased to be fashion clones of their parents and clobber shops called 'boutiques' sprang up everywhere.

(b) Cheek

Mainly refers to impudence or sauce. Never truncated, liberty-takers tend to have an abundance of it. Sometimes used anatomically, usually when a peck on the 'hide & seek' is concerned.

High as a Kite   **Tight**

A reference to being drunk, this is a piece that's been hanging around since the 1930s.

High Noon   **Spoon**

A 1950s term for a 'stirrer' based on the title of a classic Western.

High Stepper   **Pepper**

A seasoned campaigner on the table of RS.

Highland Fling   **(a) King**

At the moment this is the playing card, but when we next get a male monarch, who knows?

(b) Sing

A post-war term found on a Billy Cotton record called 'The Marrow Song', sung by Alan Breeze, the band's resident 'highland flinger'.

Hilary Swank   **Wank**

Naughty young noughties men masturbate using this term, possibly fantasising about the beautiful Oscar-winning American actress, who, had she been British, might have seen this coming and changed her name.

Hill & Dale   **Tale**

As spun by a conman or beggar to separate the gullible from their money.

Hillman Hunter   **Punter**

Based on a type of car from the 1960s and coined, unsurprisingly, by used car dealers in relation to a customer. It now applies to clients of any trade.

Hit & Miss   **(a) Kiss**

By which 'kiss me' masochistically becomes 'hit me'.

(b) Piss

Can be used in regard to urine or booze. While on the 'hit & miss', at some stage you'll have to go for one. Hit & missed – pissed (drunk).

Hit & Run   **(a) Done**

Mainly applies to being swindled. If you've been taken, you've been 'hit & run'.

(b) Sun

Once fittingly descriptive of the sun's fleeting appearances during a typical British summer, but with global warming it seems to be less shy than it once was.

Hit or Miss   **(a) Kiss**
                                   (b) Piss

Exact alternatives to hit & miss (qv).

Hobson's Choice   **Voice**

A common term that originated in the theatre, possibly when a singer was castigated for having a 'dodgy hobson's'. 'Hobson's choice' means no choice at all.

Hod of Mortar   **Porter**

Nineteenth-century term for a type of beer only seen these days at beer festivals.

Hokey-Cokey   **Karaoke**

A 1990s piece for the pub entertainment much-loved by the 'lager and I will survive' brigade. The more discerning will do the hokey-cokey, turn around and go somewhere else.

Hole in the Ground   **Pound**

An example from the days of nicker-notes when £1 was known a 'hole'. Now we have nicker-bits and well, who knows? Someone, somewhere may still dig the term. 'Dunop' – a backslang oncer.

Holler & Shout   **Kraut**

One from the 1960s package holiday when loud Germans were a feature of Spanish hotels...until someone mentioned the war.

Holler Boys, Holler   **Collar**
Originally applied to a detachable shirt collar of a bygone age and known as a 'holler, boys'. Based on a line from the traditional Bonfire Prayer:
Holler boys, holler boys. God save the King
And what shall we do with him (Guy Fawkes)
Burn Him!

Holy Friar   **Liar**
Never shortened and only used in a light-hearted manner. If someone defamed you, you wouldn't call him this: you'd call him a liar.

Holy Ghost   **(a) Host**
Possibly a theatrical term for a publican.
    (b) Post
The starting post at a racecourse, from the days before starting stalls – sometimes the winning post.
    (c) Post
A piece from the theatre for what the postman brings and from a time before junk mail turned the postie into a waste delivery agent. 'Teesopnam' – a backslang postman.
    (d) Toast
One of the Holy Trinity comes in as a slice of breakfast.

Holy Nail   **Bail**
One of those that secured Christ to the Cross becomes the money required to secure the temporary release of a prisoner.

Holy Smoke   **Coke 1**
Originally a somewhat ironic piece concerning the smokeless solid fuel made from coal. When the home fires stopped burning, the term got transferred to…
    Coke 2
…Coca Cola. The term is an exclamation of surprise, which may or may not be inspired by St Bruno pipe tobacco.

Holy Water   **Daughter**
The apple of her father's eye is his little 'holy water'.

Holyfield's Ear   **Year**

Based on the 1997 World Heavyweight title fight between Evander Holyfield and Mike Tyson, in which the latter seemingly tried to ascertain whether a boxer's ear actually tasted of cauliflower by biting a great chunk out of his opponent's 'listener'! For this act of cannibalism Iron Mike received a lifetime ban from the sport but was granted leave to re-apply for his licence 12 months later. A year therefore became known as a 'holyfield's' – although it must be said, not for long.

Home on the Range   **Strange**

Anything out of the ordinary, unusual or weird may be described as 'very home on the range'. Like Alan Brazil seen drinking from a cup, for instance.

Homer & Marge   **Large**

A modern piece of youthspeak for acting big or 'giving it homer'. Based on Mr and Mrs Simpson, and they don't come larger than Homer.

Hong Kong   **(a) Pong**

Not sure if this is apt as I've never been there, but pong is Chinese for smell, isn't it?

      (b) Wrong

When a plan has gone boss-eyed, it's gone 'hong kong' or sometimes 'hongkers'.

Hook, Line & Sinker   **Clinker**

Probably the most common piece of slang amongst the many for a piece of dried excrement attached to an anal hair has acquired a term of RS in the reduced form of 'hook-line'.

Hop it & Scram   **Ham**

Localised example that's sliced and eaten as 'hop it'.

Hopping Hut   **Slut**

This 1950s term may have its roots in reality. It was common at the time for wives and kids to go hop picking in Kent while the old man stayed behind in London to work. And with all those lusty rustics about, well, it didn't take much for a girl to get a bad name.

Hopping Pot Lot

A widely-used piece generally contracted to the first element: 'that's the hopping' means 'that's the lot', there's no more.

Hopscotch Watch

With a leap in time this children's game continues the kiddie connection with a timepiece. A 19th-century term for a watch was a 'toy'.

Horn of Plenty Twenty

One of a cornucopia of terms from the bingo hall. 'Wytnewt gaffs' – twenty fags in backslang.

Hors d'Oeuvres Nerves

Rarely used, suburban version of the cockney 'west ham reserves' (qv).

Horse & Carriage Garage

An example from the time when we bought petrol in gallons and air was free.

Horse & Cart (a) Fart

Normally employed in the past tense or when the horse has bolted, so to speak: 'Who's horse and carted?'

(b) Heart

A 19th-century term for the 'pump' that still has some life in it – especially, ironically, when discussing someone who has died because his 'horse & cart gave out'.

(c) Start

A new beginning is a new 'horse & cart'. Also used as a mocking remark to a motorist having ignition problems: 'Won't horse & cart? Get a horse and cart!'

Horse(s) & Cart(s) Dart(s)

Always curtailed to a game of 'horses', on its own a dart becomes a 'horse'.

Horse & Trap (a) Clap (VD)

A dose of the 'horse' or 'gee-gees' is usually a reference to gonorrhoea.

(b) Crap

Not as regular as the frequently passed pony & trap (qv) in regards to defecation, but rubbish or nonsense is a 'load of horse & trap'.

Horse & Trough **Cough**

Specifically a smoker's cough – when they are 'horsing' up their jiblets.

Horse Piddle **Hospital**

An example that's a pun as much as anything, either way it's older than the bugs that roam the wards these days, the oldest of these being Mister South Africa – Mr SA.

Horse's Hoof **Poof**

How a homosexual male becomes a 'horse's', as opposed to the more familiar 'iron hoof' (qv).

Hot & Cold **Gold**

Known in Hooky Street in the melted-down form of 'hot', often used to describe jewellery that's 'the other way'. 'Deelog nyach' – a backslang gold chain.

Hot Beef **Thief**

A term which, in the 19th century, was a cry of alarm, a rhyme on 'stop, thief!' Can't imagine the victim of a footpad messing about with RS whilst giving chase – so maybe it was used mockingly by amused onlookers.

Hot Cross Bun **(a) Gun**

Really only used for comic effect, it's hard to imagine a security guard feeling threatened at the idea of a 'hot cross bun' being aimed at his head.

(b) Nun

If a 'hot cross' was toting a 'hot cross bun', (a) would she be a member of the Armourlite Order?

(c) Run

The most common use of the term: to be on the 'hot cross' is to be on the run from the police, or the wife.

(d) Son/Sun

Unusual, but not unheard of in either of these settings.

Hot Dinner   **Winner**
An example from the world of racing that suggests a good meal follows a good result.

Hot Potato   **Waiter**
A 'hot pertater' sounds like an efficient table jockey, or a busy one in a curry house.

Hot Toddy   **Body**
Refers to the body beautiful and is inspired by the name of a hot alcoholic drink that's nice to go to bed with. The connection is obvious.

Hounslow Heath   **Teeth**
An early piece that has had the bite put on it by its North London rival 'hampstead heath' (qv). A betrayal is more likely to be a kick in the 'hampsteads' than the 'hounslows'.

House of Fraser   **Razor**
Originally a Scottish term where it was known as a 'hoosie', but after the journey South it became a 'howser' and was chiefly a razor when used as a weapon. Based on a retailing chain, it can also apply to a shaver.

House of Lords   **Cords**
A 1970s term for casual corduroy trousers, generally tailored to 'house-ers'.

House of Wax   **Jacks (£5)**
An example of secondary slang, see also 'jacks alive'. An obscure piece which possibly came into being after a 1953 film with this title.

House to Let   **Bet**
A piece from the 1960s when more people were 'house-to-letting' due to the opening of betting shops.

Housemaid's Knee   **(a) Key**
How the old prison officer got to hang about with a bunch of 'housemaids'.

(b) Sea
Theatrical term for the 'splash' and said of an out-of-form Chelsea striker: 'He couldn't hit the housemaids if he fell off a ship'.

Housewives' Choice   **Voice**

Based on a long-running radio request programme of yesteryear, this often applies to the shrill, raucous voice of a shrieking woman, especially a mother castigating an unruly child. Probably defunct as the show is no longer on the air and these days unruly children castigate their mothers.

Housey-Housey   **Lousy**

Never shortened, to feel unwell, run-down or itchy is to feel 'housey-housey'. Based on a slang term for the game of bingo or lotto.

How D'You Do   **(a) Shoe**

A 19th-century term for a 'trotter case', but you've got more chance of opening a Weetabix wrapper without tearing it than hearing it these days.

         (b) Stew

This is a stew in the sense of difficulty or mental agitation. When you're in a right old 'how d'you do', you're in trouble. Applies secondarily to the dish.

Howard's Way   **Gay**

A homosexual from the 1980s based on a TV series of the period.

How's Your Father   **(a) Lather**

Nothing to do with soap, but to get into a state about something is to work yourself up into a 'how's your father'.

         (b) Palava

Anything complicated or bothersome is a right old 'how's your father'.

Huckleberry Finn   **Gin**

Originally an Australian term, but 'huckleberry' or 'huck' has found its way into British glasses. Based on the eponymous hero of a Mark Twain novel.

Huckleberry Hound   **Pound**

How a cartoon dog of the 1960s became the price of everything in a 'huckleberry' shop.

Hugs & Kisses   Missus

Hardly flattering to refer to one's wife as the 'ugs', but it's meant to be.

Human Rights   Tights

Making love to a woman who is still wearing her 'humans' will start her toes a-twitching. Unless there's a breach in her 'human rights'. The term followed in the wake of the Human Rights Act of 1998.

Hundred to Eight   Plate

It's a funny fact of life that you may have a plate for many years and all the time you've got it, that's all it is: an old 'hundred to eight'. But as soon as it gets smashed, it acquires antique status. The term is bookmakers' odds of twelve and a half to one.

Hundred to Thirty   Dirty

Bookmakers' odds get a quote in reference to grubbiness, as in the saying: 'Never wear a clean shirt if your neck is hundred to thirty'.

Huntley & Palmer   Farmer

A piece from the 1990s suburbs that never made it to town – and why would it?

Huntley & Palmers   Farmers

Secondary slang for haemorrhoids. Known as 'huntleys' and based on a well-known biscuit company. See also Farmer Giles.

Hurricane Deck   Neck

The upper deck of a ship comes in for an upper part of the body. Audacious people may have 'more hurricane than a giraffe'.

Hurricane Lamp   Tramp

The second element gets blown away here, leaving vagrants, dossers, gentlemen of the road, etc. as 'hurricanes'.

Husband & Wife   Knife

Generally cut to the first element, which sees the 'husband' doing the carving.

Hush Puppy   **Yuppie**

A derogatory term from the 1980s regarding the high-earning, high-profile type, many of whom colonised London's Docklands after the demise of the dock industry. Based on a brand of footwear.

Hyde Park   **(a) Mark**

A theatrical term for an actor's mark.

(b) Nark (Informer)

Based on London's biggest park, where ears can be whispered into without being overheard. 'Narking dues' – time being served as a result of an informer.

Hydraulics   **Bollocks**

The testicles. The dictionary describes hydraulics as 'the science of the conveyance of liquids through pipes, etc. especially as a motive power'. Apt then that a well-aimed boot in the groin would have a serious effect on this. Also a colourful way to express disbelief at a nonsense or rubbish: 'What a load of hydraulics!'

I Am Back   Crack (Cocaine)

A 1980s piece that may reflect the addictive power of the drug.

I Desire   Fire

A 19th-century term for the traditional housewarmer known as an 'idey'.

I Suppose   Nose

A well-known term for the shonker that's been running since the 19th-century.

Ian Rush   Brush

An example formed in the 1980s on the name of a Welsh international footballer, which was used by painters in relation to the tools of their trade. A newspaper columnist of the time likened a paintbrush to the man's trademark moustache.

Ice-Cream Freezer   Geezer

Always shortened to the first two elements, often insultingly as in: 'cop the ice cream with the tattoos – with a bit more style he could become a chav'.

Ice Lolly   Wally (Fool)

Never sucked down to anything but the full term. A twerp is always an 'ice lolly'.

Ideal Home   Comb

An ironic term from the 1950s in that in an ideal home it

wouldn't keep getting mislaid. 'Beemoc' – a backslang 'flea-raker'.

Ille Nastase   **Carsey (Lavatory)**
A 1970s piece based on the Rumanian tennis player of the period, whose on-court antics seemed designed to take the piss out of opponents and scare the shit out of umpires.

I'll Be There   **Chair**
Early piece of RS furniture that may be heard in the pub in the form of a round of drinks: 'Who's in the "I'll be"?'

I'm Afloat   **(a) Boat**
An obvious example that was used by 19th-century dock-workers as an 'ima'.

                    (b) Coat
As old as (a) and generally an overcoat.

I'm So Frisky   **Whisky**
Usually nipped to a drop of 'I'm so'.

I'm Willing   **Shilling**
A piece that was probably obsolete before this old coin of the realm.

In & Out   **(a) Gout**
The painful affliction that comes and goes, putting the sufferer in and out of work.

                    (b) Snout 1
Refers to a snout in the guise of a nose: it's how air enters and leaves.

                    Snout 2
A cigarette or tobacco, especially in prison.

                    (c) Spout
Anything ruined or rendered useless is said to be 'up the in & out' – as is a pregnant woman.

                    (d) Sprout
Greengrocer's term for a Brussels sprout. A backslang 'green-grocer' is a 'neergresorg'.

                    (e) Stout
Beer, the 'black stuff' that's also known as 'black food'.

(f) Tout

Originally applied to a racecourse seller of tips, it now also refers to a seller of extortionately priced tickets.

In-Between　　　　　**Queen**

Originally an Australian term for a homosexual.

In the Mood　　　　　**Food**

A hungry person or a 'gannet' is always in the mood for some 'in the mood'.

In the Nude　　　　　**Food**

Jocular play on the previous entry, which may suggest a different type of 'nosh'. See 'Mouthwash'.

Indian Charm(s)　　　　　**Arms**

An eastern rival to 'lucky charms' (qv).

Inky Blue　　　　　**Flu**

A 1970s term for the illness that can be counteracted by having an 'inky' jab.

Inky Smudge　　　　　**Judge**

The man of law who can officially blot your copybook aptly becomes an 'inky'.

Insects & Ants　　　　　**Pants**

Underpants, that is – in brief, 'insects'.

Inside Right　　　　　**Tight**

An old-fashioned position on the football field relates to one whose hands are too big for his pockets.

Irene Handl　　　　　**Candle**

A piece that came to light in the early 1970s, when industrial action taken by miners forced the closure of power stations and the resulting darkness had people fumbling for 'irenes'. Based on a British actress (1902–87).

Irish Jig　　　　　**(a) Cig**

That which a smoker wouldn't have the puff to perform becomes the cause of his breathing problem: a cigarette.

(b) Wig

An 'irish' is an obvious and much-derided vanity shield.

Irish Rose Nose

Old piece, rarely picked these days.

Irish Stew (a) Blue

Refers to all things blue, including melancholia. 'Am I Irish?', as Billie Holliday may have sung, had she grown up around Maryland Point, E15 instead of Maryland, USA.

(b) True

Said in agreement: 'too irish stew, mate' – or for emphasis: 'Too bloody Irish'.

Iron Duke Fluke

A piece from the snooker hall to describe a lucky shot. The 'Iron Duke' was a nickname for the Duke of Wellington (1769–1852).

Iron Girder Murder

Not necessarily a slaying, but more relative to a liberty-taker or a spoilt child, anyone who is allowed to get away 'iron girder', in fact. 'Redrum' – a backslang slaying.

Iron Hoof Poof (Homosexual)

An extremely common piece that is always minced down to the first element: 'Actors? They're all a bunch of irons'.

Iron Hoop Soup

A 19th-century term based on a plaything of a bygone era now rolled into oblivion – although a tin of 'iron' may still put lead in your pencil, brass in your neck and steel in your nerves.

Iron Horse (a) Course

A racecourse; a term based on an old name for a train.

(b) Toss

Old cockney dialect makes this 'torse' and it's a reference to 'torsing' a coin: 'Alright, I'll iron you for it. Heads I drink, tails you drive'.

Iron Mike   **Bike**

The nickname of US boxer Mike Tyson inspires an example that would not have been out of place years ago when bicycles were great heavy beasts of iron.

Iron Tank   **Bank**

An underworld term – possibly for one that would be hard to 'knock over'.

Isabella   **Umbrella**

A piece that has been keeping rain off cockney heads every summer for over a century.

Isle of France   **A Dance**

Mid 19th-century do based on a popular ballad of the period about a shipwrecked convict, who was washed up on what was the original name of Mauritius.

Isle of Man   **Pan**

An example that is never shortened: 'You bung the bangers in the isle o' man and I'll butter the nat king coles' (qv).

Isle of Wight   **(a) Alright**

When everything's cushti, it's all 'isle o' wight'.

(b) Light

What to switch on when it gets dark and a cigarette is no good without one. Pluralised, it means traffic lights.

(c) Right

Applies in terms of direction: 'Chuck an isle o' wight at the isle o' wights'.

(d) Tight

What miserly people are said to be and if your clothes get 'isle o' wight', it's time to lose weight.

Itch & Scratch   **Match**

This has long been the cheapest way to light a fag. It's a major irritant for a smoker not to have any 'itches'.

Ivory Pearl   **Girl**

Not necessarily a fair-skinned girl.

J. Arthur Rank   **(a) Bank**

In this sense the term is uncommon and may have been gonged out.

                      (b) Wank

Self-employed extensively in the shortened term of 'J. Arthur' and based on the British film producer and entrepreneur, who became Lord Rank (1882–1972); possibly the most common term for 'playing one's hornpipe'.

J. Carroll Naish   **Slash (Urinate)**

Stopped in mid-flow at 'j. carroll', this is based on the US actor (1900–73), who played Charlie Chan in a long-running TV series.

Jack & Danny   **Fanny (Vagina)**

A well-known piece of slang for slang: 'I must have been well pissed, I kissed her jack & danny'.

Jack & Jill   **(a) Bill**

Applies to any horrible piece of paper with a charge on it, be it gas, phone, restaurant, etc. It's also a receipt so if you want to change the goods, keep the 'jack & jill'.

                      (b) Hill

Since this is what the pair in the nursery rhyme climbed, it would seem an appropriate and obvious example.

                      (c) Pill

Piece in everyday use amongst drug-users – and probably the sick.

(d) Till

A piece that has become common in regard to a cash register – especially one in a betting shop.

Jack & Joan   Alone

More correctly: on one's own. Either a misheard version of 'jack jones' (qv), or the famous Mr Jones is a century-old corruption of this. It's certainly a better rhyme, but either way it makes little difference if you are keeping yourself company, you are 'on your jack'.

Jack & Vera   Mirror

The *Daily Mirror* that is, a piece from the newspaper distribution industry. And if it's good enough for them...Based on Mr and Mrs Duckworth, stalwarts of TVs *Coronation Street*.

Jack Benny   Penny

Originally the pre-decimal penny and based on an American comedian (1894–1974), famed for his penny-pinching meanness.

Jack Dee   Pee/Wee

A 1990s term based on a British comedian of the day and later a star of stage, screen and urinal.

Jack Doyle   Boil

The painful skin eruption based on a colourful Irish boxer (1913–78), whose gimmick was to sing in the ring. Had he danced as well, would it have been the Lancer?

Jack Flash   (a) Crash/Smash

Refers to a road accident and is possibly an allusion to a speeding motorist.

(b) Hash

A drug-user's term based on the famous jumping man of the Rolling Stones' hit record.

Jack Frost   Lost

The famous iceman provides a chilly reference to an ignorance of whereabouts: 'If this isn't the B229, we're jack frost'.

Jack Horner   **Corner**

Applies to what can be stood in, turned or cut and is sometimes extended to 'little jack horner' or 'little jack' after the boy in the nursery rhyme.

Jack Jones   **Alone**

When you spend time with 'jack jones', you're on your own – or 'on your jack'.

Jack Ketch   **Stretch**

A term from prison for a 'spell in a cell', courtesy of the man who curtailed many a stay by stretching the miscreant's neck or putting an axe through it. Ketch (d. 1686) was an English executioner whose name became synonymous with the job of hangman.

Jack Malone   **Alone**

Another alternative to 'jack jones' (qv), but since it also comes down to being 'on your jack', it's no alternative at all. Thirteen and a bakers really.

Jack of Spades   **Shades**

Sunglasses, worn as 'jacks'.

Jamie Ollie   **Wally (Fool)**

Based on the celebrity chef, Jamie Oliver, whose involvement with food may lead you to suspect a pickled cucumber was involved, but no. A 'jamie' is a numbnut. Or a doughnut if you like.

Jack Randall   **Candle**

The name of a 19th-century London-born prize fighter (1794–1828) burns on with this archaic term.

Jack Sharkey   **Parky (Cold)**

An example remembered from the 1950s, but could be older as it's based on an ex-World Champion heavyweight boxer (1902–94). Sharkey ruled the division in 1932–33. Parky can be anything from nippy to 'fuckin' arctic'.

Jack Sprat   **(a) Brat**

A precocious or unpleasant child is a 'right little jack sprat'.

(b) Fat

Trim the 'jack sprat' from a greasy-spoon bacon sandwich and usually, there's not a lot left between the slices. Also applies to an overweight person, a 'stodgepot', and is ironically based on a nursery-rhyme character who wouldn't touch the stuff.

Jack Straw   **Draw (Marijuana)**

A piece from 1998 based on the then Home Secretary, an active opponent of the legalisation of cannabis, who suffered the embarrassment of his 17 year-old son, William, being arrested for selling drugs. Draw is an alternative of spliff, joint etc.

Jack Surpass   **Glass**

A 19th-century term for a glass of alcohol based on...I don't know who or what. Answers on a postcard, please.

Jack Tar   **Bar**

Not necessarily a harbour or riverside bar, even if it is based on the slang term for a sailor.

Jack the Dandy   **Randy**

Desirous of sexual gratification, or in need of one's oats. A piece from the 1960s.

Jack the Lad   **Bad**

Something that's no longer fresh: it's a fair bet that green-coloured milk has turned 'jack the lad'. Don't mess with a 'dab dratsab' – a backslang rogue or bad bastard.

Jack the Ripper   **(a) Kipper**

A well-known example based on the infamous Whitechapel mass murderer.

(b) Slipper

A term used by schoolboys when the slipper was a mode of corporal punishment that made sitting down a painful experience.

(c) Stripper

Piece from the 1970s, when it became common for pubs to put on striptease shows.

Jack Warner   **Corner**

A 1960s piece to rival 'jack horner' (qv). Based on the East London born actor (1896–1981), who found TV immortality as Dixon of Dock Green.

Jack-a-Dandy   **Brandy**

Based on an alternative name for 'will-o'-the-wisp', itself the common name for 'ignis fatuus'. This is the phosphorescent light that can be seen hovering over swampy ground at night, a connection with the blue flame of ignited brandy on a Christmas pudding.

Jackanory   **Story**

Obviously refers to a tale that is told to a child but is mainly used in the sense of lies, whereby a teller of tall tales tells 'jackanorys' and the term may become the name he is known by. In the underworld it's also the name given to an informer, one who tells stories to the police.

Jackdaw   **Jaw**

Employed anatomically but more readily associated with a scolding. To cop a 'jackdaw' is to be told off.

Jackdaw & Rook   **Book**

An old term with its roots in the theatre, where a book was a script.

Jacket & Vest   **West**

The 'Jacket' is an old reference to the West End of London.

Jackie Dash   **Slash (Urinate)**

Formed in London's docks on the name of a union official (1906–89), who found fame as a writer and artist. A council building on the Isle of Dogs, E14 bears his name, at the back of which drunks stop late at night for a 'jackie'.

Jackie Trent   **Bent**

Applies to anything that isn't straight but mainly to corruption – a crooked lawyer, a rigged result, stolen goods, etc. Based on a British singer-songwriter who had hits in the 1960s.

Jack-in-the-Box Pox (VD)
A 19th-century term which originally applied to syphilis, the 'jack' was later latched on to any of the anti-social diseases.

Jacks Alive Five
This old bingo call is also one of the most common terms for £5 (a 'jacks'). A 'pair of jacks' is a tenner.

Jackson Pollocks Bollocks
The testicles and also rubbish, it's based on an American abstract artist (Paul Jackson Pollock, 1912–56), about whose work it has probably been said: 'What a load of jacksons'. In modern parlance, however, 'the bollocks' has come to mean the best, the most excellent. A shortening of the 'dog's bollocks' pared down to the 'mutt's nuts' and now the 'dachshund's jacksons'. It's a funny old language.

Jacob's Crackers Knackers
The testicles, the fragile part of the anatomy based on a fragile biscuit. Known as the 'jacobs' and sometimes for humorous effect, the 'jacob's cream crackers'.

Jagger's Lips Chips
The singing Stone's salient features often provide late-night sustenance after a couple or 10 pints of 'mick jagger' (qv). A 'gab of piches' – a backslang bag of chips.

Jailhouse Rock Cock (Penis)
A piece from the 1950s based on an Elvis Presley film and song title, whereby improper use of the 'jailhouse' will land you in the nick.

Jam Duff Puff (Homosexual)
An early 20th-century example which sees a sweet come in for a 'sweetie'.

Jam Jar Car
A well-known piece that's been on the road of RS since the birth of motoring, although originally it applied to a tram-car. 'Rack crap' – a backslang car park.

Jam Pie   **Eye**

A 1990s version of the well established 'mince pie' (qv), which has failed to kick its predescessor off the plate.

Jam Roll   **(a) Dole**

A well-employed term regarding unemployment. 'Eelod yenom' – backslang dole money.

                 (b) Parole

An underworld term for a happy release.

Jam Tart   **(a) Fart**

Based on a sweet, but the resultant stench may be anything but.

                 (b) Heart

Has been used anatomically but the main usage is towards the suit in a pack of cards.

                 (c) Sweetheart

Originally applied to a girlfriend but somewhere along the line the 'jam' was eaten and 'tart' became a byword for a woman. On the tongue of a jealous wife, an immoral one.

Jamaica Rum   **Thumb**

The 'jamaica'; what henpecked husbands are under and hitch-hikers 'have it on'.

James Blunt   **Cunt**

A naughty piece of mid-noughties popney based on an English singer who would much rather be remembered for his songs than as a reference to a littleworth, someone with all the appeal of an ashtray full of dog ends.

James Hunt   **Front**

Applies to confidence, impudence or cheek, whereby an audacious person may have 'more james hunt than brighton'. Based on the British racing driver (1947–93), who was world champion in 1976.

James Riddle   **Piddle**

The formal version of 'jimmy riddle' (qv) is quite a common outpouring.

Jamie Dalrymple   **Pimple**

An England cricketer comes in as a modern skin eruption; a 'jamie' on the 'fireman's' will knock for six your chances of pulling. See Fireman's Hose

Jammy Dodger   **Roger**

A 1990s piece for sexual intercourse based on a popular biscuit – apt when you think about dunking it.

Jane Russell   **Mussel**

A 1950s term for the popular seafood traditionally served as a bar snack on Sunday luchtimes. Based on a voluptuous American film star of the period.

Jane Shore   **(a) Floor**

A 19th-century piece that really no longer rates a mention.

(b) Whore

A term that has long been in use as a 'jane', it was coined by 19th-century sailors who no doubt made humorous associations with shore leave. Based on the 16th-century mistress of King Edward IV.

Janet Street-Porter   **Quarter**

A 1980s term employed by drug-users for a quarter of an ounce of an illegal substance. Known as a 'janet' after a British journalist and TV personality.

Jar of Jam   **(a) Pram**

Put this down to the fact that whenever a clean baby is put in a 'jar of jam', somehow it always manages to get sticky.

(b) Tram

A 1930s example that became extinct in London when this mode of transport did.

Jasper Carrot   **Parrot**

That which sits **in** a birdcage and talks humorously as represented by a Brummie comedian, who sits **on** a 'birdcage' (qv) and talks humorously. A Birmingham City supporter for over 50 years, he must have felt as 'sick as a jasper' on more occasions than he cares to remember.

Jazz Band(s)   **Hand(s)**

Alternative to the much earlier 'german bands' (qv). Same concert, different music.

Jean-Claude Van Damme   **Ham**

Too long to be dished up as anything but 'jean-claude'. Based on a Belgian action-movie hero and used to describe what is sold on the cooked meat counter. If it has anything to do with bad acting, it didn't come from me, right?

Jekyll & Hyde   **Snide**

Very pertinent in the sense of being two-faced; also applies to fake or counterfeit goods such as a copied painting, a moody Rolex, a dodgy banknote, etc. – they're all 'jekylls'. Based on the novel *Dr Jekyll and Mr Hyde* by Robert Louis Stevenson (1850–94).

Jekyll & Hydes   **Strides**

How trousers and jeans became 'jekylls'. After they became 'strides', that is.

Jellied Eel(s)   **Wheel(s)**

Applies not only to an actual wheel but to transport in general, or more specifically a car. You always remember your first set of 'jellied eels'.

Jellybone   **Telephone**

Localised piece from the 1980s and used by some courier controllers – it was what bikers were told to use when their radios were out of range.

Jelly Tot   **Spot**

Based on a kiddie's confectionery, this is how acne sufferers get to be covered in 'jellies'.

Jem Mace   **Face**

Archaic piece based on the legendary 19th-century boxer (1831–1910). Known as the Swaffham Gypsy, he reigned supreme in pre-glove days, largely by pummelling his opponent's 'jem maces' to bloody pulps.

Jenny Hill   **Pill**
A drug taken for medicinal purposes and based on a music-hall entertainer (1851–96).

Jenny Lee   **(a) Flea**
A piece that was once as common as the bloodsucking parasite was in slum housing.

(b) Key
This old term sees 'jenny' still employed as an 'opener'.

(c) Tea
A 19th-century example now supplanted by 'rosie lee' (qv). In all three definitions, the spellings of 'Jenny' and 'Lee' are mixed and matched with 'Jennie' and 'Lea' depending on which book you read. Whichever way it's spelt, the identity of the lady is still a mystery.

Jenny Lind/Lindy   **Wind/Windy**
Can apply to the weather conditions or to internal gases that work their way out one way or another. Jenny Lind was a Victorian singer who was known as the Swedish Nightingale (1820–87).

Jenny Linder   **Window**
A 19th-century term for the casualty of a smash and grab raid – from the same source as the previous entry.

Jenny Riddle   **Piddle**
The little-known sister of the famous 'jimmy riddle' (qv).

Jenny Wren   **Ben (Truman)**
A 20th-century piece for a brand of beer, ordered as a 'pint of jenny'.

Jeremiah   **Fire**
Applies to the domestic coal fire of yore, when it was common to put a piece of 'merry' on the 'jerry'. See also 'Merry Old Soul'.

Jeremy Beadle   **Needle**
To give someone the 'jeremy' is to anger or annoy them and is aptly based on the British TV personality and practical joker (1948–2008) whose show, *Beadle's About*, seemed to be

about winding some poor unsuspecting soul up to the point of a heart attack. Secondarily, a cotton-puller.

Jericho **Po (Chamberpot)**

Named after an ancient city that was the scene of a Biblical demolition job. To save money, Joshua (the leader of the Israelites) brilliantly hired some musicians (whose hourly rate was less than the navvies of the day) to blow their trumpets and bring down the walls, thus revealing many a hapless Canaanite sitting, with fingers in ears, on their decorous chamberpots midway through fear-induced defecation. When cleaned, these pots became prized spoils of war and were known as 'Jerries'. This story was told to me by a direct descendant of Joshua who had many such family heirlooms. Due to circumstances, however, he was now forced to sell them from the back of a van on some wasteground off the Mile End Road. Not for £10, not for £8, not even £6…But to you, and I'm robbing myself…

Jerry Diddle **Fiddle**

How shady goings-on were described 100 years ago, when great-grandad was on the 'jerry'.

Jerry Lee **Pee/Wee**

There may be a whole lotta shakin' going on when you're bursting for a 'jerry lee'. A 1950s example based on US rock'n'roll singer and pianist Jerry Lee Lewis.

Jerry Quarry **Lorry**

A piece from a 1960s transport caff somewhere up the road. Based on a tough American boxer of the period (1945–99), who fought for the heavyweight title and only lost to the very best fighters of his time.

Jerry-Cum-Mumble **(a) Rumble**

If anyone's 'jerry' to what you've been up to, you've been rumbled.

(b) Tumble

A 19th-century example that originally referred to a fall. It later became widely used as 'jerry' – to fall in, to understand: 'I was "jerry" to what he was on about' – I understood (tumbled) what he meant.

Jerry Riddle **Piddle**
A 19th-century piece that may have something to do with chamberpots – or jerries.

Jerry Springer **Minger**
An undesirable person, either in a smelly mode or, more often, ugly sense. Much like those who frequently appear on the TV show of Mr Springer, a US presenter. 'Jerrys', the lot of 'em.

Jethro Tull **Skull**
Based on a British rock band, this only really applies when speaking of someone who has over-indulged in drink of drugs to the extent that they were out of their 'jethro'.

Jiggle & Jog **Frog**
A French person type of frog, that is.

Jigsaw Puzzle **Muzzle**
Heard in the late 1990s when a law was passed forbidding owners of certain breeds of dogs from walking their pets without a 'jigsaw'.

Jim & Jack **Back**
Anatomically speaking, people have been suffering 'jim & jack' pain since the 1960s.

Jim Brown **Town**
A 19th-century term for London's West End – which to Eastenders is still more likely to be known as the 'Other End'.

Jim/Jimmy Mason **Basin**
To have a portion of is to have a basinful, as in a 'basinful of porridge' – a jail sentence. Old cockney lags would have had a 'jimmyful' of it.

Jim/Jimmy Prescott **Waistcoat**
A rival to 'charlie prescott' (qv) that rarely leaves the wardrobe these days.

Jim/Jimmy Skinner **Dinner**
Since the 19th-century drunken men have staggered home and demanded their 'jim skinners', only to have it slung at them.

Jimmy Boyle   **Foil**

A drug-user's term for kitchen foil, as used for smoking heroin. Based on the name of a British writer.

Jimmy Britt(s)   **Shit(s)**

Generally used as 'the jimmys' with reference to a bout of diarrhoea. Based on an American boxer (1879–1940), who in 1902 claimed the World Lightweight title, it can also apply to a state of fear. Things that go bump in the night may give you the 'jimmys'.

Jimmy Choo(s)   **Shoe(s)**

Aptly based on a Malaysian-born fashion designer best known for his exclusive footwear. Used ironically of a scruffy pair of of workaday shoes – which may or may not amuse Mr Choo, who received the OBE in 2002.

Jimmy Floyd Hasselbaink   **Wank**

A 21st-century term for the 'beeping of one's own horn' that is simply a 'jimmy floyd'. Based on a Dutch international footballer, whose English clubs included Chelsea and Charlton Athletic.

Jimmy Grant   **Immigrant**

On its 19th-century formation this meant 'emigrant' and referred to someone leaving for the colonies. In Australia, however, the term was reversed to mean a new arrival.

Jimmy Hill   **Pill**

Based on a 1950s footballer with Fulham and later a TV pundit, this applies to a prescribed pill or an illicit drug.

Jimmy Hix   **Fix**

A drugs-related piece for a shot in the arm.

Jimmy Logie   **Bogie**

Relates to a piece of nasal residue and is based on a former Arsenal and Scotland footballer (1919–84).

Jimmy Nail   **(a) Sale**

When prices are down there must be a 'jimmy' on.

(b) Stale

A Geordie actor and musician comes in as a rival to 'british rail' (qv), but he'll never be as apt.

Jimmy O'Goblin   **Sovereign**

Not Her Maj, but £1. Seldom used, but 'sov' is very popular. 'Voss a dunop' – £1 a pound – a backslang price tag.

Jimmy Riddle   **Piddle**

By far the most common way of pumping out an overflowing 'water tank', 'jimmy' has been in business since the 19th century.

Jimmy Rollocks   **Bollocks**

As with 'johnny' and 'tommy' (see both), this represents the testicles and is what a certain alternative comedian struggling in an East End pub was said to be about as funny as a boil on. 'Eskollobs' – backslang knackers.

Jimmy White   **Kite (Cheque)**

A 1980s term based on a London-born snooker player, who in a long career has seen his fair share of big money 'jimmys'.

Jimmy Wilde   **Mild (Ale)**

Based on the former World Flyweight boxing champion from Wales and formed around the time of World War I, when both the beer and the man were in their heydays. The diminutive Wilde (1892–1969) is rated one of Britain's greatest ever fighters. 'Deelim and rettib' – a backslang pint of mild and bitter.

Jimmy Young   **(a) Bung**

A backhander or bribe, usually shortened to the Christian name. How 'palm grease' became a 'jimmy'.

(b) Tongue

Based on the name of a hit singer of the 1950s and later a beknighted radio personality.

Jingle Bell   **Girl**

A 1980s example that demands the cockney pronunciation of 'girl' as 'gel'. 'Saveloys & jingles' – boys and girls.

Joan of Arc (a) **Lark**

Not really used in the sense of having fun – the opposite, in fact. A narrow escape or a difficult situation may bring about the remark: 'Sod this for a joan of arc!' Had the Maid of Orleans (1412–31) been the Maid of Hoxton, no doubt she would have said it herself as they lit the fire.

(b) **Park**

'Even in the best-kept "joan of arc" there's a piece of dogshit' – to paraphrase a cynical cockney saying.

(c) **Shark**

This time the fiery French heroin comes in as a predatory fish and an unscrupulous person.

Joan Rivers **Shivers**

Refers to fear-induced trembling, the creeps – possibly due to the sight of this US comedienne's latest bout of plastic surgery.

Joanna **Piano**

A well-known piece from a time when every street had a pub and every pub had a 'joanna'.

Jockey's Whip **Kip**

To grab a bit of 'jockey's' is to get a 'bit of blink' – get some sleep. 'Excessive use of the jockey's whip' – a long lie-in.

Jockey's Whip(s) **Chip(s)**

May accompany a steak – or represent a stake.

Jodrell Bank **Wank**

Extensively used example for the 'polishing of one's telescope'. An act of masturbation always dislengthened to a 'jodrell' and based on the giant observatory in Cheshire. 'jodrell-line' – a telephone chat line.

Joe Baksi **Taxi**

A piece from the 1940s based on an American boxer of the period (1922–77), who found fame by coming to England to beat British Heavyweight champion Bruce Woodcock. Heard on a long, motionless bus in the Aldgate area: 'If it wasn't for all the bloody "joe baksis" in London, there wouldn't be any traffic jams'.

Joe Blake   **(a) Cake**
A 19th-century example which became obsolete after (b) and (c) gained popularity.

(b) Stake
Once heard at gambling arenas for money that is gambled.

(c) Steak
A piece that isn't in the least bit rare, possibly based on a notorious cut-throat known as Blueskin. Executed in 1724 for almost slicing the throat of thief-taker Jonothan Wild (a dull blade saving the lawman's life), he was a close ally of the legendary escaper Jack Shepherd.

Joe Blakes   **Shakes**
A reference to the DTs, the trembles of the 'well-mangled'.

Joe Brown   **Town**
A 19th-century term probably coined by itinerent entertainers, circus folk or the like.

Joe Buck   **Fuck**
Sexual intercourse from the 1970s by way of the stud character in the Oscar-winning film of 1969, *Midnight Cowboy.*

Joe Cole   **Dole**
Early 21st-century parlance for unemployment benefit, used by young out-of-workers of the period. Based on a current England footballer whose talent ensures he will never have to 'dab on'.

Joe Daki   **Paki**
A derogatory piece from the 1990s that has become common in the East End of London, but then so has the Pakistani immigrant.

Joe Erk   **Berk**
Twice-removed example (see 'berkshire hunt'), which has to be used in full to distinguish it from 'joe hunt' (qv) – which is the same, but different.

Joe Goss   **Boss**
An early reference to a foreman or guvnor based on an English bare-knuckle fighter (1837–85), who held the World Heavyweight title from 1876–80.

Joe Gurr **Stir (Prison)**

A piece that has been doing a stretch in RS since the 1930s, there are no mug shots of Joe Gurr so nobody knows anything about him, except to say that his name has been spelt 'Ghir' and 'Girr'. Put it down to another faceless criminal.

Joe Hook **(a) Book**

A 1930s example but it now seems to be a case of 'joe hook' has left the library.

(b) Crook

A perpetual law-breaker for the best part of a century, which derives from the slang word for a thief – a hook.

Joe Hunt **Cunt**

Generally reduced to a 'joey' when used in connection with a 'fool' or a 'mug', but when an obnoxious 'dog-end' of a person is involved (like a Health & Safety zealot or a council snooper, who rifles through people's dustbins looking for the 'wrong' rubbish), 'joe hunt' doesn't get shortened.

Joe Loss **Toss**

Based on the name of a British bandleader (1909–90) and used either in a sense of not caring, i.e. not giving a 'joe loss' and the 'joe lossing' of a coin.

Joe McBride **Ride**

Sexual intercourse 1990s-style and possibly based on an American jazz singer and keyboard player of the period. 'Ride' is a centuries-old piece of slang for a 'bunk-up'.

Joe Ronce **Ponce**

Another member of the family Ronce who has been living off prostitutes since the 1920s. See also 'charlie', 'harry' and 'johnny ronce'.

Joe Rook **(a) Book**

One specifically made by an on-course bookmaker. A piece that has been on the rails since bookies needed a permit rather than a licence to ply their trade.

(b) Crook

A thief, possibly based on a misheard version of 'joe hook' (qv), although to 'rook' someone is to swindle, cheat or fleece them so mayhap that's the connection.

Joe Rookie — Bookie

Time was, anyone could set themselves up as a bookmaker at a racecourse or dog track, many of whom operated outside the bounds of legitimacy. Which would explain the association with 'joe rook' (b, qv).

Joe Rourke — Fork (Hand)

Specifically, the hand of a 'dip', Mr Rourke is therefore a pickpocket.

Joe Royle — Boil

A 1980s term for a gunge-filled spot that's based on an England international footballer of the period.

Joe Savage — Cabbage

A 19th-century example that has most likely been boiled into obscurity to make way for 21st-century descendant 'lily savage' (qv).

Joe Sime — Time

'What's the "joe sime"?' A piece often heard in 1960s racing circles and based on a jockey of the period (1923–96).

Joe Skinner — Dinner

One of three J. Skinners dished up since Victorian times. See also 'jim' and 'johnny skinner'.

Joe Soap — Dope

Refers to a fool of a mug, the one in the crowd most likely to step in something.

Joe Strummer — Bummer

A 1990s example regarding an unpleasant or unlucky experience, a sickener. Based on the singer-guitarist with 1970s punk group The Clash (1952–2002).

Joe Tank — Bank

A World War II piece that's now seldom, if ever, used.

John Bull   **(a) Full**

Anything from a stadium to a stomach can be 'john bull' but the main usage is to describe being full of alcohol, i.e. drunk.

(b) Pull

Used mainly with reference to 'getting a tug' from the police but also to go out looking for a sexual encounter is to 'go on the john bull'. Based on the personification of England and Englishness. In the 1712 book *Law is a Bottomless Pit* by J. Arbuthnot, John Bull was a character representing England. It was later republished as *The History of John Bull*.

John Cleese   **Cheese**

A piece from the suburbs based on the English comedy actor and writer. Refers to any kind of cheese, be it Cheddar, Stilton or Norwegian Blue. Or is that a parrot?

John Dick   **Sick**

A 1950s rival to 'tom & dick' (qv) that is based on a West Ham United and Scotland footballer of the period (1930–2000). Over the years West Ham fans have got used to feeling 'johnny dick' at five o'clock on Saturday afternoons.

John Dillon   **Shilling**

A piece from the 1930s based on the name of a racehorse of the period, although the term has beaten the coin in the obscurity stakes.

John Hop   **Cop (Police Officer)**

They say you're approaching old age when the 'jonnops' begin to look youthful. When the judges seem younger, you're there! 'Pock-marked' – bearing bruises meted out by a backslang cop.

John Hopper   **Copper**

An early 20th-century rozzer.

John Major   **Pager**

A 1990s piece for the bleeping radio device based on a bleeping Tory prime minister of the period.

John O'Groat　　　　　　**Coat**

It makes no difference that the 's' is missing from the North-Easterly tip of Britain, for donkey's years people have been wearing their 'john o'groats'. Oh, there it is...

John O'Groats　　　　　　**Oats**

Refers to sexual gratification, when a man has had his 'johnnoes', he has 'dunked his digestive' and probably 'pumped out his porridge'.

John Peel　　　　　　**Eel**

Applies to a jellied or stewed eel, both culinary traditions of working-class London. Based on the traditional Cumberland song.

John Prescott　　　　　　**Waistcoat**

Labour Party politician, better known as 'Two Jags', becomes the latest member of the Prescott boys to represent the third part of a suit. See also 'charlie', 'colonel' and 'jim prescott'.

John Selwyn Gummer　　　　　　**Bummer**

'What a John Selwyn!' as this Conservative politician's daughter might have said when, in 1990, she was famously forced by her father, then agricultural minister, to eat a hamburger in public to prove the safety of British beef. A bummer is an unpleasant, disappointing or distressing occurrence.

John Terry　　　　　　**Merry**

Pleasantly intoxicated, that is. As used by a Chelsea fan the morning after celebrating his side's FA Cup win in 2007: 'I wasn't drunk, just a bit john terry, that's all.' Has possibly been used as 'jt' since then, as the Chelsea and England captain is widely known by his initials.

John Wayne　　　　　　**Train**

A 1950s term that seems to have run out of track since this American film star (1907–79) stopped shooting at Indians from one.

Johnnie Ray　　　　　　**Day**

A piece from the 1950s based on a popular American singer of the day (1927–90). It was used by young National Servicemen lamenting the fact that 'it had been one of those johnnie rays'.

Johnny Cash   **(a) Hash**
A drug-user's term for hashish.

                  (b) Slash (Urinate)
An American Country & Western singer and occasional actor in Westerns shows how the cowboy on the range would extinguish a ring of fire.

Johnny Cotton   **Rotten**
If it's rank, putrid or generally unfit for human consumption, it's 'johnny cotton'. Based on boy Cotton, Mrs Cotton's son.

Johnny Giles   **Piles (Haemorrhoids)**
A 1970s version of 'farmer giles' (qv) based on an Irish international footballer of the period.

Johnny Horner   **Corner**
A late 19th-century term sometimes used to signify the non-specific whereabouts of a person. Public houses were commonly found on street corners and the phrase: 'He's gone round the johnny' often meant 'He's up the pub'.

Johnny Rann   **Scran (Food)**
A largely-unheard version of 'tommy o'rann' (qv). Scran is an 18th-century term used by the poor, originally meaning scraps of food. Beggars would go 'out on the scran' – to beg for food.

Johnny Rollocks   **Bollocks**
One of a trio of 'rollocks', the others being 'jimmy' and 'tommy' (see both). A case of an extra rollock in the testicle department. 'Kaycollobs' – backslang pills.

Johnny Ronce   **Ponce**
The last of the 'ronce' boys in the prostitute-minding game. See also 'Charlie', Harry' and 'Joe' ronce.

Johnny Rutter   **Butter**
First spread in the 19th century and rarely, if ever, heard now. Based on a gentleman with the same name, height and inside leg measurement, and not the other Johnny Rutter (who is much shorter and has a speech impediment).

Johnny Skinner   Dinner

When this was first coined it would have been cooked in a scullery.

Johnny Vaughan   Porn

One of the first terms of the 21st century, which sees a British DJ, comedian and film critic turn blue.

Johnny Walker   Talker

Refers to a trappy person, a 'parrot', often an informer. Mainly though, it's someone who talks incessantly and says nothing, a 'gabbladictum'. Based on a brand of whisky, the connection with loose tongues is obvious. The Gabbladictum was a Venusian parrot with more rabbit than Smithfield from the 1960s TV series *Space Patrol*, whose name became attached to gabby people.

Joint of Beef   Chief

Refers to a boss or manager, someone from the topside of your company whose rump may need kissing if a vacancy comes up and you wish to fillet.

Jolly Joker   Poker

Strangely not the card game but the implement for poking a fire, which somewhat dates the term to the days of the coal fire – and may now limit it to a country pub.

Jolly Roger   Lodger

From a time when people supplemented their wages by letting out a spare room and taking in a 'jolly'. Based on the pirate flag, which suggests care should be taken when letting a stranger into your home.

Jolson Story   Cory (Penis)

Based on the name of a 1946 film on the life of American singer Al Jolson (1886–1950). The term appeared later as a 'jolson', regarding that which you wouldn't show your mammy.

Jonah's Whale   Tail

The wag-able part of an animal from the same poem as described in 'henry meville' (qv). Had it been a term for a 'tale', it would surely have been a whopper, like: 'Sorry I've been off work for three days, but I was swallowed by a whale'.

Jonathan Ross   **Toss**
Later version of 'stirling moss' as a term of indifference. For 'couldn't give a stirling' read 'couldn't give a jonathan'. Formed on the name of a British TV personality and journalist.

Joynson-Hicks   **Six**
A theatrical piece from the 1920s based on Sir William Joynson-Hicks (1865–1932), a Tory home secretary of the period. The number has long been up on this one: it has been hit for a 'joynson' out of the ground and now rests in the field of obsolete RS.

Joy of My Life   **Wife**
A 19th-century term probably uttered with tongue firmly in cheek for a century or so.

Joystick   **Prick (Penis)**
The control column of an aircraft has been used in this sense since pre-World War II. Some deny this as being RS, but it *is* slang and it *does* rhyme, so here it remains.

Judge Dredd   **Head**
A newspaper strip cartoon inspired a film and this late 1990s example. As the dirty fighter said just before sending the nut in: 'Here comes the judge!'

Judi Dench   **Stench**
A 1990s term based on the British actress whose numerous awards confirm this has nothing to do with her performances. Her dameship's name just happens to rhyme with a bad smell.

Judy & Punch   **Lunch**
A piece that's probably from suburbia as the working-man doesn't have 'judy', the mid-day break is dinner time. See also 'Punch & Judy'.

Jug & Pail   **Gaol**
The well-known term 'jug', meaning prison, was in place long before this. 'Jug & pail' is an early 20th-century piece that may have reflected cell furnishings.

Julian Clary   **(a) Fairy**

A 1990s term for a homosexual male, which almost wrote itself since it's based on an overtly gay British comedian.

(b) Lairy (Flash)

In regard to being gaudily dressed this is as apt as (a) given that the man's stage attire is blindingly loud. (Does that make sense?)

Julian Dicks   **Six**

A former West Ham footballer switches sports and becomes a big hit at cricket.

Julius Caesar   **(a) Cheeser**

An old diminutive of 'cheese cutter' – a flat cap – which explains why the Roman Emperor (100–44 BC) sat jauntily atop cockney heads.

(b) Freezer

Interesting that the term for what can store ice cream is based on an Italian, the original 'hokey-pokey' man, mayhap?

(c) Geezer

A late 1990s piece by which 'Who's that bloke?' becomes 'Who's that julius?'

Jumbo Jet   **Bet**

A 'jumbo' sounds like a large wager. Based on the giant aircraft, the term may be Irish as it was heard in the Guinness Village at the 2007 Cheltenham Festival. 'Lump on' – to have a large bet.

Jumbo's Trunk   **Drunk**

An infrequently used example to describe someone who has spent too much time at the water-hole.

Jumping Jack   **Black**

Refers to the black snooker or pool ball and also to a black person who, with a bit of reverse spin, is also, derogatorily, known as an 'eight-ball'. A 1960s term based on an old type of firework.

Jungle Jim(ming)   **Swim(ming)**

A piece that lived and died in the 1950s when a TV series of this name came and went. Its star, Johnny Weissmuller (1904–84), was a former screen Tarzan and US Olympic swimming champion to boot, so the term was apt at the time.

Just as I Feared   **Beard**

Always trimmed to a 'just as', this early 20th-century piece is based on a line from a limerick by Edward Lear (1812–88).

Kangaroo   **(a) Jew**

A well-known piece since the 1930s, especially on the race-course where it has long applied to Jewish bookmakers. By the looks of the term, is it mainly used in the jumping season?

(b) Screw

Prisoner's slang for a prison officer usually in the reduced form of 'kanga'. It also applies secondarily to wages: you're earning well if you're on a good 'kangaroo'.

Kate Adie   **Lady**

Based on a TV news reporter, who not only appears as one of her sex but mainly as a ladies toilet, the 'kate adie's'.

Kate & Sydney   **Steak & Kidney**

A piece from caff society of years gone by for a steak and kidney pie (or pudding). I seem to remember it from school dinner days as 'snake & pygmy'.

Kate Carney   **Army**

Well-known term based on a music-hall artiste (1869–1950). Coined by World War I soldiers and used by squaddies as the 'kate' ever since.

Kate Moss   **Toss**

A 1990s term based on a British fashion model, by which the indifferent couldn't give a 'kate'.

Katherine Docks **Socks**
Based on the dock near the Tower of London that closed in 1968, which is possibly when this term was last used.

Keith Moon **Loon**
A 1960s example based on a rock drummer (1947–78), whose outrageous exploits led to him being known as 'Moon the Loon'. This is a piece that wrote itself. London-born Moon played with The Who from 1964 until his death.

Ken Dodd **Wad**
Refers to a large roll of banknotes produced from a pocket or from under the stairs of a house in Knotty Ash. Based on a British comedian who fell foul of the taxman.

Ken Dodds **Cods (Testicles)**
'Kick 'im in the ken dodds' is an instruction to fight dirty and hard grafters work their 'kens' off.

Ken Follet **Wallet**
A rhyme from the 1990s based on a Welsh author is the reason why modern pickpockets dip for 'kens'.

Kenneth Brannagh **Scanner**
An early 21st-century example to describe part of the home PC system. Who knew when RS started that one day there would be a term for a scanner? What was a scanner back then? Oh well, that's the evolving nature of slang. Based on the Belfast-born actor, director and dramatist of the classical theatre.

Kennington Lane **Pain**
Based on a road in South London near The Oval cricket ground, this applies to physical pain rather than the mental torture of watching Australia whitewash England to win The Ashes.

Kentish Town **Brown**
Nearby rival to 'camden town' (qv) in relation to copper coinage, originally pre-decimal 'tosh'.

Kermit the Frog **(a) Bog (Lavatory)**
Based on a character from TV's *The Muppet Show*, people in danger of springing a leak and those with one in the departure lounge have been hopping to the 'kermit' since the 1980s.

(b) Snog

A passionate 'kermit' will often give rise to a 'frog spawn' (qv), which may lead to an outpouring of 'tadpoles'.

Kerry Packered　　　**Knackered**

When you're worn out and tired, you're 'kerried', as is any kind of equipment or machinery that no longer works.

Kerry Packers　　　**Knackers**

The testicles are known as 'kerrys', thanks to the Australian entrepreneur (1937–2005).

Kettle & Hob　　　**Fob**

One of many explanations as to why a fob watch is known as a 'kettle' but since there are so many theories, this has to be treated only as a possibility. Use it if you like, but don't bank on it being valid.

Kettle on the Hob　　　**Bob**

One of an elite band of male Christian names endowed with a piece of RS. Always shortened to 'kettle', but not often used these days. In old money, a shilling was also called a 'kettle'.

Keystone Cop　　　**Chop**

When the curtain came down on this crazy comedy crew of the silent screen, they endured in butcher's shops in lamb and pork form.

Khyber Pass　　　**(a) Arse**

A very familiar piece that has almost gained respectability, a kick up the 'khyber' has spurred mobility since the 19th century.

(b) Glass

An example that has been in existence since the days of the Raj, but with the popularity of (a), drinking from a 'khyber' takes on an unsavoury, if not deviant sense.

Kick & Prance　　　**Dance**

A function (and what you do when you get there). A 'lilley & kick' – a dinner and dance. See Lilley & Skinner.

Kid Creole   **Dole**

A 1980s term for unemployment benefit based on a pop group of the period, Kid Creole & The Coconuts. They had a hit with a song called 'Stool Pigeon' – which, ironically, is what the DSS want the public to become in a bid to combat benefit fraud.

Kidney Punch   **Lunch**

Always truncated to the first element, often in relation to a pie and a pint.

Kidstake   **Fake**

To be 'at the kidstakes' is to be on a wind-up, i.e. to try to con or kid someone with a phoney story.

Kilburn Priory   **Diary**

Based on a long-gone medieval convent in North-West London, this mainly applied to a police officer's notebook.

Kilkenny   **Penny**

A piece from a previous coinage which, since pennies still exist, may still be part of someone's small change.

Kilkenny Cats   **Bats (Mad)**

A reference to anyone who is mentally out of whack and based on a fabled tale of animal cruelty, whereby some soldiers in 18th-century Ireland tied a pair of cats together by their tails and threw them in a ring to fight. At the approach of an officer, a trooper sliced through the tails with his sword, causing the hapless mogs to have it on their paws. Asked to explain the two bloodied waggers, the trooper replied that the cats had eaten each other up to their tails.

King Canute(s)   **Boot(s)**

Seldom-used variation of the perennial 'daisy roots' (qv) and based on the Danish-born King of England (c. 994–1035). To prove his limited powers he is reputed to have marched onto seashore and commanded the tide to turn back. It didn't, and he ruined a perfectly good pair of 'king canutes'.

King Death   **Breath**

An old expression for halitosis is 'dodgy king death'.

King Dick   **(a) Brick**

A piece first laid on Victorian building sites.

                 (b) Thick

'Is he king dick or what?' A question asked of a king-sized puttyhead who may be a few miles short of a marathon.

King Dickie   **Brickie**

Bricklayers have probably revelled in this term since the first 'king dicks' were laid.

King Farouk   **Book**

A post-World War II term for what you're holding that's based on the last king of Egypt (1920–65).

King Kong   **Pong**

Based on cinema's greatest ape, this is an example that never gets shortened. A nasty niff is always a bad 'king kong'.

King Lear   **(a) Ear**

Well-known piece based on Shakespeare's play. Heard in a shopping mall in Ilford: 'Did you see that? A three-month-old baby with its king lears pierced. Ridiculous!'

                 (b) Queer

How a king becomes a queen. An old piece from the theatre, naturally.

Kingdom Come   **(a) Bum**

In the days when corporal punishment raised cane in the classroom, teachers were known as 'flaybottomists', which meant they would have flogged many a little 'kingdom come' to Kingdom Come.

                 (b) Rum

'A kingdom! A kingdom! My horse for a kingdom!' As Richard III might have said, had he been a cockney alcoholic.

Kings & Queens   **Beans**

Mainly refers to baked beans, whereby 'kings on holy' is a common pairing. See also 'Holy Ghost'.

King's Head   **Shed**

A garden shed, the place where the tools live – and now the only King's Head in Britain where a person can smoke in peace.

Kings Lynn   **Gin**

A piece heard in a hotel bar in Norfolk. Where else?

King's Proctor   **Doctor**

Uncommon if not obsolete piece. The 'quack' or the 'sawbones' usually suffices.

Kipper & Bloater   **(a) Motor**

Cars, vans, coaches, fish-lorries, etc...they're all 'kippers'.

(b) Photo

Refers to all types of photographs, from a holiday snap to the one that sorts out the result of a horse or dog race. And the 'kippers' being send back by the Hubble Telescope are out of this world.

Kipper & Plaice   **Face**

Always reduced to the first element, often about a moosh of no great beauty. 'Double kippered' – two-faced.

Kiss & Cuddle   **Muddle**

Never shortened. To be in a right old 'mix & muddle' is to be in a state of confusion.

Kiss Me, Hardy   **Bacardi**

The reputed last words of Lord Nelson (1758–1805) taken in jocular vein. Whether it's reduced to a 'kiss me' or not depends on the sex of the bar person.

Kiss-Me-Quick   **Prick**

More likely to be associated with a fool than the male member and based on the fact that on a beano there's always one jolly soul who dons a kiss-me-quick hat and makes a complete fool of himself. Such a person is a 'kiss-me'.

Kiss of Life   **Wife**

As used by a man whose liver has been saved by marriage, no doubt.

Kitchen Range   **Change**

Always curtailed at 'kitchen' in relation to that which is never checked by men buying drinks.

Kitchen Sink   (a) **Chink**

A Chinese person; an uncommon, and disparaging alternative to the oft-used tiddleywink. 'Kaynich' (backslang).

(b) **Stink**

An example that is often distinctly apt. 'Kaynits' (kennets) – a backslang smell. 'Kennetseeno' – stinking.

Kit-Kat   **Pratt**

A 1990s term for a fool, one who 'takes the biscuit'. Heard on a street corner as a long-legged beauty in a mini-skirt passed two stalk-eyed young lads:
1st man: Phwoahh! Look at that! It shouldn't be allowed.
2nd man: Shouldn't be allowed, you kit-kat? It should be compulsory!

Knife & Fork   **Pork**

Fairly common term for pig meat, which is usually said in full.

Knobbly Knee(s)   **Key(s)**

Asking if anyone has seen your 'knobbly knees' generally prompts a saucy response.

Knock on the Door   **Four**

Another piece of bingo-caller's slang: 'Knock on the door, the number four'.

Knocker & Knob   **Job**

May be accessories to the door of opportunity. Formed in a time when it was possible for the working-man to walk the streets, knocking on doors or gates in search of employment.

Knotty Ash   **Cash**

A 1980s term inspired by the clash between comedian Ken Dodd and the Inland Revenue. The inference being that the chief diddy-man's home in Knotty Ash, a village outside Liverpool, contained cash that was beyond the taxman's ken.

Koh-I-Noor   **Whore**

A Jewish prostitute, a clever pun on 'Cohen 'ore' and based on the famous diamond kept in the Tower of London.

Kung-Fu Fighter   Lighter

Known as a 'kung-fu' by the young generation of smokers in the 1990s.

Kuwaiti Tanker   Wanker

A term of abuse for anyone thought to be 'as low as a punch in the bollocks' or as useful as a comb might be to the Mitchell brothers of Albert Square. The piece has been heard since the Gulf War of 1991.

Kylie Minogue   Rogue

A piece of 21st-century popney. Due to the popularity of this Australian singer and actress, ne'er-do-wells are ironically known as 'kylies'.

L. K. Clark Mark

A misheard version of 'elky clark' (qv).

Lace Curtain Burton

Originally applied solely to this brand of beer but later extended so that any type of bitter became 'lace'.

La-Di-Da (a) Car

Coined when only the upper-classes owned their own 'lardys'. Based on the slang term for 'stuck-up' or 'snooty'.

(b) Cigar

Always condensed to a 'lardy', a piece that highlights the inequality of days gone by. When the officer classes smoked cigars whilst the other ranks made do with Woodbines.

(c) Star 1

Theatrical example for a star performer – the one with the la-di-da on their dressing-room door.

Star 2

An elderly newsagent's reference to the *Daily Star* newspaper.

Star 3

The Heavenly twinkler, as heard in the cockney lullabye: 'Twinkle twinkle la-di-da'.

Ladies & Gents Sense

Only really mentioned at the display of a complete lack of sense. A brainless dolt 'ain't got the ladies he was born with'.

Lady From Bristol   **Pistol**

'Stand and deliver!' yelled the highwayman as he cocked his lady' – as Dick Turpin's cockney biographer might have written.

Lady From Hitchin   **Kitchen**

A piece from the theatre based on a well-known limerick. It refers to the room where a crab-riddled Hertfordshire lass named Rose was caught scratching herself.

Lady Godiva   **Fiver**

A well-known but rarely used term for £5 based on the English noblewoman (c. 1040–80), who allegedly rode naked through Coventry market in protest at the taxes imposed by her husband, the Earl of Chester.

Lager & Lime   **Time**

A noughties term that in terms of lateness comes down to 'look at the lager!'

Lakes of Killarney   **(a) Barmy**

Generally used in a reduced form, whereby the daft are regarded as 'lakes' or 'lakie'.

          (b) Carney

A slang-for-slang term regarding a two-faced, untrustworthy person: 'What a right lakie scrote him next-door is! Says one thing to me and something completely different to someone else'.

Lal Brough   **Snuff**

Commonly known as 'lally', when snuff was commonly sniffed. Based on Lionel (Lal) Brough (1836–1909), English actor, comedian and playwright, well-known on the Victorian stage. Therefore a 19th-century term.

Lamb Shank   **Wank**

An act of masturbation, a popular pastime based on a popular joint of meat. 'Nifty-fifty' a quick 'hand jive' based on the number of strokes it should take to achieve orgasm.

Lambeth Walk   **Chalk**

An example heard as 'lambeth' in snooker halls and pubs with pool tables and dart boards.

Lame Duck   **Fuck**

A reference to sexual intercourse. Heard at a bus stop:
Woman: You are the ugliest, dirtiest, scruffiest, smelliest little man I've ever had the misfortune to meet.
Tramp: No chance of a lame duck then?

Lancashire Lass(es)   **Glass(es)**

Very old piece from the north of England that refers to spectacles and drinking glasses.

Land of Hope   **Soap**

An early 20th-century piece that seems to have been slung away with the bath water.

Lash LaRue   **Flu**

Forgotten term from the 1950s used by skivers and shirkers who felt a 'wee cough' coming on. Based on a Western film hero (1915–96) whose gimmick was to see off baddies with a bullwhip.

Last Card in the Pack   **(a) Back**

Anatomically speaking, workers have been putting their 'last cards' into it since the 19th century.

(b) Sack

To draw the 'last card' is to be dismissed from employment, perhaps from too many days off with a dodgy 'last card' (a).

(c) Snack

Old theatrical term for a bite to eat, perhaps a role to sink the teeth into.

Lath & Plaster   **Master**

A 19th-century term for a master craftsman in the building trade based on the materials used for finishing walls and ceilings. Laths are the thin strips of wood that the plaster adheres to.

Laugh & Joke   **Smoke**

Any kind of smoke, be it cigar, cigarette, pipe or one of those funny fags. A piece from the time when those who *didn't* smoke were considered anti-social. 'Eekomess' – what a backslang smoker nips outside for.

Laugh & Titter **Bitter**
Beer: the drink that cheers and makes you merry.

Laughed & Sang **Slang**
A piece from the late 1940s that possibly never made the early 1950s. Apparently it refers to RS, but I've never heard it.

Laurel & Hardy **Bacardi**
Formed on the names of the most famous comedy duo of all time, Englishman Stan Laurel (1890–1965) and American Oliver Hardy (1892–1957), generally shortened to the first mentioned. Thus Mr Laurel acquires some new partners, most commonly 'Holy Smoke' (qv), i.e. 'laurel & holy' or 'idracab and eecock' in a backslang bar.

Lay Me in the Gutter **Butter**
Spread as 'lay me' – but not for a very long time. Presumably based on the drunken instructions from one inebriate to another, but I'm guessing.

Leaky Bladder **Ladder**
A particularly high one is more likely to put a strain on the bowel than the bladder, especially in the acrophobic.

Lean & Fat **Hat**
A 19th-century term that's been swallowed up by the well-worn 'titfer'. See Tit for Tat.

Lean(s) & Linger(s) **Finger(s)**
A term that suggests loitering may have something to do with idle hands…but then it may not.

Lean & Lurch **Church**
A mid 19th-century piece for the place of worship that most of us, regrettably, visit for weddings, christenings and funerals only. As a removal man said to a vicar newly arrived in Plaistow: 'You'll find we're pretty much a matchings, hatchings and dispatchings community, Vicar – but at least you'll get your Sundays to yourself.'

Lee Marvin **Starving**
Based on the American actor (1924–87) best remembered for

his tough-guy roles and for being 'Born Under a Wandrin' Star'. Now his name will for ever be connected with a rumbling belly.

Lee Van Cleef　　　**Beef**
A piece heard in a carvery in the shortened form of 'lee van'. Certainly knows his way round a dinner plate, does this old spaghetti western star (1925–89).

Left & Right　　　**Fight**
Apt in that it's indicative of punches thrown and boots put in.

Left in the Lurch　　　**Church**
A 19th-century piece formed on the words of a music-hall song about someone being jilted at the altar. Little visited these days, as many of us tend to avoid church religiously.

Leg Before Wicket　　　**(a) Ricket (Mistake)**
When you've made a 'leg before' or more commonly an 'lbw', you've cocked up, big time.

(b) Ticket
Nearly always reduced to the initials, it refers to the obvious, be it theatre ticket, bus ticket, etc. It has also been used as praise for a task well done (that's the ticket) and anyone slightly 'off their trolley' is said to be 'not all the lbw'.

Leg of Beef　　　**Thief**
Uncommon variant of the more frequently used 'tea leaf' (qv), which seems to be based on the nursery rhyme denouncing Taffy the Welshman as a 'nicker' (thief).

Leg of Mutton　　　**Button**
A piece that may be shortened for comic effect: 'Mum, a leg's come off. Can you sew it back on for me?'

Leg of Pork　　　**Chalk**
An example heard in a pub that seems to have hopped from the dartboard to the pool table.

Leicester Square　　　**Chair**
Always restricted to the first element: 'Pull up a leicester and take the weight off your plates'.

Leisure Hours   **Flowers**

Since the 19th-century, bunches of 'leisures' have served as peace offerings, often because the presenter has spent too many leisure hours up the pub.

Lemon & Dash   **Slash**

To go for a 'lemon' is to 'splash one's boots' – to urinate.

Lemon & Lime   **Time**

Better make a dash for it when you're running out of 'lemon'.

Lemon Curd   **(a) Bird**

The feathered type is secondary to a girl, obviously a sweet and tasty one.

(b) Turd

The sweet in the street that gets under your feet and has you cursing inconsiderate dog-owners.

Lemon Drops   **Cops**

'Watch it! Lemons' – A warning cry from a lookout at the sight of the police. 'Namslop' – a policeman. 'Nammowslop' – policewoman (backslang PCs).

Lemon Flavour   **Favour**

A friend indeed may do a friend in need a 'lemon'. Also a phrase of disbelief: 'You're gonna take up exercise? Do me a lemon, you're too out of condition to get fit.'

Lemon Squash   **Wash**

Always 'lemon' your 'germans' before 'lilley' (look 'em up for yourself!). In the 1920s this became an underworld term for a public lavatory, whereby pickpockets 'working the lemon' or at the 'lemon lark' were lousy scrotes who made a living from stealing from coats hanging in public washrooms. In his 1975 *Dictionary of Rhyming Slang*, Julian Franklyn states that in the 1950s this evolved into 'lemon & dash'. Further research suggests the correct term should be 'lemon & dosh'. As my informant put it: 'A "lemon" is a mug and "dosh" is money and a fool and his money are easily parted, especially when he puts it in his coat and hangs it up in a public carsey.'

Lemon Squeezer **Geezer (Man)**
Always reduced to the first element. A naïve heterosexual's opinion of a gay bar: 'I don't like this place, it's full of lemons'.

Lemon Squeezy **Easy**
'Easy peasy, lemon squeezy', heard on TV and later at a junior football match.

Lemon Tea **Pee/Wee**
Often a colourfully apt example.

Lemonade **Spade**
Applies, offensively, to a black person. Also the suit in a pack of shufflers.

Len Hutton **Button**
Formed on the name of a former England cricket captain (1916–90), but now seems to be at the end of its innings.

Lenny the Lion **Iron (Homosexual)**
An example of twice-removed RS: 'iron hoof' (qv) became so well known that it has picked up a term of its own. Based on the name of the dummy with ventriloquist Terry Hall's hand up its back. Hall (1926–2007) and the limp-wristed Lenny were seldom off TV in the 1950s–60s.

Leo Sayer **All-Dayer**
A 1990s term based on a British singer-songwriter. When the hits dried up he re-emerged as an all-day piss-up.

Leslie Ash **(a) Gash**
Men behaving badly speak for the vagina.

(b) Slash
Urination can be known as going for a 'leslie', thanks to the British actress, a co-star in TVs *Men Behaving Badly*.

Lever-Arch Files **Piles (Haemorrhoids)**
'Lever-arches' is one of the later additions to the RS list of terms for haemorrhoids, one that seems to have been coined by an office wallah.

Levi Strauss **House**
A piece from the noughties that sees the jeans manufacturer enter the property market.

Levy & Frank   **Wank**
Formed on the name of an old London company of restaurateurs, the 'pulling of the pudden' has long been known as a 'levy'. 'Levy-mag' – a top-shelf magazine.

Life Peer   **Queer**
A homosexual, based on the stereotypical sexuality of the nobility as perceived by the working-man. Therefore disparaging.

Life & Death   **Breath**
Apt in that without breath there is no life, but this is mainly used in the case of someone's bad breath. Anyone who suffers 'dodgy life' is liable to acquire the nickname 'Ally Tosis'.

Liffey Water   **Porter**
A 19th-century term for this type of beer, very popular at the time; it also referred to any type of black beer, most famously Guinness, which is brewed near the river Liffey in Dublin.

Light & Bitter   **Shitter (Anus)**
Based on a once-popular pairing of beers, of which a bad one will get the 'l&b' working overtime.

Light & Dark   **Park**
A throwback to the days when a family day out constituted a day in the local park, arriving in the morning and leaving when they were turned out by the parkie around dusk.

Light of Love   **Guv**
An example of convict irony from the 1940s regarding the prison governor.

Light of My Life   **Wife**
Often said sarcastically of a 'battleaxe' of a woman.

Lilley & Skinner   **(a) Beginner**
Applies to someone new to a job or a novice. A 'lilley' is likely to be known as 'newbloke' until such time as introductions are made.

(b) Dinner
Based on a company of shoe manufacturers and retailers, men

have long been forced to cut short a visit to the pub for fear of their 'lilley' ending up in the dustbin or even the dog.

Lillian Gish   **Fish**

Formed on the name of an American actress (1896–1993), it applies only to a fish on a platter. Seems a pity that a woman whose film career lasted from 1912–87 should be remembered simply as a lump of fried cod, a boiled haddock or a jellied eel.

Lillian Gished   **Pissed**

A Scottish version of being drunk, given the Scots' version of pissed is pished.

Lily the Pink   **Drink**

A term that seems to have come and gone in the late 1960s, when Liverpool group The Scaffold topped the charts with a song of this title. Its slight usage was confined to going to a pub for a 'lily'. Now about as common as a 'Welcome to Kabul' fridge magnet.

Lily Savage   **Cabbage**

A 1990s example based on the tarty alter-ego of British comedian Paul O'Grady gets on the menu. Aptly, the character knows how fond men are of their greens. 'Edgabac' – backslang cabbage.

Limehouse Cut   **Gut**

Based on an East London waterway in reference to a paunch, whereby a 'boozer's belly' may be known as a 'limehouse'.

Lincoln's Inn   **(a) Fin**

A 'lincoln's' is an old reference to a hand, for which 'fin' is an even older piece of slang.

(b) Finn

A finn is an old racing term for £5, either from 'finnuf', backslang for 'funf' – the yiddish for five – or a natural corruption of (a). A fiver has also long been known as a 'handful'.

(c) Gin

A 19th-century piece pushed aside by the likes of 'vera lynn' (qv). Based on one of the four Inns of Court in London.

Linen Draper   Paper

Specifically a newspaper and always folded to a 'linen': A tale related to me by a lorry driver who, whilst delivering to an industrial estate near Dublin, entered a newsagent in a small village and asked for an English paper: 'D'you want yesterday's or today's?' asked the proprietor. 'Today's,' replied the driver.'In that case you'll have to come back tomorrow,' he was told.

Lionel Bart   Fart

An East London born songwriter (1930–99) gets on the RS stage as 'arse-music'.

Lionel Blair   Chair

A 1970s piece from the world of showbiz formed on the name of British dancer and entertainer, making him the ideal partner for 'betty grable' (qv).

Lionel Blairs   Flares

A widely used example for flared trousers since they were fashionable. Known as 'lionels', the term is now used condescendingly, especially when watching old TV shows and films.

Lion's Lair   Chair

An early 20th-century term that was probably an allusion to the old man's chair, the one no one else was allowed to sit in.

Lion's Roar   Snore

Apt example from the days before all-day pub opening hours – especially in regard to the Sunday afternoon drunk who fell asleep in front of the telly and snored all the way through the film.

Lion's Share   Chair

A corruption of 'Lion's Lair' (qv).

Lisa & Bart   Fart

An anal gust of wind known as a 'lisa' would be a blast to her rascally Simpson sibling.

Little & Large   Marge

A reference to margarine that is older than the British comedy double act who wore this handle in the 1970s.

Little Bo Peep   **Sleep**

Based on the dozy shepherdess and said as getting some 'little bo'.

Little Boy Blue   **Screw**

An early 20th-century term for a prison officer based on the horn-blowing kid in the nursery rhyme.

Little Brown Jug   **Plug**

This old song title lends itself to an electric plug or the one in the sink, but more vulgarly to a tampon.

Little Grey Home in the West   **Vest**

An obsolete piece coined by soldiers of World War I and based on the title of a 1911 song.

Little Miss Muffet   **Stuff It**

An indication of what can be done with something that's not wanted: 'You can take your advice and little miss muffet'.

Little Nell   **Bell**

Based on a character from Dickens' *The Old Curiosity Shop* and mainly applies to a doorbell.

Little Peter   **Meter**

A mid 20th-century term for a gas or electric meter that had to be fed with money and was often a target for burglars. A perfectly fitting piece, a meter being a small moneybox and a 'peter' (a safe) being a big one.

Little Red Riding Hoods   **Goods**

An underworld term – where stolen goods are known as 'little red ridings'.

Little Titch(y)   **Itch(y)**

Based on a diminutive music-hall comic and often employed when gnats and mosquitoes are doing their worst. Titch was born Harry Relph in 1868 at the time of an infamous case about a stranger's claim to be heir to the Titchborne family fortune. Nicknamed 'Titch', the name stayed with Relph until his death in 1928 and it's due to him that short people will always carry the same handle.

Live Eel   **Field**

An archaic piece of cockney coined before London became the ugly urban sprawl it now is.

Liza Minnelli   **Telly**

A 1980s rhyme based on an American actress and singer, often seen on the 'liza' at the time, especially in the oft-repeated musical, *Cabaret*.

Lloyd's List   **Pissed**

A City of London example for being 'three sheets to the wind', which makes it apt as it's based on the trade and shipping paper.

Load of Hay   **Day**

A 19th-century piece that appears to have had its 'load of hay'.

Loaf of Bread   **(a) Dead**

An example so well-known as (b) that it is seldom, if ever used in this context.

(b) Head

Most commonly used in relation to the internal workings of the brainbox hence the ultra-familiar directive to think: 'use your loaf'.

Lobster & Crab   **Cab**

Possibly coined by the taxi driver who parked outside an overcrowded mosque hoping to pick up some crushed Asians.

Lollipop   **(a) Cop**

An infrequent reference to a police officer or plurally the police, many an illegal activity has broken up after the cry: 'Scarper, lollies!' Originally applied to a copper in the form of 'slop' or 'eslop' – backslang terms for police.

(b) Drop

This is 'drop' in the form of a gratuity, therefore to give someone a 'lolly' is to tip them.

(c) Shop 1

To 'lolly' someone is to inform against them; the betrayed may claim to have been 'lollied up'.

(d) Shop 2

Occasionally used for a shop, kids on an errand were sent up the 'lollipop'. This sweetie was often their reward.

London Fog　　　　　　　　**Dog**

Probably an extinct breed now since no one ever uses anything but 'cherry' in regard to a poochimutt these days. See also 'Cherry Hog'.

London Taxi　　　　　　　　**Jacksie (Anus)**

Possibly coined when a cab driver derided a tip and got a boot up his 'london taxi'.

Londonderry　　　　　　　　**Sherry**

A piece that has been on the RS drinks list since the mid 19th century.

Lone Ranger　　　　　　　　**(a) Danger**

Never used in the sense of peril, but as a term of exasperation: 'Any lone ranger of you ever getting a drink?'

(b) Stranger

Underworld term often directed at an unknown face or someone suspected of being a plainclothes police officer. An appropriate piece because the Lone Ranger was a well-known TV Western about a masked, therefore unknown lawman.

Long Acre　　　　　　　　**Baker**

A 19th-century rhyme based on a historic London street, one that has been associated with Dickens, Cromwell, Chippendale, Pepys, various Lords and Ladies and John Logie Baird, but no famous 'masters of the rolls' – bakers.

Long & Linger　　　　　　　　**Finger**

Originally an American example for a nose-picker, earwax-remover, wife-pleasurer, etc.

Long & Short　　　　　　　　**Port**

The drink that may be served long with a mixer or short on its own – and that's the long and short of it.

Lonsdale Belt　　　　　　　　**Gelt**

Underworld term for the Yiddish word for money based on the

trophy that boxers receive after winning a British title. Used as 'lonsdale' after the sporting Earl (1857–1944), who founded the prize.

Loo-Be-Loo   **Flu**
A piece heard in the 1950s as 'looby' after Andy Pandy's girlfriend on children's TV.

Loop the Loop   **Soup**
An old term for the first course, from asparagas to zucchini it's all 'loop de loop'.

Lord & Master   **Plaster**
That which covers a wound doubles as a path in the labyrinth of terms that lead to the backside. See also 'Plaster of Paris'.

Lord & Mastered   **Plastered**
A slang term for being drunk gets a piece of RS. Plenty of married men have gone on the booze, got themselves 'lord & mastered', pulled a lady and found a mistress.

Lord Lovat   **Shove It**
Based on the aristocratic brigadier of the commandos in World War II, Simon Fraser, 15th Lord Lovat (1911–95). Pronounced 'lord love it', it is used as a suggestion as to what can be done with the unwelcome and unwanted.

Lord Lovel   **Shovel**
A navvy's term from the 19th century based on a popular 18th-century ballad, the piece was probably used ironically as the only nobleman ever to dig a hole.

Lord Mayor   **Swear**
A very common reference to bad language that may be extended to 'lord mayoring'. Heard at Royal Ascot: 'She might look like a duchess but when her hat blew off, she could lord mayor like Wayne Rooney!'

Lord of the Manor   **Tanner**
Until this coin's demise (6 pence in old money), it was one of the oldest examples of RS.

Lord Rank   **Wank**

An act of 'the lonely art' that is an extension of 'J. Arthur Rank' (qv).

Lord Sutch   **(a) Clutch**

A motor mechanic's rhyme from the 1970s based on Screaming Lord Sutch (1940–99), a rock singer turned Monster Raving Loony chief. Sutch stood for parliament many times but never made it to the House of Commons. He is, however, far more prestigiously immortalised in RS.

      (b) Crutch/Crotch

Ill-fitting trousers may be too tight round the 'lord sutch' and a kick in the 'lord sutch' is a low-down dirty blow.

Lord Wigg   **Pig**

Apart from the porker, this applies to a glutton or a discourteous person, of whom it may be said: 'You'll have to excuse my lord wigg, he's a friend'. Based on British politician George Wigg (1900–83), first Chairman of the Horse Betting Levy Board (1967–72), which dates the term to the late 1960s.

Lord(s) & Peer(s)   **Ear(s)**

Whereby a clip round the 'lords' may amount to corporal punishment, which these days could see the clipper up before His Lordship.

Loretta Young   **Tongue**

Based on an American film actress of yesteryear (1913–2000), who tongue-wrestled the leading men of her day.

Lorna Doone   **Spoon**

Only in RS can a beautiful heroine of a romantic novel end up in a bowl of spotted dick and custard.

Lost & Found   **Pound**

An old reference to £1 and heard at the Dagenham Sunday market:

Trader: Who'll give me a little lost & found for this lovely Elizabethan ashtray?

Woman: Elizabethan?

Trader: Well, Elizabeth the Second.

Lou Reed   **Speed**

A late 20th-century term for amphetamines based on the American singer-songwriter who walked on the wild side in 1973 and enjoyed a perfect day in 1997.

Loud & Clear   **Dear**

Expensive. Anything overpriced is 'too loud' and that's how we should complain.

Lousy Lou   **Flu**

I have no idea who the 'Lou' in question is, but he or she must be knocking on a bit as this is a pretty old example.

Love & Hate   **Weight**

Refers to the constant battle between the human being and the scales whereby we love to eat, but hate to get fat.

Love & Kisses   **Missus**

Everyman's reference to his dearly beloved...right up to the end of the honeymoon.

Love & Marriage   **Carriage**

A probable allusion to the horse-drawn conveyance once used at a traditional wedding.

Lover's Tiff   **Syph**

Despite the rhyme, this is not restricted solely to syphilis but to venereal diseases in general, although there might be more than a tiff if one partner infected another.

Lucky Charm   **Arm**

Based on that which is supposed to give evil the elbow and keep you from 'arm.

Lucky Dip   **Whip(Round)**

A collection of money, usually up the pub. Lucky the 'dip' who picks the pocket of the one holding the 'lucky dip'.

Lucky Dip(s)   **Chip(s)**

May be based on the traditional way of eating a bag of chips and the luck involved in not picking up and munching a green one.

Lucozade   **Spade**
A derogatory term for a black person, often reduced to 'luke'.

Lucy Locket   **Pocket**
Refers to where one's hands are happy to linger, often to the annoyance of a foreman, from whom: 'Take your bleedin' hands out of your lucys and do some work!' was a common rucking. At least it was with my old foreman.

Luger Lout   **Kraut**
A World War II German, as described by a wag watching *The Great Escape* for the umpteenth time.

Lumberjack   **Back**
Anatomically speaking, this is a clever reworking of the word 'lumbar', especially when crying off work with an 'iffy lumber'.

Lump of Coke   **Bloke**
Large gentlemen are often referred to as 'big lumps' and have been since the 19th century. Coke is coal with the gasses removed and in backslang the term becomes a 'pemmul of eekoc'.

Lump of Ice   **Advice**
Often needed when you're in hot water.

Lump of Lead   **Head**
A 19th-century example that aptly describes a weighty bonce after a heavy bevvy.

Lump of School   **Fool**
An ancient term that may sound familiar when shortened, as in: 'You stupid great lump!' When compulsory education started in the 19th century, going to school was seen by some as a hindrance, which is why doing a 'lump of school' sounds like a punishment.

Lumpy Gravy   **Navy**
The Royal Navy, as termed by members of other services.

Mac Gimp   **Pimp**

A prostitute's bully, known as a 'mac' or 'magimp'; an early 20th-century example, originally from the US.

Macaroni   **Pony 1**

A long-established term for £25, especially in betting circles where a 'maca' each-way bet costs a 'lobster' (a £50 note is red).

Pony 2

A piece of twice-removed RS referring to excrement and defecation; the reduced form of 'pony & trap' (qv) has become a byword for 'crap' so people may go for a 'maca' – or step in a lump of it.

Macaroon   **Coon**

An offensive reference to a black person.

Mackerel & Sprat   **Pratt**

As usual the 'sprat' gets swallowed up and a fool becomes a right 'mackerel'.

Mad Hatter   **Natter**

A term that can't be shortened – friends and neighbours stop for a 'mad hatter'. Based on a character from *Alice in Wonderland*.

Mad Max   **Tax**

A piece from the 1990s relating to income and, at that time, betting tax. Based on a series of popular films which grossed millions of dollars, incurring a lot of 'mad max'.

Mad Mick   **Pick (Axe)**

An example heard on building sites at least since World War II, whereby the archetypal Irishman strikes up an unlikely partnership with the aristocratic 'lord lovel' (qv).

Madame de Luce   **Spruce (Deceive)**

Extensively employed in the first element, a con artist will try to 'madame' you and a liar will give you a 'load of old madame'. The word 'spruce' comes from an imitation beer made of twigs and needles from the spruce tree.

Madame Tussaud   **Bald**

Aptly used when describing someone with less hair than a waxwork model. A piece of useless advice: Worrying about losing your 'barnet' will make you go 'madame tussaud'.

Madonna   **Sconner**

An early 21st-century piece that sees an American singer-actress become a person with a 'shaven haven' – a shaved pubic area.

Mae West   **Breast/Chest**

Based on the American film actress (1892–1980), who is remembered as much for her one-liners and bawdy persona as for her films and 'mae wests'. 'Gib teesurbs' – big breasts of the backslang variety.

Maggie May   **Gay**

A 1980s rhyme based on the eponymous heroine of a couple of popular songs. Applies mainly to gay men who may be known as 'maggies'.

Maggie Thatcher   **Scratcher**

A 1990s term for a scratchcard, the game that promises winners instant capitalist status. Aptly based on Britain's first female prime minister.

Magistrate's Court   **Short**

Drinker's reference to a measure of spirit, a 'drop of magistrates' – which is appropriate since it's where a lot of people end up as a result of a few too many.

Mahatma Gandhi　　　　　**(a) Brandy**
Generally reduced to the first element, which from a cockney comes out as 'me'atma'.

(b) Shandy
A bit confusing really seeing as the same piece is also used for brandy, but since the Indian nationalist (1869–1948) was teetotal, this seems most apt.

Maidstone Jailer　　　　　**Tailor**
An ancient piece that seems to have fallen off the peg – along with the made-to-measure suit.

Major Loder　　　　　**Soda**
A piece from the racing fraternity based on a once-famous owner and breeder Major Eustace Loder. His most celebrated horse, Pretty Polly, won 22 of her 24 races between 1903–06. The term gets on the card as the natural partner of whisky.

Major Stevens　　　　　**Evens**
The only time that odds can be evens is in the betting game.

Malcolm Scott　　　　　**Hot**
A term from the theatre based on a long-forgotten female impersonator (1872-1929), known in his day as a dame comedian.

Man & Wife　　　　　**Knife**
A cutter from the early part of the 20th century, specifically a penknife.

Man Alive　　　　　**Five**
A piece of bingo-caller's jargon that sometimes serves as £5 as a 'man aliver' – fiver. Eevif kews' – five weeks of a backslang 'ray' (year).

Man in the Moon　　　　　**Loon**
A mad person or an eccentric, someone about whom it is often said: 'There's more out than in'.

Man o' War　　　　　**Bore**
Apt when applied to the old soldier who trots out tales of heroism in the Western Desert, etc., ad infinitum.

Man on the Moon　　　Spoon

This piece must have begun to cause a stir after Neil Armstrong's giant leap for mankind in 1969.

Man Trap　　　Crap

To defecate but mainly the putrid pile of pavement purée that lies in wait for an unsuspecting foot to be drawn into it.

Manchester City　　　Titty

'Manchesters' is a rare alternative to the commonly mouthed 'bristols'. See also 'Bristol City'.

Manfred Mann　　　Van

A piece from a 1960s haulage company based on a British rock group of the period, which took its name from their South African keyboards player. Their live recording of 'My Old Man Said Follow The Manfred' is much sought after.

Mangle & Wring(er)　　　Sing(er)

Normally used of a singer with no great vocal talent, like the karaoke clown who takes the stage and 'mangles' 'My Way'.

Mangle & Wringer　　　Finger

A underworld term based on a device that can be used as a finger-flattener; an informer will 'put the mangle on' – and if caught by the informee, he may have the mangle put on his finger.

Manhole Cover　　　Brother

A piece only used in the third person when speaking of one's 'manhole'.

Mantovani　　　Fanny (Vagina)

Based on bandleader Annunzio Mantovani (1905–80), whose orchestra had several hits in the 1950s, this applies to women as sex objects. Boys go out to pull a bit of 'manto'. At least they did back then.

Maracas　　　Knackers (Testicles)

A fairly common rhyme, most often employed as a mock threat: 'You're gonna get a kick in the maracas before you get much older'.

Marble Arch Starch

An old term for an old product based on an old construction in London. Starch is used as a stiffening agent for fabrics.

Marble Halls Balls (Testicles)

An old expression which comes down to 'marbles'. Probably based on the famous Marble Hall, which was the entrance hall at Highbury, Arsenal FC's former stadium.

Marbles & Conkers Bonkers (Mad)

Based on two games of childhood, this is always reduced to the first element – which is fitting enough in that adults who continue to play such games and enter championship events are considered by the rest of us to be 'quite marbles'.

Margaret Rose Nose

A piece from the 1940s which may be based on the given names of HM The Queen's sister, the Princess Margaret Rose (1930–2002).

Margate Sand(s) Hand(s)

Based on the Kent resort that for generations has been a popular destination for beanos, the boozy coach trips on which drunken men try to get their 'margates' on drunken women. And vice versa.

Maria Monk Spunk 1 (Semen)

'Custard', 'yoghurt', 'gravy' or 'cream', whatever else you call it, in RS it's 'maria' and inspired by the eponymous heroine of a pornographic novel from 1836.

Spunk 2

Applies to courage, but has been beaten down by time.

Marie Corelli Telly

A piece from the very early days of television, based on the pseudonym of romantic novelist Marie Mackay (1855–1924) – whether any of her works have appeared on the 'marie corelli' or not, I don't know.

COMPLETE COCKNEY RABBIT

Mario Lanza Cancer
An Australian import for the 'Big C' based on an American opera singer (1921–59), who became a star of Hollywood musicals.

Marmite Shite
Rubbish, nonsense, shoddy gear – or to give it a name 'crap' – becomes a 'load of marmite'. Based on the spread, which may seem visually apt.

Marquis of Lorne Horn (Erection)
A 19th-century example that has probably reached its climax in that those men who originally described their standing member as a 'marquis' will now be long-departed or in need of a vanload of Viagra. Based on John Campbell (1845–1914), who married a daughter of Queen Victoria and became the Duke of Argyll, Governor General of Canada.

Mars & Venus Penis
Used jokingly as a 'mars bar', especially in relation to oral sex: 'If you're hungry, I've got a nice mars bar for you to get your teeth round'.

Mars Bar Scar
A 1970s piece of yob yab normally used about a facial scar caused by a knife or glass: 'You can't miss him, he's got a mars bar down his boat the size of a...er...mars bar' (see Boat Race).

Martin Luther King String
Used in the newspaper distribution business as 'martin luther' and based on the American civil rights campaigner (1929–68).

Martin-le-Grand(s) Hand(s)
Slapped down to 'martins', a cut-down version of 'st martin-le grand' (qv).

Marty Wilde Mild (Ale)
Had a slight currency in the 1950s when this British singer was making hit records and the beer was still popular.

Mary Ann   **(a) Fan 1**
Originally a hand-held, but later an electric cooler, 'mary ann' is a popular girl during a heatwave.

(b) Fan 2
A vagina, 'fan' has long been a slang term for a woman's hot-spot.

(c) Hand
Old term that was often employed as a fist. In an old cockney hand the 'd' is silent, as is the 'h'.

Mary Blane   **(a) Rain**
Drought conditions have probably set in on this 19th-century piece.

(b) Train
A 19th-century underworld term that seems to have come off the rails and is based on the title of a popular song from 1847. Thieves and con men would 'meet a mary blane' and fleece new arrivals to the big city.

Mary Ellens   **Melons (Breasts)**
A 1980s term for the larger bra-fillers, ones that Page 3 girls aren't shy about displaying. From the music-hall song, 'I'm Shy, Mary Ellen, I'm Shy'.

Mary Green   **Queen**
In short, the 'mary' only applies to the playing card.

Mary Rose   **Nose**
Often associated with a 'super snozz', one whose owner is said to be able to smell his own breath. Seems to be based on Henry VIII's flagship, famously raised from the Solent in 1982 after 437 years on the seabed.

Marylou   **Glue**
A girl to get stuck on, but not to be sniffed at.

Mashed Potato   **Waiter**
Another spud gets on the menu, along with 'roast', 'hot' and 'cold', for the man who'll bring them to you.

Match of the Day   **Gay**
The BBC's long-running football programme gets on the ball

as a term for homosexuality. The term doesn't seem to get shortened: anyone that way inclined is 'match of the day'.

Matheson Lang   Slang

A 1920s example that belongs here and is based on a Canadian actor (1879–1948), a matinee idol and silent film star of the day.

Maud & Ruth   Truth

A rhyme from the pens of TV scriptwriters of the 1970s and that's the 'maud', the whole 'maud' and nothing but the 'maud & ruth'.

Max Factor   Actor

Not necessarily someone who treads the boards in make-up, but a person who feigns injury, illness or innocence to gain an advantage. A premiership footballer is a classic example and you're as likely to see a 'max factor' at Old Trafford as the Old Vic. Based on a well-known cosmetics company.

Max Miller   Pillow

Based on the great English comedian, who, according to his act, 'pillowed' every barmaid in Brighton. Miller (1895–1963) is reckoned to be the guv'nor of stand-up comedy.

Max Walls   Balls (Testicles)

Used as 'maxies' after a Londoner considered by many to be a comedy genius. Towards the end of his career, Wall (1908–90) proved to be a fine serious actor.

Maxwell House   Mouse

A 1960s term for a verminous house-guest based on a brand of coffee. In this book, 'mice' become 'mouses' as 'maxwell houses', which in turn become 'maxwells'.

Mazawattee   (a) Potty 1

Formed on the name of an old brand of tea in relation to anyone thought to be two ounces short of a pound.

                    (b) Potty 2

A baby's waste collector; a 'sprog-bog'. When there's a piece of 'maca' in the 'maza', empty it or it'll attract 'meat pies' (qv). See 'Macaroni'.

Me & You   **(a) Menu**
A piece long thought to be RS but it would appear to be a play on words.

       (b) Screw
An example that relates to sexual intercourse, but apparently not in group sex.

       (c) Two
A seaside resort bingo caller's rhyme since the days when players covered the numbers with bottle tops.

Meat & Two Veg   **Reg**
The diminutive of Reginald is 'meat'.

Meat Pie   **Fly 1**
Old transport cafes were often known for the wrong type of 'meat pies'.

       Fly 2
That which should be adjusted before leaving, be it button or zip, it's a trouser fly. Many a man in a hurry has brought tears to his 'mince pies' (qv) by zipping his 'meat' up in his 'meat pie'.

Mechanical Digger   **Nigger**
A derogatory term for a black person.

Meg Ryan   **Iron**
Based on an American film actress, this 1990s piece is an example of secondary slang. See 'Iron Hoof'.

Melody Linger(s)   **Fingers(s)**
A rhyme that's been in the air for many years as 'melodies'; an informant, one who may 'sing like a canary', will put the 'melody' on a culprit.

Melvyn Bragg   **(a) Fag**
A cigarette, a piece that got fired up in the late 1990s, but in 2007 a 'melvyn' was barred from public places.

       (b) Shag
Based on a popular TV presenter and author whose novel – *A Time To Dance* – was made into a television serial in 1992. The production contained many sex scenes and the act of lovemaking immediately became known as a 'melvyn'.

(c) Slag

A contemptible person, one considered to be 'lower than an ant's left bollock'.

Men of Harlech   Garlic

Some 'men of harlech' hanging around a room will, apparently, keep vampires away. Once they start singing they'll keep everyone away. Formed in the wake of a million cookery programmes on TV, which raised the profile of garlic in British kitchens.

Merchant Banker   Wanker

A 1980s term of abuse levelled at the contemptible or the useless. Someone thought to be lower than a child molester in a coal mine or as much use as a digital wristwatch on a one-armed man.

Merlin the Magician   Pigeon

Only known as 'merlin' because of the number of syllables involved.

Merry & Bright   (a) Light

Fittingly applies to illumination. It was once a big thing for Londoners to go to Southend to see the 'merrys'.

(b) Tight (Drunk)

Being a 'bit merry' is a familiar expression for being tipsy.

Merry-Go-Round   Pound (£1)

From a time when a 'merry' would get you about 200 goes on a merry-go-round, now it won't get you into the funfair.

Merry Monk   Spunk (Semen)

A johnny-come-lately rival to the long-known 'harry monk' (qv). Based on the jolly friar – who, given his vows of abstinence, may wake up with a messy habit.

Merry Old Soul   (a) Coal

When coal fires were all the rage it was common for folk to put a bit of 'merry' on them.

(b) Hole

From the nursery rhyme about Old King Cole, this applies to any orifice, including the anus.

Meryl Streep   Sleep
An American film actress comes in as an alternative to the long-serving 'bo peep' (qv). Someone with no conscience may tell you they have no trouble 'meryling', that they can do it with their eyes closed.

Metal Mickie   Sickie
A moody day off work since the 1980s when this robot first appeared in a TV programme bearing his name, it's also down to him that any male thought to be 'rowing a bath up the Thames with the plug out' may be known as 'Mental Mickie'.

Mexican Wave   Shave
A 1990s example based on that stand-up-and-wave thing that spectators do at sporting events. A face-scrape gets cut to the first element which doesn't seem very apt as every south-of-the-border baddie in every Western film needed a 'mexican'.

Miami Vice   Ice
Based on a US television series from the 1980s, this was heard in a West End nightclub when a customer wanted some 'miami' in his scotch.

Michael Caine   Pain
Based on the beknighted south London born actor, this is how a friend-in-need can become a 'michael in the khyber'.

Michael Hunt   Cunt
The formal name of Mike: the bloke in the schoolboy prank, who gets a girl to innocently ask if they've seen 'Mike Hunt'.

Michael Miles   Piles (Haemorrhoids)
One of a daffy of terms for the dirtbox disorder, this is based on a New Zealand born television quiz show host (1919–71), who was seldom off the box in the 1950s–60s.

Michael Schumacher   Tobacco
A 1990s example based on a German racing driver who had a long association with Marlboro cigarettes, in a business largely sponsored by tobacco companies. The term was coined in the wake of rising domestic prices for cigarettes when cut-price smokes from the continent flooded the market.

Michael Stoute   Shout

The knighted racehorse trainer is to be found in the pub when it is someone's turn to buy a round: 'Get your money out, Roger, it's your michael stoute'.

Michael Winner   Dinner

Like many terms of the 1990s, this, based on a British film director and food critic, was first served up in suburbia.

Mick/Micky Bliss   Piss

Seldom used in relation to urination but in terms of 'taking the piss' meaning to deride or insult. 'Taking the micky' is supremely common in this guise and is used by people who do not realise it's RS. Sometimes extended to 'extracting the michael'.

Mick Jagger   Lager

A term used by Scots but then you would have to be a jock to make a rhyme between the Rolling Stone and what to real ale-drinkers is known as 'sex on a riverbank' because it's 'fucking near water'.

Mick O' Dwyer   Fire

An old domestic fire based on an Irishman, about whom nothing is known except that his name is O'Dwyer and he is of Irish descent – if it wasn't for RS, even that would be forgotten.

Mickey Mouse   (a) House

The giant rodent of Disneyland has become the most common term for living quarters. In show-biz circles it also applies to a theatre.

                                 (b) Scouse

An example mockingly used by London football supporters against their Merseyside rivals. The derision stems from non-RS meaning of the term, which is second rate or inferior. 'Mickey mouser' – scouser.

Mickey Rooney   Looney

An American film actor gets a role as somebody who is mentally out of focus, one thought to be 'not a full deck of cards'.

Mickey Rourke   **Pork**

A 1990s example from the meat market that's based on an American film actor – although only in a small way. The backslang 'kayrop' is still the favoured expression at Smithfield.

Mickie Most   **Toast**

A piece from the 1970s when this record producer (1938–2003) was a regular critic on the TV talent show, *New Faces*. For a while cafes sold a lot of 'beans on mickie most'.

Micky Blisser   **Pisser (Penis)**

To 'pull someone's micky' is the same as 'taking the micky' – same boots, different laces really.

Micky Duff   **(a) Puff**

A piece that relates to drugs: for the smoking of. 'Puff' is a slang term for cannabis.

(b) Rough (Unwell)

Based on an English boxing trainer and promoter, this is generally used about the appearance of someone after a night's carousing. The more you drink, the bigger the hangover and the more 'micky duff' you look.

Microchip   **Nip (Japanese)**

Shortened to 'micro', this is relevant as the Japanese have long been at the forefront of microchip technology. It's also indicative of the widespread perception of the size of your average son of Nippon.

Midland Bank   **Wank**

A fairly well-known example of a 'handshag'.

Midland Banker   **Wanker**

An objectionable or ineffectual person, one thought to be lower than a dungeonful of wheel clampers or as much use as a hydrophobic duck.

Mike/Michael Bliss   **Piss**

Exactly the same as 'mick/micky bliss' (qv).

Mike Dickin   **Chicken**

An English radio presenter (1943–2006), generally regarded as Britain's angriest man, gets on board as poultry, usually when cooked. He may have raised a smile though at a Mrs Malaprop of my acquaintance who went into a butcher's shop and asked for a 'free-lance chicken'.

Mike Malone   **Phone**

Sounds like it's based on a tough Irishman but he can't get the better of the 'dog' (see Dog & Bone).

Mile & A Quarter   **Daughter**

From the racecourse comes the reason why some daddies have referred to their little girls as their 'ten furlongs'.

Mile End   **Friend**

After an area of east London where a 'mile end' in need is a 'fuckin' nuisance'.

Milk Jug   **Mug**

An early 20th-century term for a simpleton, someone easily duped, a person who 'stands the broads' (falls for the three card trick).

Milkman's Horse   **Cross (Angry)**

Old cockney pronunciation of 'crorse' dates this example to the late 19th century and is probably obsolete.

Milky Bar Kid   **Yid (Jew)**

How a Jewish person became a 'milky bar' in the 1990s. Inspired by a long-running TV ad for a chocolate bar. Said with humour rather than malice.

Milky Way   **Gay (Homosexual)**

Based on the sweetie that can be eaten between meals. Seems apt enough.

Millennium Dome   **Comb**

A 1990s rhyme coined when this multi-million pound building was being constructed. Now re-named the 'O2', but will forever be known locally as the 'Dome' and people will continue to 'rake their barnet' with a 'millennium'.

Miller's Daughter   **Water**

'She was only a miller's daughter but she certainly knew how to grind,' so says a mid 19th-century comic folk song. Probably. Folk songs about millers and their daughters, as well as other country tradesmen, were common at that time.

Millwall Reserves   **Nerves**

South London rivals of the once more common 'west ham reserves' (qv). In Bermondsey a pest will get on someone's 'millwalls'.

Milton Keynes   **(a) Beans**

Any beans can be 'miltons' but usually it's the ones that sit comfortably on 'holy ghost' (qv).

(b) Queens

Refers to homosexual men and is a reference to an establishment catering for them, e.g. a 'miltons' bar.

(c) Jeans

A noughties term for denims based on the town in Buckinghamshire; all types, all shades, cheapo, rip-off or knock-off, they're all 'miltons'.

Mince Pie   **Eye**

A very well-known piece, it's common for gogglers to be termed 'minces' or 'mincers'. There's a story of a pal of mine, Big Edgy, who was staring in disbelief at a pair of drunken idiots making complete wallies of themselves in a pub in Bermondsey. 'You got a problem, pal?' asked a drunken Wally. 'I've got trouble with my minces,' replied Edgy. 'I'm seeing twots before my eyes.'

Mini Moke   **Smoke**

A 1990s term for cigarettes and tobacco, which may (or may not) be drugs-connected. Based on a small car, which may (or may not) have a dodgy exhaust.

Minnie the Minx   **Jinx**

Someone seen as being a bad luck charm, a bock; one whose mere presence seems to put the mockers on you, that's a 'minnie'. Based on a dastardly schoolgirl character in the *Beano* comic, who, were she allowed to act her true age, would be terrorising fellow passengers on Saga cruises.

Misbehave   **Shave**

When a man goes into the bathroom saying he's going to 'misbehave', you now know what he's going to do! Or do you? 'Ain't misbehavin', gonna grow a beard for you' – the lyric Fats Waller may have written, had he been born in New Cross instead of New York.

Miss Fitch   **Bitch**

An elderly reference to a spiteful woman. No information exists on who Miss Fitch was, mayhap she was an actual nagwitch.

Miss Piggy   **Ciggy**

A 1970s piece for a cigarette whereby the porcine siren of *The Muppet Show* becomes smoky-bacon.

Mister Ed   **Bread**

A piece from the stable of forgotten terms of the 1950s, Mister Ed was the eponymous star of an American sitcom who just happened to be a talking horse: 'You can't make a decent sandwich with stale bread.' As the bar-stool philosopher said to the football manager, who was prone to buying older players: 'Nothing to do with the nattering nag, I just thought it was worth repeating.'

Mix & Muddle   **Cuddle**

One of life's little ags, is when you're lying in bed on a cold night, having a nice 'mix & muddle' and you have to get up for a 'cuddle & kiss' (qv).

Moby Dick   **(a) Nick**

Refers to a prison or police station, convicts get banged-up in, and drunks sleep one off in the 'moby'. Based on the novel by Herman Melville.

(b) Prick (Penis)

Doesn't necessarily have to be like the whale in the novel, i.e. a great white one. A 'moby' is also a fool, much the same as a 'plonker'.

(c) Sick

Time off work through illness is known as being on the 'moby dick'. It may sound like a venereal disease, but it needn't be.

Mockingbird   **Word**
An old piece from the theatre killed off by 'dicky bird' (qv).

Mods & Rockers   **Knockers (Breasts)**
Based on rival youth cultures of the 1960s, this applies to those of a fuller variety, the type that have caused men to wax lyrical down the ages: 'Look at the mods on that' is a phrase that springs to mind.

Mogadored   **Floored**
Refers to being baffled, stumped or beaten by a problem. The assembly instructions to anything bought from a DIY store 'mogadors' most people. Mogador is a place in Morocco, so the term may have been coined in the Forces.

Molly Maguired   **Tired**
Possibly Irish in origin as the widow Maguire was the leader of anti-landlord activists in 1840s Ireland. Her name was taken 30 years later by a group of militant miners in Pennsylvania, about whom a film was made in 1970, *The Molly Maguires*. It may be then that the term is based on the film title. Oh well, at least you've had a history lesson.

Molly Malone   **Phone**
The seafood-seller from the fair city of Dublin has for years been seen off by the 'dog'. See 'Dog & Bone'.

Molly O'Morgan   **Organ**
Originally a 19th-century barrel organ but later applied to any organ, musical or otherwise.

Mona Lisa   **(a) Freezer**
Where else but in RS could a great work of art be mentioned in the same breath as a fishfinger?
                     (b) Pizza
One Italian dish for another.

Monica Rose   **Nose**
A term for the bugle, which came and went in the 1960s with the rise and fall of this London-born quiz show hostess. 'Much Bugle on the Moosh' is an imaginary village inhabited by people with big hooters.

Monkey's Cousin   **Dozen**
A rhyme from the game of bingo.

Monkey's Tail   **Nail**
A 1930s example from the carpentry trade, specifically by joiners working on film and stage sets.

Montezumas   **Bloomers**
An old term for the type of underwear that would have been consigned to history, had it not been for the seaside postcard. Based on the 15th-century Aztec ruler.

Montgomery Clift   **Lift 1**
An elevator, the one mode of transport never to have been involved in speed contests, thus elevator racing will never be an Olympic event.

     Lift 2
A ride, as in: 'Give me five minutes and I'll give you a montgomery'. Based on a US film star (1920–66).

Moody & Sankey   **Hanky-Panky**
Applies to deception, something that isn't quite what it seems is referred to as 'moody'. The week off work with a 'moody' backache isn't for real, a 'moody' banknote is a forgery and a con man will give you a 'load of old moody'. Dwight Moody (1837–99) and Ira Sankey (1840–1908) were a pair of American revivalists, who toured Britain in 1875 so people have been making up 'moody' excuses for well over a century.

Moonlight Flits   **Tits**
'Moonlights' are obviously breasts that men would do a bunk for.

Mop & Bucket   **Fuck it**
If you're ever in the company of nuns and you hit your thumb with a hammer, this is the thing to holler.

More or Less   **Dress**
Applies to the garment and is probably based on the shifting necklines and hemlines of fashion.

Morecambe & Wise   Rise

A pay rise, courtesy of the popular British comedy double act of Eric Morecambe (1926–84) and Ernie Wise (1925–99). If you need more dough, ask your boss for a 'morecambe' – and good luck to you!

Moriarty   Party

Often reduced to a 'morry' and based on the arch-enemy of Sherlock Holmes and Neddy Seagoon.

Mork & Mindy   (a) Indy

The *Independent* newspaper, an example from that industry.

(b) Windy

From a 1970s American sitcom comes this term for a blow.

Morning Glory   Cory (Penis)

Would appear to refer to one that stands tall and erect on waking. Cory is from the Romany word 'kori', meaning a 'thorn', hence a 'prick'. 'Corystory' – a cocktail. Geddit?

Morris Minor   Shiner (Black Eye)

A 1950s term to describe a 'dipped headlamp'. Based on a once-popular car, this minor sign of battle is known as a 'morris'.

Mortar & Trowel   Towel

A 19th-century piece not often heard outside a building site washroom and now unlikely to be found anywhere but within these pages.

Mother & Daughter   (a) Quarter

An old term used by rivermen in regard to a riverside post to which boats are tied.

(b) Water

In the first element, an archaic term for the wet element, which caused chaos and misery in the floods of 2007.

Mother Brown   Town

The star of an East End knees-up is sometimes used as a reference to London's West End.

Mother Goose Juice

The old bird who puts in an appearance on stage during the panto season keeps your motor running in the form of fuel. Juice is either petrol or diesel and the term was heard in a London taxi.

Mother Hen Ten

A 1990s tenner (£10) or in backslang 'net dunops'.

Mother Hubbard Cupboard

A fairly obvious piece from the world of nursery rhymes concerning a provisionless woman and her hungry dog.

Mother Kelly (a) Jelly

Applies to the sweet and that which covers an East End eel. It's also what one's legs turn to when gripped by abject fear, as testified to by a bar punter when he ordered a large brandy: 'This vicious-looking dog came bounding towards me, barking its stupid head off. Well, my legs turned to mother kelly'.

(b) Telly

The appliance that now has more channels than good programmes to fill them. Based on the woman with the famous doorstep.

Mother Machree Tea

An early 20th-century example based on a 19th-century Irish ballad. Who'll be mother? The one who pours the 'mother machree'.

Mother-in-Law Saw

A chippy's term for the tool of his trade based on she who would cut his legs off with her bare teeth should he upset her daughter.

Mother of Mine Nine

A popular song title gives the bingo caller another example, sometimes £9. 'Eenin eenin eenin' – the number of the backslang emergency services.

Mother-of-Pearl Girl

Often preceded by 'the old' or 'my old', meaning 'the wife'. A lot of older men refer to their other halves as 'mother' or 'mum'.

Mother's Pride   **Bride**
Apposite term for the radiant star of the wedding especially if she resembles a loaf of bread.

Mother's Ruin   **Gin**
A very familiar example from the early 20th century; throughout history, gin has been regarded as a woman's drink so this is a fitting piece even though it isn't a great rhyme.

Motor Boat   **Throat**
A rival to the older 'nanny goat' (qv) that may be used threateningly: 'If I get my hands round his motor, I'll give it full throttle'.

Moulin Rouge   **Stooge**
Theatrical term for a comedian's foil that's based on the world-famous theatre in Paris, but pronounced the London way: 'moolyn'.

Mountain Bike   **Dyke (Lesbian)**
A 1990s variation on the older 'raleigh bike' (qv) regarding a 'todger dodger'.

Mountain Passes   **Glasses**
Scenic routes for spectacular viewing.

Mountains of Mourne   **Horn (Erection)**
Probably inspired by appearances above the sheets due to stirrings beneath. Based on the title of an Irish song.

Mouse Trap   **(a) Jap**
An alternative to the World War II term 'rat trap' regarding a Japanese person.

                                          (b) Nap
Refers to 40 winks – or in Nelson's case, 20.

Mouthwash   **Nosh (Fellatio)**
A 'beejay' – an example that goes down well when it comes to aptness. Said of a pest: 'I wish his old man had settled for a mouthwash'.

Mozart & Liszt   **Pissed**
A piece composed in the theatre and performed on TV and

radio before gaining a wide usage. Based on composers Wolfgang Amadeus Mozart (1756–91) and Franz Liszt (1811–86).

Mozzle & Brocker   **Knocker**

Originally used in association with door-to-door salesmen whose job it was to go 'on the knocker'. The term now lends itself to borrowing – a neighbour may be 'on the mozzle' for a cup of sugar. From Yiddish 'mazel' – good luck, and 'brocha' – good health.

Mr Hyde   **Snide**

A variant of 'jeckyll & hyde' (qv), but this relates to a person rather than an object. If someone is two-faced, he's a 'mr hyde'. A cowardly snide is known as a 'kipper' because he's two-faced and gutless.

Mr Magoo   **(a) Clue**

Aptly based on a myopic cartoon character, who never knows what's going on, it relates to the ignorant, naïve or plain stupid: those who 'don't have a mr magoo'.

(b) Poo

To defecate or the resultant mess it produces. This is a piece from suburbia: cockneys don't take up residence in the throne room for a 'mr magoo', they have a 'tom tit' or a 'game of nap' (see both).

Mrs Chant   **Aunt**

A 19th-century term that bears no relation to the relative but to the toilet for which 'aunt' is a polite old euphemism. When your ancestors 'had one in the waiting room' they'd go to the 'mrs chant', which would have been one in the eye for Mrs Ormiston Chant (1848–1923), a moral crusader of her day.

Mrs Doyle   **Boil**

A 1990s zit based on the much-blemished housekeeper in the TV sitcom, *Father Ted*.

Mrs Draper   **Paper**

Based on one of the three old ladies who got stuck in the

lavatory, it therefore applies mainly to toilet paper, but occasionally to a newspaper.

Mrs Ducket   **(a) Bucket**

A piece common in the fishmonger trade and also employed on building sites.

(b) Fuck It

Seldom used as an expletive unless a mishap befalls one in the presence of the vicar. More a comment on whether or not something should be done, like when grass needs cutting: 'Oh mrs duckett! I'll do it tomorrow'.

Mrs Mopp   **Shop**

The place to do the 'mrs mopping'. Based on a character in the legendary wartime radio show, *ITMA*.

Mrs More   **Floor**

One can walk on, sit on and when drunk, fall on the 'mrs more'. From the music hall song, 'Don't Have Any More, Mrs More'.

Mud in Your Eye   **Tie**

A 'mud' is an old example that's been consigned to the wardrobe of oblivion.

Muddy Trench   **French**

Possibly a World War I double rhyme on 'bloody french', which is how the English have been known to regard 'them over the channel'.

Muffin Baker   **Quaker**

A 19th-century example that applies to constipation. A 'quaker' is a name given to a piece of 'hard-baked' excrement that causes a blockage, thus causing the sufferer to tremble and quake in their straining attempt to force it out.

Muffin the Mule   **Fool**

A 1950s term based on a TV puppet of the period, it refers to the sawney (foolish) type who is 'painting the ceiling in their best hat'. What a muffin!

Mulligan Stew   **Two**

Based on services slang for Irish stew, this has been put forward as an explanation as to why a 'mulligan' is the name given to a second attempt at a mis-hit golf shot.

Mulligatawny   **Horny**

A hot, tasty dish would seem like a pretty appropriate term for sexual arousal, when he has a 'knob-throb' for her and she has a 'clit-wobble' for him.

Mum & Dad   **Mad**

As well as applying to someone with his 'boots on the wrong feet', this also relates to a loss of temper. Taking a regular liberty with someone will eventually make them go 'mum & dad'.

Mumble & Mutter   **Butter**

People have been spreading 'mumble' on their 'uncle fred' (qv) for nigh on 100 years.

Mums & Dads   **Pads**

Those protecting the little legs of cricketers.

Murray Mint   **Skint**

The 'too good to hurry mint' does a 'too broke to worry stint'. Why worry about money you haven't got?

Mustard & Cress   **Dress**

Always a 'mustard', perhaps in relation to a hot little number.

Mustard Pickle   **Cripple**

An imperfect rhyme, but a mustard was the 1990s equivalent of the widely used 'raspberry ripple' (qv).

Mustard Pot   **(a) Hot**

The contrary nature of the British is never more apparent than when talking about the weather. It's too 'taters' in winter and too 'mustard' in summer.

          (b) Twat (Vagina)

As owned by an alluring woman who has men wishing they could 'dip their sausage in her mustard pot'.

Mutt & Jeff   **Deaf**

A very well-known example commonly employed as 'mutton'. Based on a couple of cartoon characters from the 1930s who regularly featured in newspaper strips for decades later.

Mutter & Stutter   **Butter**

Alternative ''breadspread' to 'mumble & stutter' (qv).

Mutton Pie   **Eye**

A 19th-century term that is well in the shadow of 'mince pie', but a person with an eye defect is known as 'mutton-eye'.

My Word   **Turd**

Just the right exclamation when you slip on one, crack your head on the pavement and get dog's mess all over your best suit. I should think so!

Mylene Klass   **Arse**

An early 21st-century example based on a British singer, classical pianist and TV presenter. It's too early to say if a kick up the 'mylene' will ever replace one up the 'khyber' (qv).

Myrna Loy   **Saveloy**

Not a great rhyme but one that was widely used as a 'myrna' in the double act with pease pudding. Based on an American film star (1905–93), once known as the Queen of Hollywood. Now known as a sausage.

Mystic Meg(s)   **Leg(s)**

A piece that's been kicking around since this spaced-out crystal gazer first materialised on TV's National Lottery show in the 1990s.

Nails & Tacks   **Fax**

A 1990s term for what no office can do without, a 'nails' machine.

Nancy Lee   **(a) Flea**

A 19th-century example that was common when poverty caused fleas to be common.

         (b) Tea

Older, but less familiar than arch rival 'rosie lee' (qv). Nancy Lee is the title of a best-selling 19th-century sea shanty.

Nanny Goat   **(a) Boat**

A World War II term that never saw a lot of usage after London's docks closed.

         (b) Coat

'Nannies' are frequently worn on building sites in the guise of donkey jackets.

         (c) Throat

The first sign of a cold or flu is often a sore 'nanny'.

         (d) Tote

Possibly the widest usage of the term is in racing circles for the totalisator: 'The favourite paid evens a place on the nanny'.

Nanny Goating   **Courting**

Not a great rhyme but a very old term for an old-fashioned word.

Nantucket   Bucket
Had a limited employment on a building site in the 1970s, when a brickie used to call for 'another nanny of muck' – bucket of mortar.

Nap & Double   Trouble
A 1930s piece that seems to have its roots in the turf, possibly from the financial trouble of losing bets.

Naseem Hamed   Spam'ead (Bald)
Based on a World Featherweight boxing champion of the period, this 1990s piece relates to the insult aimed at the prematurely bald, especially those men whose forehead extends to the top of their heads, resembling slices of spam.

Nat King Cole   (a) Dole
A piece from the 1950s that was an update of the older 'old king cole' (qv), thus 'on the nat'.

(b) Mole
Although gardeners may be plagued with 'nats', this mainly applies to a mole on the skin.

(c) Roll
A bread roll based on the American singer-pianist. A couple of pints and a 'nat king cole' was the staple lunch of the labouring classes.

Nat West Bank   Wank
Another 'hand-shandy' courtesy of another high-street bank.

Nat West Banker   Wanker
An habitual 'hand-shagger' can be known as a 'nat wester'. The name is also given to the profoundly useless, someone considered to be as useful as a square marble.

Nathaniel   Hell
An ancient piece and pronounced as in: 'What the nathan-iell are you on about?'

National Debt   Bet
A reference to gambling that would be more appropriate if it were 'personal debt' – but it ain't!

National Front   Cunt

A 1970s rhyme for the vagina, but mostly a contemptible person, someone deemed to be 'lower than a scabby rat's arsehole'. Based on a right-wing political movement formed in the 1960s.

National Hunt   Front

People with a lot of cheek, audacity or nerve are said to have 'more national hunt than cheltenham'.

Naughton & Gold   Cold

A rare alternative to 'taters' (qv) as far as temperature is concerned this mainly applies to illness, whereby a sufferer is 'down with a naughton'. Based on Charlie Naughton (1887–1976) and Jimmy Gold (1886–1967), a British comedy duo who formed part of The Crazy Gang.

Nautical Miles   Piles

Normally shrunk to 'nauticals', this is another reference to the condition that non-sufferers find amusing.

Navasota   Motor

A piece from London's long-vanished docks industry, based on a ship that used to sail between the capital and Argentina, carrying refrigerated beef.

Navigator   Potato

A 19th-century term for a spud that was once employed in the cry of itinerate baked potato vendors as 'navigator scot' – potatoes, hot!

Nazi Spy   Pie

A 1940s example for a meat pie, predominantly.

Near & Far   Bar

A 19th-century piece for a bar room, either saloon or public bar and the counter (timber) that runs through them.

Near Enough   Puff

A homosexual male, an example from pre-politically correct days when the close approach from behind of someone so inclined would draw the remark: 'That's near enough!'

Ned Kelly   **(a) Belly**

Based on the name of an Australian outlaw (1855–80), this import generally applies to a beer gut.

(b) Telly

A 1970s term rarely switched on outside 'kangaroo valley', the part of West London renowned for its accumulation of Aussies.

Ned Skinner   **Dinner**

A 19th-century piece from the old cookshops, old 'ned' is one of several 'skinners' to make the table. See also 'Jim', 'Joe' and 'Johnny'.

Needle & Cotton   **Rotten**

Applies to anything that is less than pleasant, from a maggot-ridden apple to a nasty person. It may also apply to the gases emitted by the nasty person after eating the apple.

Needle & Pin   **(a) Gin**

An old piece usually crashed down to 'a drop of needle'.

(b) Thin

An apt example heard recently at the Royal London Hospital after an outbreak of Clostridium difficile in one of the wards: 'Aunt Doll's hardly been off the carsey for a fortnight. She's so fuckin' needle & pin you can hardly recognise her'.

Needle & Thread   **Bread**

When used in conjunction with 'stammer & stutter' (qv) to form a convoluted example, it's impossible for the uninitiated to work out that a slice of 'needle & stammer' is a slice of bread and butter.

Needles & Pins   **Twins**

Like the well-dressed dwarf who sat on a tack, this is short, sharp and to the point. Pins and needles are identical, except around the eyes.

Nell Gwynn   **Gin**

The mistress (1650–87) of Charles II lends her name to 'the Spirit of the East End', often as a glass of 'nell' or 'nellie'.

Nellie Bly   **Fly**

Applies to the flying pest of summer and also to that which is left undone on a flasher's trousers. Based on an American reporter (1864–1922) who, in 1890, circled the world in a record 72 days.

Nellie Dean   **(a) Green**

A 1950s rhyme for a green snooker ball, the next colour up from the 'cinderella' (qv).

(b) Queen

A reference to a homosexual male, especially an older one, hence 'old nellie', based on the title of a music-hall song that was in the repertoire of every drunk who ever walked home late at night.

Nellie Deans   **Greens**

A greengrocer's term for green vegetables, which is usually boiled down to 'nellies'.

Nellie Duff   **Puff (Breath)**

Through breath we get life, hence the well-known phrase 'not on your nellie' – not on your life. There is no trace of a famous person of this name but the schooner, *Nellie Duff*, sank in Lake Erie in 1895 and if, as suggested by Julian Franklyn in his *Dictionary of Rhyming Slang*, this is an American import, maybe it's based on that.

Nelson Eddy   **Ready**

Formed on the name of an American singer and actor, this is an expression normally borne out of the frustration of waiting for someone: 'ain't you nelson eddy yet?'

Nelson Eddys   **Readies**

Cash, ready money; what's needed to seal a dodgy deal. Bungs are handed over in 'nelsons'.

Nelson Mandela   **Stella (Artois)**

The former president of South Africa lends his name to a brand of lager, sharing a pint with 'paul weller' and 'uri geller' (see both).

Nelson Riddle   **(a) Fiddle**

Based on the name of an American musician and composer (1921–85), but this has nothing to do with violins. People who make a living on the very edge of legality are said to have a few 'nelsons' going.

(b) Piddle

A 'nelson' is another example of water production, or 'chasing the dog-end', as men did before fags were banned in pubs.

Nervo & Knox   **(a) Box**

Mainly applies to a 'goggle box' – a television – and has been around since the old black-and-white days. Generally turned down to a 'nervo', this is based on the comedy pairing of Jimmy Nervo (1890–1975) and Teddy Knox (1896–1974), who formed part of The Crazy Gang.

(b) Pox (VD)

Usually truncated to the name of the first partner, which is a result for the one who actually makes the rhyme. He may have craved a clap in his professional life but wouldn't have wanted to be remembered as a dose of one.

(c) Socks

A piece that's been separating feet from their shoes since the 1940s, post-war children often went to school with 'spuds in their nervos' – holes in the heels of their socks.

Nervous Wreck   **Cheque**

What many a pools winner has reportedly been whilst waiting for the man from Littlewoods to arrive to confirm their good fortune and present them with a nice big 'nervous'.

Never Again   **Ben (Truman)**

An example for a brand of beer that seems to be based on the words every hungover person speaks, every time they get drunk.

Never Fear   **Beer**

A 19th-century bevvypint that may be based on the bravado that often comes with an excessive booze-up.

New Delhi   **Belly**

An appropriate rhyme for the rumbling one that may follow a powerful curry.

Newgate Gaol   **Tale**
A 19th-century term for a hard luck story, often one of a beggar, based on London's notorious, but long-demolished prison.

Newington Butts   **Guts 1**
The name of a road in South London is a 19th-century term for the stomach. Always cut short at the first element, whereby one can take a punch or get a disease in the 'newingtons'.

      Guts 2
Applies to physical courage, the gutsy have the 'newingtons' to fight the puncher and the disease at (1). Strange how in standard English, 'guts' stands for 'backbone'.

Newton & Ridley   **Tiddley (Drunk)**
A 1990s piece comically based on the fictitious brewery in TV's *Coronation Street*.

Newton Heath   **Teeth**
A piece regarding the choppers of northern England and formed on the original name of Manchester United FC.

Niagara Falls   **(a) Balls 1**
The testicles, mens 'hangings' – 'niagaras' for short. A recent derivation is for courage: 'His old woman walks all over him and he hasn't got the niagaras to stand up to her' – an overheard conversation on a train.

      Balls 2
Spoken nonsense; if an excuse sounds a load of 'niagaras', it probably is.

      (b) Stalls
Theatrical term for that part of an auditorium.

Nice Enough   **Puff**
A homosexual male – widely known as 'one of those nice boys' or 'he seems nice enough'.

Nice One, Cyril   **Squirrel**
Based on a catchphrase of the early 1970s, started by Spurs supporters and directed at their England defender, Cyril Knowles (1944–91). It was taken up and used in an advertising

campaign for a brand of bread and soon it seemed as if everyone was saying it. It even became the title of a song that reached the charts in 1973. Squirrels have become a common sight in parks and gardens in and around London, which is why the 'tree-rat' has become known as a 'nice one'.

Nick Cotton　　　　　**Rotten**

As a term for a thoroughly bad person, this just had to happen. 'nasty nick' was one of the meanest, rottenest characters ever to disgrace the streets of Walford in TV's *EastEnders*.

Nickel & Dime　　　　　**Time**

A piece from the US that found its way over here during World War II and promptly disappeared when peace broke out.

Nicker Bits　　　　　**Shits**

The £1 coin was introduced in 1983 and immediately christened a 'nicker bit'; this term for diarrhoea appeared shortly afterwards.

Nicky Butt　　　　　**Nut**

A late 1990s example that sees a bag of peanuts become a bag of 'nickys' and an animal lover will feed a 'nicky' to a 'nice one' (qv). Formed on the name of an England international footballer.

Nicky Butts　　　　　**Nuts (Testicles)**

A knee in the 'nickys' could be seen as a high tackle. If it's performed in the bar after the game, it's a bloody late one as well!

Nigel Benn　　　　　**Pen**

Based on a former world Super-Middleweight champion boxer from Ilford, this 1990s term was seen as a serious contender to the long-reigning champion 'bill & ben' (qv). The knockout blow never came and the flowerpot men are still ahead on ballpoints.

Nigh Enough　　　　　**Puff**

A homosexual male – close enough to 'near enough' (qv), but not enough to make any difference.

Night & Day   **(a) Grey**

A reference to the ageing process – as seen in a mature head of hair. Never cut, in ghost stories people have been known to turn 'night & day' overnight.

(b) Play

A 19th-century application to a theatrical performance.

Night Boat to Cairo   **Giro**

A term relating to a cheque from the DSS and mainly concerning dole or sickness benefit. A piece that was coined by young unemployed people of the 1980s and based on a 1980s' song by the British band, Madness.

Nig-Nog   **Wog**

An abusive term mainly used against black or Asian people, although it originally applied to any foreigner of any skin tone.

Niki Lauder   **Powder**

The name of an ex-Formula One champion from Austria was never one to be sniffed at in his heyday. Sadly though, it is now – and will be for as long as he does the rounds on the drugs circuit as any powdered narcotic.

Nits & Lice(s)   **Price(s)**

An example from the racecourse coined by odds-layers from around a century ago.

Noah's Ark   **(a) Dark**

A piece that's been around since they illuminated the 'noah's ark' with gas-lamps.

(b) Lark

A 19th-century term for fun, a laugh. A trick or wind-up against someone who, when told it's only a 'noah's ark', is supposed to laugh rather than punch his tormentor's nose in.

(c) Nark

Possibly in its most common form as an informer, the term also spoonerises very cleverly as 'oah's (whore's) nark' and represents extreme despicability and lack of trust.

(d) Park 1

An old example still in use: people walk, play and allow their dogs to soil the footpaths in the 'noah's ark'.

NOBBY HALLS

Park 2
A late 1990s derivation heard in the congested streets surrounding West Ham United's ground on a match day: 'Where the fuck are we supposed to noah's ark around here?'

Nobby Halls   **Balls**
Based on the eponymous, unitesticular subject of a comic traditional folk song ('Oh his name was Nobby Hall and he only had one – arm'). A huge disappointment is a 'kick in the nobbys'.

Nobby Stiles   **Piles**
Haemorrhoids, courtesy of the hard-tackling member of England's victorious World Cup team of 1966, who was a constant pain in the arse of opponents. 'Nobbys' for short.

Noddy Holder(s)   **Shoulder(s)**
A piece from the 1970s based on the lead singer with the hit band, Slade. He later became an actor and was awarded the MBE in 2000, but unlike several beknighted hitmakers of his era, he has yet to feel the tap of the sword on his 'noddy'.

Non-Skid   **Yid**
A 1940s term for a Jew, which seems to have slid out of use.

Nook & Cranny   **Fanny (Vagina)**
The dictionary gives 'nook' as a secluded place and a 'cranny' as a crack. Apt or what? 'Wynaff' – 'fanny' by backslang.

Nora Batty   **Tatty**
A 1990s term for anything in bad condition, most commonly a car that has seen better days. Can also apply to old ladies in wrinkled stockings, like this character in TV's *Last of the Summer Wine*.

Normandy Beach   **Speech**
The D-Day destination often sees action at wedding receptions, when the best man goes over the top with a 'normandy' designed to embarrass the groom.

North & South   **Mouth**
A very famous piece immortalised in the music-hall song,

'What a Mouth'. Unlike most terms this is never shortened, as in: 'Just 'cos you've got hairs round your north and south, there's no need to talk like a cunt'.

North Pole　　　　　**Hole (Anus)**

An old example that has lost out to 'south pole' (qv), which has the edge in directional relevance.

Northants　　　　　**Pants**

Underwear; a piece probably based on the County Cricket Club rather than the county itself. The fearful may soil their 'northants'.

Northern Rock-up　　　　　**Cock-up**

A fiasco, a 2008 term based on the government's handling of the crisis surrounding the Northern Rock bank in 2007. A big mistake is now an almighty 'northern rock-up'.

Nose & Chin　　　　　**(a) Gin**

A 19th-century term for what may make a nose red and a chin wag.

(b) Win

Not uncommon for a gambler to have a bet 'on the nose' – that is to win, rather than each-way. The term originally applied to a 'winn', which was a 19th-century piece of slang for a penny.

Noser My Knacker　　　　　**Tobacco**

Reduced to 'noser' or 'nosey', the term literally means 'smell my testicles'. This is an old cockney reply to an admonishment, much the same as 'Balls!' or 'Bollocks!' is today. The 19th-century term is said to have originated as a smoker's retaliation to complaints by non-smokers.

Novices Chase　　　　　**Face**

In the race for the best-looking fizzog, a 'novices' is a faller at the first fence, therefore an ugly mug.

Now & Never　　　　　**Clever**

An example from the 19th century which may have been used ironically at a display of stupidity. In games of street cricket there was always someone who would hit the ball on a roof, thus bringing the game to a pemature ending. The culprit would be deemed 'fuckin' now & never'.

Now or Never   **Clever**
The same as the above and used in the useless piece of homespun philosophy: 'You don't have to be now or never to be a dunce'.

Nuclear Sub   **Pub**
A modern piece used by modern youth about a modern drinker.

Nun's Habit   **Rabbit (Talk)**
A piece of secondary slang, 'rabbit' has become so common that it has acquired its own term just to make things interesting. See also 'Rabbit & Pork'.

Nuremberg Trials   **Piles (Haemorrhoids)**
Bottom nasties based on the place top Nazis faced their accusers in 1945–46. Known as 'nurembergs'.

Nursery Rhyme   **Crime**
An example from the 1990s that was a reflection of the fact that lack of control and discipline had led to a rise in child crime.

Nursery Rhymes   **Times**
Refers to the top people's newspaper…which may cause 'Angry of Tunbridge Wells' to dash off a letter to the editor.

Nutcrackers   **Knackers**
Seems to be an extension of 'nuts' where the testicles are concerned, but it's a term to bring tears to the eyes of the hardest of men.

Nutmeg(s)   **Leg(s)**
A piece of football slang, where to push the ball through an opponent's legs is to 'nutmeg' him.

Oak & Ash   **Cash**

A term emanating from the theatre, where a couple of trees take the stage as 'nelson eddys' (qv).

Oars & Rowlocks   **Bollocks**

Can be used anatomically but is mainly applied when the smell of bullshit is in the air, when someone is talking a load of 'oars'.

Oats & Barley   **Charlie**

A 19th-century term that in its time has referred to all things 'charlie-ish', it's one of the few Christian names to be endowed with a piece of RS and in the days when construction companies hired nightwatchmen instead of security guards, those old chaps who sat around a brazier all night were called 'charleys', thus a 'watchie' was known as an 'oats'. It has been used as secondary slang on a couple of occasions, as a fool (see 'charlie hunt') and as a ponce (see 'charlie ronce') and most recently 'oats' has been used as a reference to 'cocaine charlie'.

Oats & Chaff   **Path**

A 19th-century term for a footpath; a piece that's been overgrown or paved over.

Obadiah   **Fire**

An 'obey' refers to the domestic coal fire of yore. Based on a biblical prophet, the term has been reduced to ashes.

Ocean Liner　　　**Shiner (Black Eye)**
A fairly old term for what is also known as 'half a surprise', this is due to the words in the music-hall song 'Two Lovely Black Eyes' – altogether now, 'Oh what a surprise…'

Ocean Pearl　　　**Girl**
A 19th-century example relating to a girlfriend. It doesn't seem to have made it to the 21st.

Ocean Wave　　　**Shave**
Since the 1940s an 'ocean wave' has been one way of destabilising the 'boat'. See 'Boat Race'.

Oedipus Rex　　　**Sex**
Doesn't sound particularly wholesome since it's based on an ancient Greek who killed his father and married his mother.

Office Worker　　　**Shirker**
An example used by manual workers, originally dockers, who find the phrase 'a hard day at the office' amusing and scornfully remark: 'Call that bloody work!' Therefore anyone seen to be not pulling their weight is called an 'office worker'.

Oh My Dear　　　**Beer**
A 'pint of oh' was a 19th-century bar order and a 'pot of oh' was a carryout from the off-licence. It's now as rare as a plausible plot in a soap.

Oh My Gawd　　　**Bald**
A long-lost aquaintance whose hair loss is apparent may be greeted with: 'Oh my gawd, he's gone oh my gawd!'

Oi, Jimmy Knacker　　　**Tobacco**
Pipe or rolling tobacco was known as 'oi, jimmy' or just 'oi'. Based on the same old street game as at 'hi, jimmy knacker' (qv).

Oil Lamp　　　**Tramp**
Doesn't necessarily apply to hobo scruffians, any ragged-arsed, couldn't-care-less-how-they-look scruffbucket can be labelled an 'oil lamp'.

Oil Leak   **Sikh**

A 1990s term for he who wears a 'napper wrapper'.

Oil Slick   **Spick (Spaniard)**

Formed in the early days of the package holiday to the Costas, when young Spanish males typically used masses of hair cream and, with copious amounts of Latin smarm, greased their ways into the beds of female tourists. Used disparagingly by jealous young British lads.

Oil Tanker   **Wanker**

An abusive term used against the obnoxious and the useless, like the pilot of one of these oversized vessels who, through rank bad navigation, hits something or runs aground, causing colossal damage to the environment.

Oily Rag   **Fag**

A cigarette – from a time when non-smokers were seen as the anti-social members of society. People are still smoking 'oilys', but not inside public places any more.

Okey Doke   **(a) Coke**

In the 1980s this innocently applied to Coca Cola, but in the following decade, when cocaine became easily available, the descended into the world of drugs as 'okey'.

                                (b) Poke

Condensed to 'okey', this refers to a wallet, or more specifically, to what it contains. A low-life term used by a pickpocket.

Old Bag   **Hag**

In its original form this applied to an old or infected prostitute. It has since become a supremely common term for any disagreeable woman.

Old Fogey   **Bogey**

Refers to nasal residue, or 'nose-shit' and is based on an old term for an invalid soldier. Lusting after a Page 3 girl, a *Sun* reader was heard to remark: 'I'd eat her old fogeys!'

Old Iron & Brass   **(a) Grass**

Applies to the green, green stuff of Tom Jones' home. Overly officious parkies used to delight in keeping people off the 'old iron'.

(b) Pass
An old military term for what is required to leave barracks.

Old Jalopy **Poppy 1**
'Poppy' is an old slang term for money and the term relates to a required loan between friends: 'Got any ol' jalopy till Friday?'

Poppy 2
Wear your 'old jalopy' with pride on Remembrance Day.

Old Jamaica Rum **Sun**
Always decreased to the first two elements, this old naval term has probably sunk below the horizon.

Old King Cole **Dole**
The nursery rhyme monarch has long been associated with unemployment benefit, but the merriest old souls in the dole queue are the ones employed in the black economy.

Old Kit Bag **Fag**
A cigarette – based on the piece of equipment into which World War I soldiers packed up their troubles, at a time when getting a smoking-related disease was considered preferable to stopping an enemy-related bullet.

Old Nag **Fag**
A long-since stubbed-out cigarette that was first ignited by WWI tommies, who probably smoked until they were hoarse soldiers.

Old Oak **Smoke**
Refers to London, long known as 'The Smoke'.

Old Pot & Pan **Old Man**
Originally a term of endearance for a father when young men would take the 'old pot & pan' for a pint. And when the gloss of matrimony had worn off, wives used it about their husbands, often as the 'old pot'. In backslang he's the 'deelo nam'.

Old Rag **Flag**
A piece that was flying long before it became 'offensive' in

some quarters to run the Union Jack or the Cross of St George up the 'old ragpole'.

Old Whip   **Ship**
An early seaman's term for his own ship, that is, the one he is serving on.

Oliver Cromwell   **Tumble (Understand)**
An example from a time when cockney dialect would have produced a rhyme: just as Bromley and Romford were pronounced 'Brumley' and 'Rumford', so Cromwell would have been 'Crumwell' or 'Crummell', a suitable match for 'tumble'. 'Now do you, oliver?' Like the man (1599–1658), the term is long dead.

Oliver Reed   **(a) Speed**
A young drug-user's term from the 1980s that relates to amphetamines. Known as 'olly' and based on a well-known British actor and boozer (1938–99), this originally applied to another habit (b).

(b) Weed
Tobacco. Known only as the dreaded 'olly', it applies to all forms of smokes including the illicit kind.

Oliver Twist   **(a) Fist**
A 19th-century piece that is always shortened to the Christian name of Dickens' orphan.

(b) Pissed
Descriptive of people who have presented their glasses and asked for more…and more.

(c) Wrist
Rarely used in any other sense than masturbating, whereby 'one off the wrist' becomes 'one off the oliver'.

Ollie Beak   **Sikh**
Just what the connection is between people of this religion and a television glove puppet of the 1960s I don't know, but someone had a hand in it. 'Ollie' was a cheeky owl with a scouse accent, voiced by singer and musician Wally Whyton (1929–97).

Omar Sharif   **Grief**

This is grief in its slang form of trouble or problems. Those who don't want any comebacks may hope they won't get any 'omar'. Based on an Egyptian-born film star and renowned bridge player.

On & Off   **Cough**

Obviously not based on the consumptive pest who always seems to sit behind me at the cinema and goes on and *on*, coughing his pipes up.

On the Floor   **Poor**

Very common piece that has transcended the ranks of RS because of its total suitability. To be 'on the floor' is as low as you can get.

Once a Week   **(a) Beak (Magistrate)**

An example that seems to have been coined by an habitual ne'er do well.

(b) Cheek

Alludes to non-edible sauce, as poured on by a liberty-taker or a lippy nipper. Used as 'oncer'.

One & Eight   **Plate**

Takes in all kinds of plate, including crockery, a forger's plate and what is passed around in church. Sometimes used as secondary slang for feet, as in: 'my one & eights are killing me'. See 'Plates of Meat'.

One & Elevenpence Three Farden   **I Beg Your Pardon**

A humorous phrase used, apparently, by the hard-of-hearing. Based on a sum of pre-decimal money, a farthing short of two shillings (10p). 'Farden' was the common pronunciation of a farthing, which was a quarter of an old penny.

One & Half   **Scarf**

Either a headscarf or a choker can be a 'one an' arf'.

One & Other   **(a) Brother**

Exactly the same as 'one & t'other' but pronounced 'one another'.

COMPLETE COCKNEY RABBIT

(b) Mother

Exactly the same as at (a).

One & T'Other   **(a) Brother**

A bit confusing really, as this is also used for…

(b) Mother

…In either case it's always employed in full and in the third person, when speaking of one's 'one an' t'other'.

One For His Nob   **Bob**

A once-common reference to a shilling (5p), the term represents something extra and was used in the guise of a tip. Older folk still give taxi drivers 'one for his nob' but it no longer has to be 5p – at least it better not be, if they don't want a mouthful of abuse!

One(s) & Two(s)   **Shoe(s)**

'One gets one's "ones" from one's personal "one" maker': As Princess Anne might say if she were a Pearly Princess Royal.

Ooh La La!   **Bra**

A coy piece from a less permissive era – possibly from the stage, when boys on their twelfth date might have got a feel, but not under the 'ooh la'.

Open the Door   **Four**

The number 4 on a bingo card.

Opportunity Knocks   **Fox**

A piece in existence since the wily one became the urban dweller it now is. Always an 'opportunity' – why use one syllable when you can use five? Well, that's slang! Presumably based on a long-running TV talent show.

Orange Pip   **Nip**

A Japanese person has, since the 1990s, been an 'orange'.

Orange Squash   **Dosh (Money)**

An example of 1990s youthspeak, whereby those holding some 'orange' enjoyed the fruits of their labours, whilst those suffering from skintitis declared themselves to be in an 'orange-free state'.

Orchestra Pit(s) **Shit(s)**
Defecation, but mainly diarrhoea. A theatrical term so probably connected to stage-fright. Many actors get the 'orchestras' before a perfomance.

Orchestra Stalls **Balls**
Whereby the scrotal area is commonly known as the 'orchestras'.

Organ Grinder **Minder**
A reference to a bodyguard that brings tears to the eyes if the organ involved is not a musical one.

Orinoko **(a) Cocoa**
The popular bedtime drink has long been known as an 'ori'.
(b) Poker
An old piece for the fireside implement and burglar-basher, always cocknified to an 'orinoker'.

Orphan Annie **Fanny (Vagina)**
Based on a cartoon character whose adventures were turned into a stage and film musical, this has been heard as a cautionary warning against anything that should be given a wide berth. Roadworks on the M25, for example, or a pub where the landlord drinks lager should be avoided like an infected 'orphan'.

Oscar Asche **Cash**
Always curtailed to 'oscar', this time-honoured piece is formed on the name of a long-forgotten actor (1871–1936).

Oscar Wilde **Mild (Ale)**
Not often heard now that this beer has all but disappeared in London. Based on the Irish writer and wit (1854–1900), who may or may not have been partial to a drop of 'oscar'.

Otis Redding **Wedding**
A piece of early popney based on an American soul singer (1942–67) whereby a 'splicing' is known as an 'otis'.

Ounce of Baccy **Paki**
With the prevalence of the Asian tobacconist this piece just

had to happen. And it did, in the 1970s, when a Pakistani person became known as an 'ouncer'.

Over the Stile **Trial**
A 19th-century example employed as being sent, or having to stand 'over the stile'.

Overcoat Maker **Undertaker**
An obvious allusion to a 'wooden overcoat' – a coffin.

Owen Nares **Chair(s)**
A 1930s rhyme that originated in the theatre and is based on an actor (1888–1943) from the early days of cinema. Although his name was Nares, one chair was an 'owen'.

Oxford Bag(s) **Fag(s)**
You're getting old if you can remember when 20 'oxfords' cost an 'oxford scholar' (qv). Based on wide, baggy trousers, the height of fashion for the 1920s well-to-do.

Oxford Scholar **(a) Collar**
An early 20th-century term from a time when shirt collars were detachable. 'Oxfords' have come in all shapes and sizes since. 'God rollack' – what a backslang vicar wears – a dog collar.

(b) Dollar
An English dollar; five shillings in old money – some die-hards still use the term for the modern equivalent of 25p, but they are now few and far between.

Oxo Cube **Tube**
The London Underground system has long been known as 'The Oxo'.

Paddington Bear   Chair

A 1970s rival to 'teddy bear' as a market trader's cry. Based on the Peruvian bear, created by writer Michael Bond, who became a TV 'star' in 1976.

Paddy & Mick   (a) Pick (Axe)

Again, on the two typical Irish partners in grime on a building site.

(b) Thick

Based on the names of the two typical Irishmen who, for years, have kept a host of comedians in business.

Paddy O'Rourke   Talk

Possibly based on the legendary sweet-talker whose lip-prints are all over the Blarney Stone, the bloke who could talk a nun out of her knickers.

Paddy Quick   (a) Kick

A 19th-century boot in the head, groin or up the jacksie, presumably supplied by a fleet-footed Irishman.

(b) Stick

What manner of stick is not recorded, but possibly an aid to walking, as used by the Irishman at (a) who put the boot *in*, before putting his boot *on*, thus injuring his foot.

(c) Thick

Stupid, dull-witted; a 19th-century 'doon' who, in modern times, could be ironically known as 'mastermind'.

COMPLETE COCKNEY RABBIT

Paddy Rammer **Hammer**
Early 20th-century piece that has probably knocked in its last nail.

Padlock **Cock (Penis)**
A 1970s term that was trapped in the phrase: 'She could pick my padlock anytime'.

Pain in the Neck **Cheque**
An example that may have been coined by a recipient who had been 'bowled a bouncer' – passed a dud cheque.

Pall Mall **Gal**
A 19th-century term that's no longer heard as cockney dialect has changed. 'Gals' are now 'gels'.

Pampas Grass **Arse**
A piece seen in a newspaper article following England's defeat by Argentina in the 1986 World Cup, when Diego Maradona punched the ball into the English net, an action he later put down to the 'Hand of God'. It was suggested he should take his holy hand and shove it up his 'pampas grass'.

Pancake Roll **Hole (Anus)**
An item from a Chinese food menu comes in as the place it will eventually emerge from. And if it's inedible, tell the waiter to lodge it up his 'pancake' or for effect, his 'crispy pancake'.

Panorama **Hammer**
A navvie's term from the 19th century that seems to have dropped out of site.

Panoramas **Pyjamas**
Parents get their kids washed and into their 'panoramas' at bedtime. They also get them into 'jimmys' 'jammies' and 'jamas'. *Panorama* is a long-running current affairs programme on TV.

Pantomime Cow **Row**
A light-hearted variation of 'bull & cow' (qv) that refers to the type of argument where nothing gets thrown but insults and threats, much to the amusement of onlookers. Oh yes, it *is*!

274

Pants & Vest   **Best (Bitter)**

An old beer-drinker's shout seldom, if ever, heard now. In modern slang 'pants' means bad, so if you get a 'pants' 'pint of pants', send it back.

Paper Bag   **Nag**

To verbally larrup somebody; many a last pint has been refused because, 'I couldn't stand the old woman papering me all night'.

Paper Doll   **Moll**

A piece from the 1960s that refers to a prostitute or a girl used to decorate the arm of a villain. Probably based on the title of a song made famous by American vocal group, The Mills Brothers.

Paper Hat   **Prat (Fool)**

A typical 'paper hat' is someone who thinks a judo expert is an Israeli financial consultant.

Paraffin   **Gin**

A term used humorously to confuse new bar staff: 'paraffin & supersonic with miami and st clement'. Look 'em up!

Paraffin Lamp   **Tramp**

Always reduced to the first element, often as an insult to people with truggy inclinations, like 'soap dodgers' and 'dirtywacks'. Also those who don't bother with fashion or dress codes, who turn up for social events looking like 'paraffins'.

Parker-Bowles   **Rolls**

As Lady Penelope might have said, had International Rescue operated out of the Isle of Dogs instead of an isle in the Pacific: 'park the parker, parker'. See also 'Camilla Parker-Bowles'.

Parlamaree   **Gee**

An underworld term for the member of a team of street traders who 'gees-up' a crowd by rushing to buy what's on offer.

Partick Thistle   **Whistle**

The Scottish football team comes in for what a referee blows;

and what the crowd do to get him to blow at the end of 90 minutes when their team is winning by the odd goal. Presumably, informants also 'blow the partick' on those responsible.

Pat & Mick   **Prick**

A 19th-century example for the penis that may also have been employed as a fool, possibly by English navvies against their Irish counterparts on London's many building sites.

Pat & Mike   **Bike**

Those two Irish lads in tandem again; in another term from the 19th century.

Pat Cash   **Slash**

Urination based on an Australian tennis player, the 1987 Wimbledon champion. A typical 'pat cash' in a urinal will take in the time-honoured ritual of 'going for the gilbert', in which, by water power alone, that great, green glob of phlegm reclining there is washed towards the drain. Skilled men can get it around the disinfectant blocks without touching them.

Pat Malone   **Alone**

An alternative to the better-known 'jack jones' (qv), but in the same way as being 'on your jack'; if you are 'on your pat' you have only yourself for company.

Patrick Swayze   **Crazy**

A piece from the 1990s, which sees the mad, eccentric or ultra-violent as 'patrick'. Based on an American film star of the period.

Patsy Cline   **Line**

Although based on an American country singer (1932–63), this has nothing to do with dancing. The 'patsy' in question is a line of white powder: cocaine. For the snorting of.

Patty Hearst   **First**

Student slang for a first-class honours degree, based on an American heiress and bank robber. Kidnapped in 1974, she later joined her captors in the urban guerilla game.

Paul Anka   **Wanker**

A 1960s term based on a Canadian singer-songwriter, a 'paul anka' is someone deemed to be lower than a burglar down a coal 'ole or as useful as a bent nail.

Paul Ince   **Mince**

A 1990s rhyme for the main ingredient of a spagbol. Based on an England international footballer, the piece has also been used as a slang-for-slang term for an eye. See 'Mince Pie'.

Paul McKenna   **Tenner**

£10, courtesy of a well-known TV hypnotist. A piece of noughties popney.

Paul Weller   **Stella (Artois)**

A British singer-songwriter gets up the ramp as a popular brand of lager.

Pavarotti   **Potty 1**

What a toddler tiddles and turdles into, a chavvy lavvy, courtesy of big Pavvy – Italian tenor Luciano Pavarotti (1935–2007), that is.

Potty 2

Refers to someone thought to have failed quality control in the brain department. Also anyone who loses control is said to have 'gone pavarotti'.

Peace & Quiet   **Diet**

Some endure the battle of the bulge and fight the flab to shed some suet just to get some peace and quiet from a loved one.

Peanut Butter   **Nutter**

A mad, crazy person; someone said to be 'fourteen numbers on a bingo card' – one number short of a full house, that's a 'peanut'.

Pearly Gate   **Plate**

A dinner plate or one that is passed around in church, as represented by Heaven's Door.

Pearly King   **Ring (Anus)**

'Ring' or 'ringpiece' are old slang terms for this part of the anatomy, hence the choice expression of rejection: 'poke it up your pearly'. 'Pearly burner' – a particularly hot curry; one that may induce an attack of the 'orchestras', leaving one's ring looking like the Japanese flag. See 'Orchestra Pits'.

Pea Shooter — Hooter (Nose)

Not to be confused with 'pee shooter', which is a different extremity altogether. Has been used as a car horn.

Peas in the Pot — Hot 1

Applies to temperature, sweaty old Londoners would complain that 'It's too bloody peas'.

Hot 2

An alluring or sexy female; a tasty bird from around the turn of the 19th/20th centuries was labelled 'peas'.

Hot 3

Used to describe a highly skilled or talented individual, be it in the arts, sport, or just brainy or shrewd, whereby someone who 'knows his onions' is said to be 'well peas'.

Pease Pudding Hot — Snot (Nasal Mucous)

Reduced to the first two elements, this is how a hanky gets gets full of 'pease pudden' during a cold. Based on a nursery rhyme.

Pebble Mill — Pill

Based on a long-running BBC TV programme, *Pebble Mill at One*, these are pills that are popped, rather than taken as directed on the label – a case of 'pebbles' getting you stoned. The show ran from 1973–86, which somewhat dates the term.

Peckham Rye — Tie

A piece encircling cockney necks since the 19th century; based on an area of South London, a 'peckham' supposedly creates a good impression when worn, especially with a 'whistle & flute' (qv). A formal occasion requires an 'oxford & peckham'. See 'Oxford Scholar'.

Pedigree Chum — Come/Cum

A term for the unromantic clod in that it applies to semen and orgasm. This tasteless example was formed on a brand of dog food.

Pedlar's Pack   **Sack**
Dismissal from work, an uncommon rival to the older 'tin tack' (qv). Either based on the wares of an itinerant trader or a drug dealer. Whichever way, you're 'up the road' when you get the 'pedlars'. 'The kaycass' – the backslang shove.

Peggy Sue   **Clue**
A 1970s term aimed at anyone lacking street credibility, the naïve soul who 'ain't got a peggy sue'. Based on a hit song for Buddy Holly in 1957.

Peg-Legger   **Beggar**
A cruelly apt rhyme that came into being after World War I, when limbless ex-soldiers, unable to find work, were reduced to begging in their 'home fit for heroes'.

Pen & Ink   **Stink**
An old and very common expression for a bad smell; also to complain loudly is to 'kick up a pen & ink'.

Pen & Inker   **Stinker**
Dated term for a scoundrel or a particularly tough problem – a fiendishly cryptic crossword puzzle, for example.

Pencil-Rubber   **Scrubber**
A woman of doubtful virtue, courtesy of a clever term that doubles as a metaphor in a masturbatory sense. A 'pencil' is a slang term for the penis, so a female described as 'an old pencil' may be a dab-hand at the wristic art.

Penholder(s)   **Shoulder(s)**
It's hard to write with a dislocated 'pen'.

Penn'orth of Bread   **Head**
A stale reference to the 'turret' from the days when bread could be bought for a penny – a pre-decimal penny, that is.

Penn'orth of Chalk   **Walk**
Always shortened to the first element, when something is mislaid or gone missing, it has 'gone for a penn'orth'.

Penny Banger   **Clanger (Mistake)**

Appropriate piece from the days when fireworks were cheap. Drop a 'penny banger' and it may blow up in your face.

Penny Black   **Back**

Based on Britain's first postage stamp and used only in an anatomical sense, this fits as a work dodger's excuse. He'll phone in sick with a dodgy 'penny', then stick it to his bed.

Penny Bun   **(a) One**

Only really used in connection with gambling, whereby odds of 'a cockle to a penny bun' is 10/1. See 'Cockerel & Hen'.

       (b) Son/Sun

One of several examples from the baker's shop, making the same connections – the term's age is given away by the price of the bun.

Penny-Come-Quick   **Trick**

Originally a fitting term for a con trick that for a good spieler was a quickly-earned coin. It later came to represent any trick before disappearing.

Penny For the Guy   **Pie**

Seems a much more reasonable request down the chip shop than a 'smack in the eye' (qv).

Penny Locket   **Pocket**

The thirsty may be as dry as a snooker player's 'penny locket'.

Penny Stamp   **Tramp**

An old term for the vagrant, who may be worth slightly more than the 'halfpenny stamp' (qv).

Penny-a-Mile   **(a) Tile (Hat)**

A 19th-century example of secondary slang, a 'tile' sits on one's 'roof' (head).

       (b) Smile

If this was the price of a 19th-century cab ride you can see how out-of-touch the term is. These days it costs about a penny-an-inch plus tip. No tip, no 'penny-a-mile' from the cabbie.

Penny-a-Pound   **Ground**

Terra firma has, for over a century, been known as the 'penny'. To knock someone down is to 'penny' him.

Peppermint Flavour   **Favour**

A 1960s term of disbelief: 'Do me a pep'ment!' is another version of 'You must be joking!'

Peppermint Rock(s)   **Sock(s)**

'Peppermints' (pronounced 'pep'ments') may be the preferred 'plate covers' in cold weather, unless you hate hot trotters, of course. See Plates of Meat.

Percy Thrower   **(a) Blower**

Even with today's technology, telephones are known as 'blowers' so you are still likely to be stuck on the 'percy' for ages, pressing numbered options.

     (b) Mower

Totally suitable term from the suburbs based on the original TV gardening expert (1913–88). If it cuts grass, it's a 'percy'; if it eats it, it's a goat!

Perry Como   **Homo**

An old term for the old-fashioned shortening of homosexual, based on the name of an American singer (1912–2001) for no other reason than its rhyming factor.

Persian Rugs   **Drugs**

A 2000s example taking in all sorts of junk.

Pete Murray   **Curry**

Formed on the name of a British radio and TV personality, a 'pete murray' is sometimes dished up as an alternative to his renowned namesake 'ruby'. See also 'Ruby Murray'.

Pete Tong   **Wrong**

Applies to a worsening situation, one that's going 'pete tong'; after a British DJ.

Peter Cook   **Book**

A 1960s term for a 'reader' that never really caught on. Based on a comedian and writer (1937–95), once rated Britain's funniest man.

Peter O'Toole   **Stool 1**

Mainly applies to a bar stool, which is fitting enough, given this Irish actor's bar fly reputation. Incidentally, how come when famous actors get out of their skulls on drink and wreak havoc on pubs and hotel bars, they're called 'hellraisers' while the rest of us are 'drunken yobbos'?

Stool 2

A piece of excrement, an example that's only heard in connection with taking a 'peter o'toole' sample to the doctor.

Peter Pan   **Van**

A 1980s piece from the light haulage business seems to have taken off in the courier trade. Like J.M. Barrie's creation, 'peters' are flying all over the country.

Peters & Lee   **(a) Pee/Wee**

Lennie Peters (1939–92) and Di Lee were a hitmaking duo of the 1970s and the term came and went with their records, a slash in the pan, you might say. Some may still go for a 'peters' in deference to Lennie, a great East End singer.

(b) Tea

Too many cups of which will lead to an overwhelming need to (a).

Petrol Tank   **Wank**

From the vulgarly sung first line of the song 'Granada': 'I once had a wank in an old petrol tank in Granada'. Applies to an act of masturbation and a loathsome or ineffective person is deemed to be 'not worth a petrol'.

Petrol Tanker   **Wanker**

A base individual, like a crack dealer in an ice-cream van or a hopeless one, someone thought to be less effective than one-legged tightrope walker. Or tightrope hopper, I suppose.

Petticoat Lane   **Pain**

Based on East London's famous Sunday market at Aldgate, this applies to physical pain or a nuisance, whereby a pain in the neck becomes a 'petticoat in the gregory peck' (qv).

Peyton Place   **Face**

A 1960s example based on a long-running American soap on British TV at the time. The show made famous 'peytons' of its stars.

PG Tips   **Lips**

'Pee Gees' refers to thick lips, as worn by the chimpanzees in the famous TV adverts for this brand of tea, which incidently became known as 'monkey brand'.

Pheasant Plucker   **Fucker**

Not too sure if this well-known spoonerism qualifies as RS. It is used in the same context as: 'He's a nice bastard', meaning the opposite. A 'pheasant plucker' therefore is not the same as a 'pleasant fucker!'

Phil MacBee   **Flea**

A pre-World War I term that doesn't seem to have survived the second lot. Given in BritSlang as 'Phil McBee' – who is as equally unknown as this bloke.

Phil the Fluter   **Shooter (Gun)**

A post-war term from the National Service barrack room, jokingly known as a 'phil' after the song about an Irish musician who had a celebrated ball.

Philharmonic   **Tonic**

The perfect accompaniment to 'vera lynn' (qv).

Photo Finish   **Guinness**

The world-famous 'black food' is sometimes downed to a 'photer'. The National Hunt Festival at Cheltenham sees plenty of both.

Phyllis Dixie   **Pixie (Homosexual)**

'Pixie' is a 19th-century variation of 'fairy' and this 1940s term is inspired by a wartime dancer (1914–64) billed as the Queen of Striptease.

Physical Jerk   **Berk (Fool)**

An example of secondary slang that sees an idiot become a 'physical'. See 'Berkshire Hunt'.

Piccadilly   **(a) Chilly**
Cold weather brings on much grumbling about how 'piccadilly' it is.

(b) Silly
Anyone or anything found wanting in the sense department is said to be 'picca'.

Piccalilli   **Willie (Penis)**
A case of a pickle representing the 'schnickel'.

Piccolo & Flute   **Suit**
A 19th-century alternative to the equally old, but more widely worn 'whistle & flute'.

Piccolo(s) & Flute(s)   **Boot(s)**
An example from between the two World Wars, when the working-man would scuff and the soldier would polish his 'piccolos'. And fathers could deliver a well-aimed one to their son's backside without fear of prosecution.

Pick & Choose   **Booze**
A piece from the theatre that seems to reflect the number of alcoholic drinks available to pick and choose from. Going 'on the pick' is a more polite version of going 'on the piss'.

Pick Up Sticks   **Six**
Another rhyme from the bingo hall.

Pickle & Pork   **Talk**
The verbosely vocalacious 'can't half pickle!'

Pickled Onion   **Bunion**
In normal circumstances, pickled onions sit nicely on plates of meat, but not at this table! See 'Plates of Meat'.

Pickled Pork   **(a) Chalk**
A 19th-century term for the then much used scribbling stick.

(b) Talk
An unheard example, which seems to be based on drunken pigs.

Pie & Liquor   Vicar

The man of the cloth becomes a man of the scoff sold in pie and mash shops. The liquor in question is the green gravy made in those establishments.

Pie & Mash   (a) Cash

In the minicab and courier games, a 'pie & mash' job is a fare or delivery not on account. Based on a traditional London dish.

(b) Flash

An ostentatious, trappy, big-headed know-all may be a 'bit too pie & mash' for many people's liking.

(c) Slash (Urinate)

Very common for those 'about to blow a washer' to disappear behind whatever cover is available for a 'pie & mash'.

Pie & One   (a) Son

Based on the same fare as at 'pie & mash', i.e. a pie and one portion of mashed potato.

(b) Sun

How hopes of having a decent summer depend on 'pie' in the sky.

Pieces of Eight   Weight

The aim of the dieter is to 'do some pieces'. A piece of eight was a Spanish dollar, a coin much sought after by pirates.

Pig & Roast   Toast

An example coined by soldiers of WW2, a piece heavy on irony due to the lack of cordon bleu dishes served up on front line. A slice of pig sounds better than a slice of burnt bread gone cold.

Pig in the Middle   Piddle

Used in full or condensed to a 'pig', but never a 'piggy'. An announcement of 'I'm going for a piggy' means something completely different. See 'Piggy Bank'.

Piggy Bank   Wank

A piece usually rubbed down to the first element, a 'piggy' is the activity of a 'solo yachtsman', one who takes on the horn single-handedly.

Pig's Ear   **Beer**

By far the commonest term for 'brown food', the original pub grub. A 'top o' reeb' – a backslang pot of beer.

Pig's Fry   **Tie**

A seldom used alternative to the common 'peckham rye' (qv). 'Trish and Ite' – a backslang shirt and tie.

Pig's Trotter   **Squatter**

A 1970s rhyme for someone who dips their snout in someone else's trough.

Pillar & Post   **Ghost**

Whereby the Holy Trinity becomes the 'Soap, Currant and Holy Pillar & Post'. See also 'Soap & Lather' and 'Currant Bun'.

Pimple & Blotch   **Scotch (Whisky)**

A couple of skin blemishes come in for a drop of short, a surfeit of which may have brought them on in the first place.

Pimple & Wart   **(a) Quart**

A 19th-century example for a quarter of a gallon, a measurement that beer was sold in as a carry-out. A quart pot would be taken to a beer shop, filled, taken home and emptied.

     (b) Port

A piece that should be used in full to avoid confusion with 'pimple & blotch' (qv).

Pin & Needle   **Beetle**

An old term for the insect that has long been cocknified to a beedle.

Pineapple Chunk   **(a) Bunk 1**

A naval term from World War I seamen, who slept on 'pineapples'.

     Bunk 2

An example used by WWII prisoners of war, whose main aim was to 'do a pineapple' – escape.

     (b) Drunk

A 1990s piece from suburbia, where middle-class boozers get 'pineappled'.

(c) Junk

Heard at a noughties car boot sale: 'You'll be lucky to find anything valuable amongst all this old pineapple'.

(d) Spunk (Semen)

A Scottish example for what is ejaculated north of the border.

Pink Lint   Skint

An infrequent interloper into the popularity of 'boracic lint' (qv) as an expression for being devoid of a receptacle into which to urinate.

Pinky & Perky   Turkey

What is traditionally eaten on festive occasions, courtesy of a brace of TV puppets from the 1950s/60s, who happen to be pigs. A slice of 'pinky', however, is not a chunk of pork.

Pipe & Drum   Bum

The anus and therefore the basis of the charming expression: 'push it up your pipe', an indication of where the unwanted should be despatched to.

Pipe Your Eye   Cry

It's debatable whether or not this is genuine RS, but it has been given as an example for so long that it warrants inclusion as such.

Piss in the Pot   Hot

Low, vulgarist's version of 'peas in the pot' (qv). Or is that term an expurgated rendition of this?

Pisspot   Sot

An enduring example of a drunkard, although maybe a rhyme of convenience in that 'pisspot' along with 'pisshead', 'piss-artist', etc. may just describe a habitual boozer.

Pitch & Fill   Bill

Originally applied to men of this Christian name, later to a poster or hand-bill, as used to describe a beggar's disability.

Pitch & Toss   Boss

A reference to the person in charge based on an old gambling game. 'Can't do enough for a good pitch & toss' – the tenet of a jobsworth. Which draws a layabout's reply: 'You can't do enough for any bloody gaffer!'

Pizza Hut   Slut

Based on a chain of pizza restaurants, this is how a promiscuous woman becomes a 'pizza'.

Plain & Gravy   Navy

The 'plain' is an old reference to the Royal Navy, courtesy of that culinary delight the dumpling and gravy.

Plain & Jam   Tram

A piece that is sitting on the backburner, just waiting for this form of transport to make a major comeback.

Planet of the Ape(s)   Grape(s)

'Beulah, peel me a planet' – as Mae West might have said, had she been in Cricklewood instead of Hollywood. A 1960s piece of limited use when a film of this title was showing at a cinema near you.

Plaster of Paris   Aris

Thrice-removed piece that leads eventually to the backside, 'aris' is the shortened form of 'aristotle', which in turn is RS for bottle. This is a reduction of 'bottle & glass' – we have now arrived at the arse.

Plate of Beef   Chief

A convict's term for a chief warder.

Plate of Ham   (a) Gam (Fellatio)

Always reduced to the first element, this is supremely well known, whereby to 'plate' becomes a verb. 'Gam' is an abbreviation of 'gameroosh', a corruption of a French word for the performance of oral sex, *gamahucher*. Many a filthy comment was raised in the early days of betting shops when it was announced over the blower that a race was delayed due to a horse being plated (re-shoed): 'Good job jockey's are little, it saves 'em getting their knees dirty' is one I seem to remember.

(b) Tram

When trams went out of sight in London, this went out of mind.

Plate of Meat **Street**

The original meaning before the term was pluralised to dance to a new tune. See also 'Plates of Meat'.

Plate(s) & Dish(es) **Wish(es)**

As written on greetings cards and inscribed by authors of books on slang: 'Best plates & dishes'. Originated in the theatre, probably as part of a pantomime script.

Plate Rack **Hack**

A 19th-century piece for this type of horse. Not sure if it has ever applied to a journalist.

Plates & Dishes **Missus**

An early 20th-century reference to a wife, the 'plates' was the one who did the washing-up.

Plates of Meat **Feet**

The fame of this is legendary and the leg-ends are always known by the first element: 'My plates are so hot I could do the ironing with them'. Technically the term should only be used in the plural, but such is not always the case – a sore foot can be a dodgy 'plate'.

Platters of Meat **Feet**

Rarely used variant of 'plates' except maybe in matters of the patter of tiny 'platters'.

Pleasure & Pain **Rain**

Apt since the umbrella-maker's pleasure is the holidaymaker's pain.

Plink-Plonk **Vin Blanc**

A term coined in the battlefields of World War I. 'Plonk' was soldier's jargon for mud, which was likened to the cheap wines available, as a result of which 'plonk' has become a common hand-me-down for any dodgy wine, white or red.

Plough the Deep **Go to Sleep**

An archaic piece that hit rocky ground years ago.

Plum Duff **Puff (Homosexual)**

A 1970s example of an unmanly man, hence to act 'plummy' is to behave effeminately.

Plymouth Argyle **File**

The football team comes in as an underworld term for the tool that gets smuggled into prison in a cake in countless cartoons and comedy sketches.

Plymouth Argyles **Piles (Haemorrhoids)**

A double painful condition, people with 'plymouths' have 'grapes the size of footballs'.

Plymouth Cloak **Oak**

A 19th-century term for an archaic piece of slang for a cosh or cudgel; a piece which shows that early slangstas knew their history since it's based on the garment that the well-known Plymouth lad, Sir Walter Raleigh, reputedly threw across a puddle for Elizabeth I to walk on.

Pogo Stick **Prick (Penis)**

A toy with which to jump with becomes something else that enjoys a jump. And much the same as a 'plonker', a 'pogo' is also an idiot.

Poison Dart **Fart**

The smell of poison gas may demand the question: 'Who's fired a "poison dart"?'

Polish & Gloss **Toss (Masturbate)**

A piece that generally gets off at the first element: 'She said she never goes the whole way on a first date so she gave me a quick polish'.

Polish & Spit **Shit**

This is the word in rubbish mode, anything considered crappy is said to be 'polish'. 'This referee's polish' – a disgruntled Crystal Palace supporter.

Polly Flinder **(a) Cinder**

With the demise of the coal-fire this is mainly used as a humorous put-down of overcooked food, which may be burnt to a 'polly'.

(b) Window

An early 20th-century example used by glaziers and window cleaners. Based on the little girl in the nursery rhyme who obviously felt the cold.

Polly Parrot **Carrot**
A piece from the fruit & veg market, which could be off-putting to a vegetarian. 'Torrack' – a backslang 'polly'.

Polly Wolly Doodles **Noodles**
The popular fast-food, pot polly wollys, for example, or crispy ones at the Chinese. Inspired by a well-known song.

Polo Mint **Skint**
The mint with the less fattening centre comes in as a protest of the potless, who may be 'polo' till payday.

Pompey Whore **Four**
A streetwalker from Portsmouth gets the bingo-caller treatment.

Pony & Trap **Crap 1**
Oft-employed example for defecation, 'ponies' are a common cause of tardiness – and lumps of 'pony' on a shoe are a common cause of anger when brought indoors.
Crap 2
Rubbish or bad merchandise, whereby anything crappy is 'pony'.

Poor Relation **Station**
Presumably formed when rich relations had cars but hardly relevant these days when virtually every family has means of transport and even the rich find rail travel expensive.

Pop Goes the Weasel **Diesel**
A bit of a mouthful, so always reduced to 'pop', a piece from the haulage trade. Based on a nursery rhyme, the meaning of which is open to speculation.

Popcorn **(a) Horn (Erection)**
Aptish in that both term and definition may be found in a Soho cinema.

(b) Porn
Commonly associated with dirty books, blue films and sex on the Internet.

Pope of Rome **Home**
A 19th-century rhyme for where the heart is, there's no place like 'pope-a'.

Popeye the Sailor **Tailor**
The old spinach-munching cartoon man of the sea becomes a needle-bashing man of the cloth.

Pork & Beans **Portuguese**
A development coined by soldiers of WWI.

Pork Chop **Cop**
A police officer, a piece that goes hand in cuff with the common slang term for plod & co. – 'pigs'.

Pork Pie **Lie**
The staple diet of those who speak with a 'double tongue' – politicians, for example, who rarely get through the day without a few 'porkies'. Sometimes said as 'porky pie'.

Porky Pig **Big**
Used in terms of size and as a mild rebuke against someone who has done you no favours but thinks he has: 'So you put me down for a fiver's worth of raffle tickets, did you? Well, that was porky pig of you!' Based on a Loony Tunes cartoon character.

Port & Brandy **Randy**
An appropriate piece since this concoction has long been used by the saloon bar lothario as a knicker loosener for his girlfriend.

Posh & Becks **Sex**
A piece from millennium year based on the celebrity couple that famously had sex in Brooklyn, New York. Victoria and David Beckham were not the first to name their child after his place of conception – I once had a classmate called Bikeshed.

Postage Stamp **Ramp**
The ramp is a common expression for the bar of a pub, hence: 'get up the postage' means 'it's your round'.

Postman Pat **Pratt**
A complete fool becomes a 'prize postman', thanks to a mail deliverer from kids' TV.

Postman's Knock **Clock**
Probably formed in the days when you could set your 'postmans' by the arrival time of the post. Now you may meet him on your way home from work.

Pot & Pan **(a) Man**

For use when speaking of a bloke in the third person, a man with a beard, for example, is the 'pot with the whiskers'. See also 'Old Pot & Pan'.

(b) Van

With so many vans currently on the road, 'peter pan' had to acquire a rival and this 21st-century piece is it.

Pot of Glue **(a) Jew**

More familiarly known as a 'potter'.

(b) Queue

Particularly fitting term since it's not unusual to get stuck in a 'pot o' glue' at the post office on pension day.

Pot of Honey **Money**

A 19th-century term whereby the penniless have long been 'potless'.

Pot of Jelly **Belly**

A term of derision for a fat, wobbly gut – which should be used in full as a reference to a 'pot' speaks for itself.

Potash & Perlmutter **Butter**

A play of this name was produced in London in 1914 and the term duly followed. You now have more chance of getting sunstroke in a cave than ever hearing it again.

Potato Chip **Zip**

Only ever used as a 'tater' and most commonly in relation to a fly. Most men know the agony of catching an unsuspecting willie in a 'tater'.

Potato Mashers **Gnashers**

An example that would work equally well in a non-RS context, teeth are perfectly adapted for mashing spuds.

Potato Peeler **Sheila (Woman)**

An old piece from Down Under which has a currency among ex-pat Aussies in London, where women are more likely to be known as 'janes' 'jills' and 'renes'.

Potato Pilling   **Shilling**
How this amount of old money became a 'tater'.

Potatoes in the Mould   **Cold**
Very well known and only ever known as 'taters'. Refers to temperature, not illness.

Pot(s) & Dish(es)   **Wish(es)**
Alternative to 'plates & dishes' (qv), also from the theatre and maybe even from the same panto.

Pound Note   **Coat**
An elderly piece which was based on the banknote that is consigned to the memory bank.

Pound of Butter   **Nutter**
Applies to any loon, from the wildly dangerous to the mildly strange; the eccentric who lives in a world of his own because he doesn't like the only alternative – the real one.

Pound of Lead   **Head**
A pounding 'pound' may have described a 19th-century hangover.

Pounds & Pence   **Sense**
A piece generally used to have a go at those lacking common sense.
Foreman: Ain't you got any pounds & pence?
Worker: Sorry, my mind is somewhere else today.
Foreman: Well, as long as you know where it is.

Powdered Chalk   **Walk**
A less exercised version of the more common 'ball of chalk' (qv).

Power & Glory   **Cory (Penis)**
What a proud man feels about his standing member.

Prawn Crackers   **Knackers (Testicles)**
Currently in use and always in the first element, a low blow is a punch up the 'prawns'. Based on a number on a Chinese menu.

Press & Scratch   **Match**
Cigarettes are rarely lit by 'presses' these days.

Pride & Joy   **Boy**
Mainly a reference to a newborn son and in use as long as he's the apple of his parents' eyes.

Princess Di   **Pie**
Current among the younger generation, this took a respectful dip after the death of Diana Princess of Wales (1961–97), but soon returned to your friendly neighbourhood chip shop. Just goes to show, you can't keep a good woman down. You can't keep a bad 'princess di' down either!

Principal Skinner   **Dinner**
The head teacher from *The Simpsons* TV series gets in as a piece of noughties youthspeak, which is fitting if applied to school dinners.

Private Ryan   **Iron (Homosexual)**
An example of secondary slang based on the Oscar-winning film of 1998, *Saving Private Ryan*. Here referred to as a 'raving private ryan'. See 'Iron Hoof'.

Prune & Plum   **Bum**
From one of nature's laxatives comes a term for the breech.

Prussian Guard   **Card**
A playing card and also a bingo card from the days when bingo was called housey-housey.

P(s) & Q(s)   **Shoe(s)**
To mind your ps & qs in normal speech is to be careful of what you say and do, not to put your foot in it. In RS, however, if you don't put your feet in your ps & qs, it's not worth having them.

Psychopathic   **Traffic**
A most appropriate example that has come into being in the exhaust-filled wake of the motor car and the personality disorders driving can engender, turning normally rational people into would-be killers at the first whiff of a traffic jam. A

condition known as 'road rage' has entered the language and used in connection with several well-publicised murders.

Pudding & Beef　　　　　**(a) Chief**
The 'pudden' was the chief warder in an old prison.
　　　　　　　　　　　　　　(b) Deaf
A piece that is as it sounds, Scottish.

Pudding & Gravy　　　　　Navy
The 'pudden' is a 1940s rhyme for the Senior Service.

Pudding Basin　　　　　Mason
One of the 'funny handshake mob', whereby freemasonry becomes 'freepuddingry'.

Pudding Chef　　　　　Deaf
A piece heard in a 1960s sitcom that seems to have left the kitchen.

Pudding(s) & Pie(s)　　　　　Eye(s)
Doesn't appear à la carte as often as 'mince pie' (qv), except perhaps in the form of a shiner, when it becomes a 'black pudding'.

Puff & Dart　　　　　**(a) Heart**
A mid 19th-century example based on the forerunner to the game of darts in which a blowpipe was used to propel a dart at a target.
　　　　　　　　　　　　　　(b) Start
Commencement from the 1930s when engines were harder to 'puff' on cold mornings.

Puff & Drag　　　　　Fag
Apt allusion to what office workers congregate outside the buiding for – and why factory workers kept nipping to the toilets.

Pull Down the Shutter　　　　　Butter
A late 19th-century piece probably alluding to a slice of bread and butter as well as the spread itself. Either way, the shutters have been well and truly pulled down on this one.

Pull Rank **Wank**
To masturbate – sounds like one off a military wrist.

Punch & Judy **Moody**
An example of secondary slang (see 'Moody & Sankey') and used in disbelief at an obvious lie or con, when someone gives you a load of old 'punch & judy'. From the traditional puppet show seen on beaches the length and breadth of Britain before some PC wally deemed it unseemly.

Punk Rockers **Knockers (Breasts)**
Shortened to 'punks', this 1970s rival to the youth cultures of the previous decade, 'mods & rockers' (qv), needn't have safety pins through the nipples.

Push in the Truck **Fuck**
Applies only to coitus and was seemingly coined in the transport industry, conjuring up visions of long distance lorry drivers and hitch-hikers who go all the way.

Pussy Willow **Pillow**
Sounds like a nice way to drop off to sleep, with your head on a 'pussy'.

Put & Take **Cake**
An early 20th-century term based on a gambling game thought to have been invented by World War I soldiers to help pass the time in the trenches.

Put in the Boot **Shoot**
A World War I piece that is no longer afoot.

Pyramid **Yid**
A piece that's hardly appropriate given that unlike Jews, these great tombs are in Egypt.

Quaker Oat   Coat
Based on a brand of porridge which, like a coat, is synonymous with warmth.

Quarter Past Two   Jew
One of a multiple of terms for the non-gentile, this is a later version of 'quarter to two' (qv), but only by half an hour.

Quarter To Two   Jew
Earlier and better-known version of the previous term.

Quasimodo   Soda
Reduced to 'quasi' or pronounced 'quasimoda', this is the traditional partner of (Bells?) whisky and is based on Victor Hugo's *Hunchback of Notre Dame*.

Queen Mum   Bum
The anus, courtesy of Queen Elizabeth the Queen Mother (1900–2002), which was heard as a drunk's put-down of the acting profession: 'Actors? They all take it up the queen mum!'

Queen of the May   Gay (Homosexual)
A 1990s term that has to be used in full since queens are already known as 'queens'.

Queen of the South   Mouth
Lippy people may be advised to watch their 'queens', courtesy of a Scottish football team which, to the English, is just a place on a pools coupon.

Queen Vic   **Sick**

Ill or perverted, a 1990s example based on the fictional pub in TVs *EastEnders*. 'Kaykiss' – sick in backslang.

Queenie Watts   **Trots (Diarrhoea)**

It's down to this London-born actress and entertainer (1926–80), who was also the owner of some popular public houses in the East End, that when your anus resembles a brake light, you've been stricken by the 'queenies'.

Queens Park Ranger   **Stranger**

Although employed as a variant of 'glasgow ranger', this has a wider range of usages. It is a non-regular punter in a betting shop who strikes a large bet, the mysterious face in the local, the man that children mustn't takes sweets from and it's the little star of a happy event.

Queensbury Rules   **Balls (Testicles)**

Ironically, a kick in the 'queensbury's' is totally at odds with the rules of fighting as laid down by the Marquis of Queensbury (1844–1900). Cockney dialect affects a rhyme.

Rabbit & Pork   Talk

One of the superstars of RS, especially since my book *Cockney Rabbit* hit the shelves. When I coined the title, little did I realise that it would become the Internet term for cockney rhyming slang. Ironically, cockneys tend to say 'bunny' rather than 'rabbit', whereby garrulous gasbags are said to have 'a lot of bunny'.

Rabbit Hutch   Crutch 1

The groin area, a piece that gives a new slant to a rabbit punch.

Crutch 2

And the lame shall walk with the aid of a 'rabbit'.

Rabbit's Paw   Jaw

With 'rabbit & pork' (qv) already established, this seems an unnecessary term in the sense of to talk, so is better placed in terms of a telling-off, whereby to jaw is to scold. To 'catch a rabbit's paw' then is to get a rucking.

Racehorse   Sauce

An alternative to 'rocking horse' (qv) as a condiment – same thing, really; it just runs out the bottle faster.

Racks of Meats   Tits

'Racks' for short, on a rhyme on teats.

Radio One's   Runs (Diarrhoea)

Known as 'the radios', this just has to have something to do with the verbal outpourings of your average DJ. Radio One, a BBC music station since 1967.

Radio Rental **Mental**

A well-known piece based on a High Street TV rental company now no longer trading. It describes a crazy, mad person; someone said to 'have his hat on inside out'.

Raffle Ticket **Ricket (Mistake)**

No prizes when you make a 'raffle' – although a lucky 'raffle ticket' is a mistake that comes in your favour.

Rag & Bone **Throne**

A reference to a lavatory seat and nothing to do with where Her Majesty sits, at least not when she's being regal. Strange to think of the Queen sitting on the other throne – of course she does, though. We've all heard of the royal flush and the royal 'wee' is legendary.

Rain & Pour **Snore**

Always reduced to the first element, many a night's sleep has been interrupted because of a partner's 'raining'. But does she believe you?

Rainbow Trout **Kraut**

A 1990s piece used by the Club Med set when they can't get near the pool for 'rainbows'.

Rajputana **Banana**

An obsolete piece based on a P&O passenger and cargo ship that commuted between the Far East and London's Royal Docks. Launched in 1925, it was torpedoed and sunk in 1941.

Raleigh Bike **Dyke (Lesbian)**

Possibly based on a saying that purports to sum up a lesbian: 'I bet her bike's got a crossbar'.

Ralph Lynn **Gin**

This predecessor of 'vera lynn' (qv) is based on a British actor (1882–1964), who was noted for his performances in farce. The term seems to have died along with the man.

Ramsgate Sand(s) **Hand(s)**

The beach of this Kent resort is well-known in connection with the maulers, so if anyone mentions a dirty 'ramsgate', you now know it has nothing to do with a scandal involving an MP caught in a compromising position with a couple of male sheep – they just needed a wash. 'Deenah' – another backslang mitt.

Randolph Scott   Spot

The perennial goodie in countless Westerns (1898–1987) is reborn as a skin eruption now starring on the face of a young person near you.

Rangitiki   Tricky

An old docker's term for an awkward situation that's based on a refrigerated cargo ship that used to berth in London's Royal Albert Dock. The ship was broken up in 1962.

Rangoon   Prune

Probably based on the effect that both the place and the fruit are said to have on the bowels.

Rank & Riches   Breeches

A 19th-century piece that shows the ruling classes and their jockeys wearing legholders for riding.

Raquel Welch   Belch

Just goes to show that nothing and no one is sacred in RS. This glamorous American film star, the sex goddess of her era, lends her name to an expulsion of gas from the stomach.

Rasher & Bubble   Double

Mainly applies to a double on a dartboard but sometimes two selections in a bet. The term is the dish of bacon and bubble'n squeak.

Raspberry Ripple   (a) Cripple

An unkind reference to a mentally or physically disabled person.

           (b) Nipple

That of a woman, a term used solely by men for whom it's a bit of a mouthful so it's always a 'raspberry'.

Raspberry Tart   (a) Fart

A piece that has joined the ranks of mainstream English but as an oral impression of an anal emission: 'raspberries' are now blown rather than dropped.

(b) Heart

The original 19th-century meaning of the term but now obsolete in this sense.

Rat & Mouse   **(a) House**

A 19th-century example that's verminously as relevant today in some areas as it was on its formation.

(b) Louse

Refers to a human louse, someone universally disliked even by their own dog,

Rat Trap   **Jap**

Reduced to a 'rat', this World War II piece, which was directed at an enemy, will survive for as long as there remain ex-prisoners of the Japanese.

Ratcatcher's Daughter   **Water**

A late 19th-century term based on a popular music-hall song of the period, which contained the classic line: 'Her father caught rats and she sold sprats, the pretty little ratcatcher's daughter'.

Rats & Mice   **(a) Dice**

A 1930s example used by gamblers in the mournful: 'The rats ain't running for me tonight'.

(b) Rice

Served up in curry houses, where chicken and 'rats' is a popular dish. Ask for it at your peril.

Rattle & Clank   **Bank**

Onomatopaeic example from the days when the working classes dealt mainly in coins.

Rattle & Hiss   **Piss**

The 'draining of the tank', another version of 'snake's hiss' (qv); a night on the 'rattle' is a drinking bout.

Rattlesnakes   **Shakes**

A case of delirium tremens (DTs), whereby the 'rattles' follows a night on the 'rattle & hiss' (qv).

Ravi Shankar　　　**Wanker**

An unspeakable rotter or a person of little or no talent, it's based on the Indian sitar player who popularised the instrument in the late 1960s by playing at rock venues. It matters not how his name should be pronounced, in RS it's 'ravvy shanker'.

Rawalpindi　　　**Windy**

Based on the name of a passenger liner that regularly berthed at London's Royal Docks. With the advent of World War II she was commandeered by the Royal Navy and converted into an armed merchant cruiser. On 23 November 1939 she gallantly, but suicidally engaged two of Germany's most powerful battlecruisers, *Gneisenau* and *Scharnhorst*. With the sinking of the *Rawalpindi*, 265 members of her crew were lost. The term therefore refers to weather conditions, not cowardice.

Razor Blade　　　**Spade**

An offensive term for a black person.

Razzmatazz　　　**Jazz**

Refers to this type of music and the noisy excitement once generated by it, especially when played traditionally. The term has been around since the late 19th century in one form or another and was hooked on to jazz in the 1920s.

Read & Write　　　**Fight**

An example never truncated, two people having a 'read' doesn't exactly conjure up visions of violence.

Ready, Steady Go　　　**Po**

A chamber pot from the 1960s based on a TV music show of the period. Also known as a 'p-p' (piss-pot), it was standard issue in the basic holiday-camp chalet. So if you needed a middle-of-the-night 'pee-pee' in the 'p-p', you'd grab the 'ready, steady' and go.

Rear Ender　　　**Bender (Homosexual)**

An appropriate if offensive, example: a backside for a 'backside enthusiast'.

Red Devil   **Level**

A building site term relating to a spirit level; an important tool of a bricklayer, carpenter, floor-layer, etc.

Red Hots   **Trots (Diarrhoea)**

During a bout of the 'scatters', this may aptly describe the muzzle of one's 'scatter gun' – the anus – which is likely to resemble your car's cigar lighter.

Red Rum   **Dumb**

Most commonly used in admonishment of someone who doesn't speak rather than a person who can't: 'Why didn't you say something? You're not red rum!'

Red, White & Blue   **(a) Flu**

A piece that seems apt if red stands for temperature, white for pallor and blue for melancholia.

                                   (b) Shoe

An example from the late 1960s, when psychedelic 'red whites' were all the rage.

Reelings & Rockings   **Stockings**

A 1950s example that was heard much later when an East End villain walked into the lavatory of a local pub and was stopped in his tracks by the sight of the performing drag act putting on a stocking: 'What's the matter, never seen a man putting on a reeling before?' asked the performer. 'Only over his head' came the reply.

Reels of Cotton   **Rotten**

Applies to all things that have gone bad, from the putrification of food to a state of affairs that has changed for the worse. As the poker player said: 'I started off getting good hands then it all went reels and I lost everything'.

Reggie & Ronnie   **Johnny (Condom)**

A case of the brothers Kray still offering protection, this was inspired by the twin Kings of the London Underworld, Reggie (1933–2000) and Ronnie (1933–95).

Reginal Denny   **Penny**

An example from the 1940s that was probably as well known

as the British actor (1891–1967) it was based on. Didn't make the transition to decimal coinage, though.

Reverend Ronald Knox　　**Pox (VD)**
Refers to all types of the disease that this Catholic priest could never have caught, given that he did his job properly. Shortened to the 'reverend ronald', it is based on a priest (1888–1957), who also wrote detective stories.

R.G. Knowles　　**Holes**
A piece that lived and died in the theatre, possibly when well-worn costumes became full of 'argees'. Based on Canadian-born comedian Richard George Knowles (1858–1919), a star turn of the British music hall.

Rhubarb　　**Sub 1**
Cocknified to 'rhubub', this applies to a loan or an advance on an expected income.

Sub 2
A substitute – especially in a football match, where disgruntled fans may call for the manager to send on the 'rhububs'.

Rhubarb & Custard　　**Mustard**
Pork pie for lunch? Steak for dinner? OK, pass the 'rhubub'. (Serving suggestions.)

Rhubarb Pill　　**Bill**
That which must be paid based on a type of purgative. Heard in a restaurant:
Customer: Get the rhubarb, please.
Waiter: There's no rhubarb, sir.
Customer: No rhubarb? Lovely-lovely! Get my coat then.

Rhubarbs　　**Subs 1**
Refers to subscriptions, as paid by members of social and sports clubs.

Subs 2 (Suburbs)
London taxi-driver's slang for the outer boroughs that form part of The Knowledge, the learning process that all drivers of black cabs must go through before becoming licensed to clog up the streets of the capital.

Rhythm & Blues   **Shoes**

A 1980s term that leads to 'crabshells' being known as 'rhythms'.

Ribbon & Curl   **Girl**

A term for a little lady, probably one under seven – older than that and ribbons and curls are snubbed as childish.

Richard & Judy   **Moody**

An update of 'punch & judy' (qv) regarding deception and lies and based on TV presenters Richard Madeley and Judy Finnegan. See 'Moody & Sankey'.

Richard Briers   **Pliers**

An electrician's term heard on a building site in the 1990s. Used as 'richards' after a British actor, the star of some of our best sitcoms. Coined when British sitcoms were funny.

Richard Burton   **Curtain**

Drawn on the name of the Welsh actor (1925–84), this applies to domestic and more relevantly, stage curtains.

Richard Gere   **Queer**

Based on an American actor, one that women have been known to swoon over. As far as I know the term only exists because it rhymes.

Richard the Third   **(a) Bird 1**

A one-term-fits-all piece from the 19th century for all species of bird, from sparrows and pigeons to those you can't put a name to – except 'richard'.

Bird 2

More recent than (1) but widely used in relation to a young woman who is strangely always a 'richard'.

Bird 3

This is 'the bird', as meted out to second-rate performers. Actors dread being given the 'richard'.

(b) Turd

Quite a common piece – especially dog's mess when stepped in.

(c) Word

A rarely used alternative to the oft-stated 'dicky bird' (qv).

Richard III (1452–85) ruled England from 1483 until his death at Bosworth.

Richard Todd　　　**Cod**
Based on a British actor, this applies to a piece of fried cod. Overfishing has placed the cod on the endangered species list, so who knows how much longer 'richard & chips' will be on the menu?

Riddle-me-Ree　　　**Pee/Wee**
A piece everyone understands, in full or truncated to a 'riddle'.

Riff-Raff　　　**(a) Caff**
A greasy spoon – as represented by the Great Unwashed.
　　　(b) Taff
One of the hoi polloi specifically becomes a Welsh person.

Rifle Range　　　**Change**
Always check your rifle: women do, men don't, children spend it and taxi drivers keep it.

Rikki Tikki Tavi　　　**Lavvy**
A lavatory courtesy of the snake-killing mongoose in Rudyard Kipling's *Jungle Book*. A public 'rikki tikki' is likely to be frequented by homosexual men intent on getting their trouser snakes 'eaten'.

Ringo Starr　　　**Car**
After writing in *Cockney Rabbit* that I wouldn't be surprised if this term existed, I received a letter saying that it did. Based on a former Beatle, it had a short spell in the RS chart in the 1960s, but failed to knock 'jam jar' off the Number One spot.

Rinky Dink　　　**Pink 1**
Colourwise this is only used in connection with the pink snooker ball.
　　　Pink 2
An old reference to a state of wellbeing, fit people are in the 'rinky dink'.

Rin-Tin-Tins　　　**Pins (Legs)**
A 1950s example based on a canine star of early film and TV

Westerns, who was a bit lively on his 'rintys' but never seen to cock one.

Rip & Tear   Swear

A piece that has escaped beyond the bounds of RS, to sound off with a barage of bad language is to 'let rip'.

Rip Van Winkle   Tinkle/Sprinkle

To 'rip van' is to urinate. 'Tinkle' is a childish euphemism and 'sprinkle' is the adult version. Based on a slumberous character in Washington Irwin's *Sketch Book* (1819).

Rip-Rap   Tap (Borrow)

Generally known as being on the 'rip-rap', a state not unfamiliar to scroungers and the permanently skint.

Rise & Shine   Wine

Not a particularly apt example, as anyone who ever awoke with a bacchanalian hangover will confirm.

Rising Damp   Cramp

A 1970s term based on a popular TV sitcom, which was commonly heard on Hackney Marshes whenever members of pub football teams went down with this painful condition.

River Lea   Tea

A 19th-century term based on East London's other river. What a lousy cuppa is said to taste like.

River Nile   Smile

What the 'boat' of an unemployed person breaks into when their 'nightboat to cairo' (qv) arrives. See 'Boat Race'.

River Ouse   Booze

A common expression for a drinking session is to be 'on the river ouse' or just 'on the ouse'.

River Tyne   Wine

Refers to a bottle from the cheaper end of the wine list or the bottom shelf at the supermarket. It wouldn't do to label a vintage claret a bottle of 'River Tyne'.

Riverina   **Deaner (5p)**

A rhyme from the days of our previous currency when a 'deaner' was a shilling, the term survived decimalisation for a while as 5p but seems to be dying out, much like those who once used it.

Roach & Dace   **Face**

A rarely used alternative to that other fishy pairing 'kipper & plaice' (qv).

Roast Beef   **Teeth**

An example that is sometimes used instead of the well-known 'hampstead heath' (qv): 'I'll knock your roast beef so far down your throat you'll be able to chew your dinner again'.

Roast Joint   **Pint**

Old cockney dialect would have made this 'roast jint' and since the rhyme is no longer heard, neither is the term.

Roast Pork   **(a) Fork**

Applies to cutlery but could conceivably be used to confuse a lost motorist: 'Keep going till you come to a roast pork in the road and chuck an isle o' wight' (qv).

      (b) Talk

A rare alternative to 'rabbit & pork' (qv) that has been around since World War I. An expert on backslang may give a 'kaylat' on the subject.

Roast Potato   **Waiter**

One of several terms rhyming waiters with potaters, this one gets cut to a 'roastie'.

Roasted Duck   **Fuck**

A 1930s term for sexual intercourse, which most slang-users haven't given a 'roasted duck' about since.

Rob Roy   **Boy**

A piece that entered the RS catalogue in the late 19th century but seems to have been been dropped when 'saveloy' (qv) came on the scene. Inspired by Robert Roy MacGregor (1671–1734), a Scottish folk hero who, in this book, was eventually bested by a sausage.

Robert E. Lee   **(a) Key**
Seems to have taken over from its soundalike version at (d) to take part in one of life's little mysteries: Why are 'roberts' never where you left them?

(b) Knee
Usually heard in connection with a painful one, most famously in George Formby's song, 'My Auntie Maggie's Remedy'.

(c) Pee/Wee
Another famous Lee gets in for 'the straining of the greens'. This is the commander (1807–70) of the Confederate Army during the American Civil War.

(d) Quay
An elderly piece from London's docks and, like Docklands, has been redeveloped. See (a).

Roberta Flack   **Sack**
An American singer comes in to put people out of work, but mainly she represents a bed. The knackered long to 'hit the roberta'.

Robertson Hare   **Pear**
An old street market example inspired by a long-expired British actor (1891–1979). The term is long gone too, replaced by 'teddy bear' (qv).

Robin Cooks   **Looks**
Ironic piece from the 1990s based on an MP of the period (1946–2005), much ridiculed for his less than handsome features. Bachelors were advised to strike whilst they've still got their 'robin cooks'.

Robin Hood   **Good**
Based on the legendary baddie-but-goodie and seemingly almost as old, this turns up in various guises. It's what children are told to be; also anything praiseworthy – a used car, for example – may be a 'robin hood'un'. On the other hand, it may be 'no robin hood'.

Robin Hoods   **Goods**
Merchandise, often illegal; a warehouse or 'slaughter' may be full of hooky 'robin hoods'.

Robin Hoods(s)   Wood(s) 1

Fittingly applies to a collection of trees or a chopped-up one. When coal fires were the norm, greengrocers would sell penny bundles of 'robin'.

Wood(s) 2

A World War I term for Woodbine cigarettes. Hard-up smokers could once buy single cigarettes, whereby a tobacconist would break open a packet of fags and sell them for a copper or two. In the 1950s kids starting on the road to addiction could buy 'tup'ney Wood'. No 'elf 'n safety then, they'd even light 'em for you.

Robinson & Cleaver   Fever

A 19th-century example based on a firm of Irish linenmakers who had stores in Belfast and London. You are more likely to see a tap-dancing gout-sufferer than to hear this again.

Robinson Crusoe   Do So

A piece of 19th-century defiance based on the eponymous hero of novel and pantomime: 'If you don't move your car from in front of my gate, I'll call the police.' 'Well, robinson crusoe then!'

Rock & Roll   (a) Dole

A piece that first signed on in the early 1960s, which saw the unemployed as being on the 'rock'.

(b) Hole

What boots, clothes and excuses may be full of; also a crude expression of sexual intercourse, 1950s teddy boys were probably the first to brag about 'getting their rock & roll'.

Rock of Ages   Wages

Often shortened to 'rocks' and based on an old hymn, this is what people originally thanked God it was Friday for.

Rock of Gibralta   Water

Post-World War II sailors may have spent their lives on the water, but they never put 'rocka' in their rum.

Rock(s) & Boulder(s)   Shoulder(s)

Symbolic of strength, the sort of 'rocks' on which a friend in need may need to lean on.

Rockford Files   **Piles**

One of a bunch of terms for haemorrhoids, this one formed on the name of an American TV cop show seen in Britain in the 1980s and heard as 'rockfords'.

Rocking Horse   **Sauce 1**

The condiment. The 'rocking horse' was commonly passed in caffs.

Sauce 2

Cheek or impertinence, kids of yore expected a clip round the ear from the old man for their 'rocking horse'. And they got one!

Rod Laver   **Saver**

An Australian tennis player, four-times Wimbledon champion in the 1960s, comes in as a bet made to safeguard another. For example, if, at the start of a tournament, you back a player to win and he reaches the final, you can then back the other player as a 'rod laver' to put you in a no-lose situation.

Rogan Josh   **Dosh (Money)**

An early 21st-century example used by young curry-house frequenters, who trim it down to 'rogan'. Based on a Kashmiri dish of lamb curry and yoghurt.

Roger Hunt   **Cunt**

It seems that anyone with this surname comes in for the same treatment in RS and this England footballer of the 1960s is no exception. Refers to a fool, a rat or a vagina.

Roger Moore   **Snore**

When a woman hasn't slept because of the non-stop 'rogering' of her old man, she won't necessarily wake up with a smile on her face. Based on a knighted British actor who may, or may not be prone to noisy 'bo peeping'.

Rogue & Villain   **Shilling**

An old monetary piece that is well and truly spent.

Roland Rat   **Prat**

Since the 1980s an idiot has been known as a 'roland' down to a TV puppet.

Roland Young   **Tongue**

A 1940s example based on a British actor (1887–1953), who made his name in Hollywood and had it hijacked in London's East End. A man with one of those faces, whose name is on the tip of your 'roland'.

Roll Me in the Dirt   **Shirt**

Doubtful if anyone has worn a 'roll me' since the 19th century.

Roll Me in the Gutter   **Butter**

A piece from World War I that was probably last heard some time before World War II.

Rolling Billow   **Pillow**

A piece that has ebbed and flowed for 'donkeys' but is probably washed up now.

Rolling Stone(s)   **Bone(s)**

An example from the 1970s, before the boys in the band made old 'rollings'.

Rollmop(s)   **Cop(s)**

The police – as represented by pickled herrings.

Rolls-Royce   **Voice**

Applies, you might think, to a superior singing voice but not necessarily.

Roman Candle(s)   **Sandals**

An old piece that fits like a glove in relation to the footwear of the ancients.

Romantic Ballad   **Salad**

Based perhaps on 'The Green Leaves of Summer' or 'The Green, Green Cress of Home'.

Ronan Keating   **Meeting**

Business people go from one 'ronan' to another, courtesy of the Irish singer; a piece of early 21st-century popney.

Ronnie Barker   **Marker (Pen)**

A piece that was used in betting shops in the 1970s, when this British comedian (1929–2005) was at the height of his comic powers and the board-man hadn't been replaced by a wall full of television screens. Results and prices were marked up with a 'ronnie'.

Ronnie Biggs   **Digs (Lodgings)**
Named after one of the Great Train Robbers of 1963 who, dissatisfied with his own living conditions in Wandsworth prison, escaped to find fresh 'ronnies' in Brazil.

Ronnie Scott   **Hot**
An East London born jazz musician (1927–96), known as a cool saxophonist, gets on the chart as the temperature soars. Best known as the co-founder of Ronnie Scott's Jazz Club in London's Soho.

Ronson Lighter   **Shiter (Anus)**
The 1990s term that is responsible for the delightful expression 'up your ronson!

Rookery Nook   **Book**
A 1920s rhyme inspired by an Aldwych farce of the period. Apart from what you are holding, 'rookerys' were also made at racecourses by 'joe rookies' (qv).

Rory McGrath   **Laugh**
A 2000s piece whereby piss-takers, wind-up merchants and practical jokers are said to be 'having a rory' after a British comedian.

Rory O'More   **(a) Door**
An ancient entry that's still in use. Probably coined by Irish navvies on 19th-century building sites in London as it is based on one of the leaders of the Catholic rebels of the Ulster revolt of 1641 (c.1620–55).

(b) Floor

Apart from what you stand on and what elevators stop at, this is used in a sense of destitution. Those 'on the rory' are as low as they can go. This can be taken as secondary slang (see 'On the Floor') and so, by extension, Rory O'More – who also gave his name to an early Victorian poem and a street ballad from 1888, also gets in as (c).

(c) Poor

See (b).

(d) Whore

A 19th-century prostitute; working girls no longer walk the streets as 'rorys' – 'T'is pity she's a rory', as English playwright John Ford may have written had RS been about in 1633.

Rose of Tralee   Pee/Wee

Inspired by an Irish ballad, this can go down as a female water release whereby she may be in the 'rosie's' having a 'rose of'. See 'Rosie O'Grady'.

Roseanne Barr   Bra

A 1990s example based on a larger-than-life American comedienne with larger-than-average underwear.

Rosebud   Spud 1

A 19th-century piece that sees potatoes mashed to 'roses'.

Spud 2

An example from the 1950s concerning a hole in the heel of a sock, long known as a 'spud'.

Roses Red   Bed

Probably more romantic as a love nest than 'uncle ned' (qv)...Careful, though, thorny relationships start in beds of roses.

Rosie Lee   Tea

Evergreen term for the drink with which the English wash down theirs' and the world's troubles.

Rosie Loader   Soda

A rhyme from the 1950s that generally relates to a whisky and soda.

Rosie O'Grady   Lady

From a 1940s film and song title comes a piece that mainly applies to the ladies toilet, the 'rosie's'.

Rotten Row   (a) Bow 1

A 19th-century piece probably used ironically about an area of East London. Rotten Row in London's Hyde Park would have been full of swells on horseback and Bow packed with scruffbags in bare feet. Not sure why Bow should be singled out for a piece of RS, but it's obsolete anyway.

Bow 2

A century-old example, when it was fashionable for girls to wear bows in their hair. Later, it transferred to a bow tie.

(b) Blow

An early 20th-century reference to a whack and in the 21st century, the police still fetch 'rotten rows' down on the heads of rioters.

Round me Houses   **Trousers**

See next entry.

Round the Houses   **Trousers**

A well-worn piece from the mid 19th century, usually dropped to 'round de's'. Sometimes said as 'round me houses', which gets cut down to 'round me's'.

Rowton Houses   **Trousers**

A piece that gets tapered to 'rowtons', after Baron Rowton (1838–1903) and the lodging houses he founded for ragged-arsed men.

Roy Castle   **Arsehole**

The name of a British entertainer (1932–94) lives on as the 'reeking roy castle' of a persistent wind-breaker.

Roy Hudd   **(a) Blood**

Only heard this once, but the story's worth repeating: A less than funny comedian was struggling to get laughs at an East End pub on a Sunday lunchtime. He was heckled, abused and harassed by an unruly audience and somebody or other would yell out the punchline of every joke he tried to tell. In the end it all became too much. Unable to take any more he waved his handkerchief as a white flag of surrender, which incurred even more derision. With a tear in his eye he pleaded with his tormentors: 'Look,' he said, 'I'm doing my best. What do you want, Roy Hudd?' 'Yes,' replied a wag, and promptly launched a light ale bottle in the direction of the funny man's head. He never appeared there again.

(b) Spud

Baked or boiled, roasted or raw, any potato is a 'roy hudd'. Based on a British comedian, actor, writer and life-long devotee of the theatre. A former King Rat, he now achieves a kind of immortality as a King Edward.

Roy Race   **Face**

A 1960s term that's based on the ultimate English hero, the cleaner-than-soap footballer, Roy of the Rovers of *Tiger* comic fame. Never take an honest 'roy race' on trust – it may house a dishonest mouth.

Roy Rogers   **Bodgers**

Applies to rogue tradesmen or inferior workmen and is aptly based on the name of a Western film star (1912–98), billed as 'the King of the Cowboys'. Bodge, Fleece and Leggit – that well-known company of rogue builders.

Royal Docks   **Pox 1 (VD)**

Applies to any form of the disease and is probably inspired by infected seamen.

Pox 2

To 'have the pox' of something is an old London expression for being fed-up with a situation. Long-stationary motorists on the M25 may utter: 'I've the right royal docks of this'. The Royals in Silvertown, E. London – once the major source of income in the area – have been redeveloped with, amongst other things, the ExCel exhibition centre, the London City Airport and the University of East London occupying the site.

Royal Mail   **Bail**

Almost exclusively the property of the criminal fraternity, but then I suppose it would be.

Royal Navy   **Gravy**

An alternative to the more common 'army & navy' (qv) and may be connected to the adage: 'The Navy gets the gravy but the Army gets the beans'. Then again, maybe not.

Rub-a-Di-Dub-Dub
A slightly different version to the next entry that breaks down to a 'rubbidy'.

Rub-a-Dub-Dub
(a) Club 1
Applies to any type of club, including a social, working-man's or drinking club.
Club 2
A playing card of this suit pluralised to the shortened 'rubbadubs'.
(b) Pub
Inspired by the nursery rhyme about three men in a tub, this was in more use than (a1) – simply down to the higher number of boozers in the East End and usually in the cut-down versions of 'rubba' or 'rubbadub'.
(c) Sub
An infrequent rival to 'rhubarb' (qv) relating to a loan or an advance on wages.

Rubber Duck　　　　　**Fuck**
Mostly used in a sense of not caring; for 'couldn't give a fuck', read 'couldn't give a rubber duck'.

Rubber Glove　　　　　**Love**
This 1990s example smacks of fetishism.

Rubik's Cubes　　　　　**Pubes**
A famous puzzle from the 1970s finds its way into people's underwear as pubic hair: 'Mess with us and we'll string you up by your rubiks' – an underworld threat.

Ruby Murray　　　　　**Curry**
Based on the name of an Irish singer (1935–96), as famous today as a vindaloo as she was in 1955 when she had five records in the charts at the same time.

Ruby Red　　　　　**Head**
A World War I term which may have something to do with vin rouge and the hangovers it would have given the soldiers who drank it.

Ruby Rose   **Nose**

An old term that's always truncated to a 'ruby', which may be apt in a case of a beery bugle, claret conk or boozer's beezer.

Ruck & Row   **Cow**

Refers to a disagreeable woman, not the animal. Usually reduced to the first element and prefaced with 'old', as in 'the old ruck next door'. In backslang she's a 'delo wock'.

Rudolf Hess   **Mess**

A post-war term based on the high-ranking Nazi (1894–1987), which is representative of failure: 'He's made a right rudolf of that!' – as Hitler might have bellowed after his deputy's bid for Anglo-German peace failed when Hess was bunged in the Tower in 1941.

Ruin & Spoil   **Oil**

Fittingly shortened to 'ruin' and probably coined in the wake of the environmental damage caused when an oil tanker runs aground.

Rumptitum   **Bum**

An early 20th-century rhyme for the buttocks, known as the 'rumpty', the term may be an extension of 'rump'.

Runner & Rider   **Cider**

Sounds as though this could have been formed on a West-Country racecourse. 'Redis' – backslang cider.

Rupert Bear(s)   **Share(s)**

A 1980s example, which arose after the sell-off of some nationalised industries, putting 'ruperts' in the hands of people who had never before had any dealings in the Stock Exchange. Based on an ever-popular children's book and cartoon character with a name easily associated with stockmarkets.

Russell Crowe   **Dough**

A 21st-century term for money based on an award-winning Australian actor whose success ensures he will never be short of 'russell'.

Russell Harty 　　　　　**Party**

A knees-up, courtesy of a TV personality (1934–88), who hosted a long-running chat show in the 1970s.

Russian Duck 　　　　**(a) Fuck**

A 1950s expression for sexual intercourse, when couples caught having a 'russian' never came to a satisfactory conclusion.

(b) Muck

An early 20th-century term for dirt or grime that got scrubbed long before the 21st.

Russian-Turk 　　　　　**Work**

A mid 19th-century piece, which seems to have been based on immigrant labour. Now unemployed.

Ruud Gullit 　　　**Bullet (Dismissal)**

A late 20th-century example which reflected this Dutch international footballer's headline-making sacking from his post as Chelsea's player-manager in 1998.

Ryan Giggs 　　　　**Digs (Lodgings)**

A 1990s piece based on a Welsh international footballer, who will never have to scour the streets in search of 'ryans'.

Ryan's Daughter 　　　　**Water**

A film of this title was released in 1970 and soon afterwards people were having a splash of 'ryans' in their whisky and filling their kettles with it.

Sacha Distel   **Smell**
A 1970s example for any type of odour, a 'sacha' can be a nice or nasty smell. Based on a French singer (1933–2004), who was often seen on British TV.

Sack Race   **Face**
No nice mooey this, a miserable or angry face may draw the comment: 'Look at the sack race on it'.

Sacks of Rice   **Mice**
An old term from the docks, where ships carrying the term would have given passage to stowaway rodents.

Sad & Sorry   **Lorry**
A rueful-sounding piece that may touch on the loneliness of the long-distance lorry driver.

Saddam Hussein   **Pain**
A 1990s example based on the former president of Iraq (1937–2006), who had long been a 'saddam' in the arse of the world.

Safe & Sound   **Ground**
Possibly coined by a nervous air traveller whose only wish was to be back on the 'safe'.

Sailors at Sea   **Tea**
Long-winded piece only ever poured as 'sailors'.

Saint & Sinner   **Dinner**
Has connotations of Sunday dinner: whilst the 'saint' cooks it,

the 'sinner' goes up the pub, has a skinful, staggers home, wolfs down the meal and then crashes out in the armchair and drowns out the TV with his snoring.

Saint Moritz   **Shits**

The Swiss ski resort becomes a 1960s term for diarrhoea. Possibly something to do with the nervousness felt by novice skiers staring down a mountain with a couple of planks of wood strapped to their feet. And do tobogganists come down with the cresta runs?

Salford Dock(s)   **Rock(s)**

Piece of nautical slang for those navigational hazards around a coastline.

Salisbury Crag   **Skag (Heroin)**

A 1980s piece based on a landmark outside Edinburgh.

Sally Gunnell   **Tunnel**

Mostly, but not exclusively the Blackwall Tunnel, which runs beneath the Thames between Poplar and Greenwich. Based on a world-beating athlete from Essex who, despite her retirement from the track, now runs underground.

Salmon & Prawn   **Horn (Erection)**

A fish-dish gets on the scran-chart as a show of length.

Salmon & Shrimp   **Pimp**

A piece that seems to be based on a fish paste, which is apt when you consider the 'fishy money boxes' he looks after.

Salmon & Trout   **(a) Gout**

As long as there's gout, its victims will suffer from 'salmon'.

(b) Snout 1

A slang-for-slang term for the nose: 'Get your salmon out of my business' – as the prostitute said to the midget when they slow-danced.

Snout 2

An informer, all the best rozzers have them.

Snout 3

Rolling tobacco or a cigarette, an old term from prison.

(c) Stout

Refers to this type of beer rather than the waistline that may occur through drinking it.

(d) Tout

Originally a racecourse term for someone who sells tips, it now applies to those who sell overpriced tickets too.

Salt Beef　　　　　**Thief**

A sometimes-used alternative to the common 'tea leaf' (qv).

Salt Fish　　　　　**Dish**

An extremely attractive woman; as Delboy Trotter once said of a prospective blind date: 'She's got to be a salt.' And I'm assured this is the origin of it.

Salt Junk　　　　　**Drunk**

Well known in the reduced form of 'salted', the term dates from the 19th century and is based on the salted beef fed to soldiers of the time.

Salvador Dali　　　　　**Charlie (Cocaine)**

Based on the Spanish artist (1904–89) and known only as 'salvador', this originally went up the noses of arty types before the great unwashed took to snorting it.

Salvation　　　　　**Station**

The railway or underground variety; a 19th-century reference to where the Lord's name is uttered in temper more times and by more people than anywhere else.

Salvation Army　　　　　**Barmy**

Nearly always dislengthened to 'sally army' in relation to someone who may be a bit on the mad side or, as they say, 'has his hat on backwards'.

Sam Cooke　　　　　**Book**

A 1960s example based on an American soul singer of the period (1931–64). Read any good 'sam cookes' lately? Only this one!

Sam Cory　　　　　**Story**

An old example from London's docks apparently based on an

actual dock worker who probably had a reputation for telling whoppers.

Samantha Eggar   **Beggar**

A 1990s term inspired by a British actress, which relates to the professional beggars who haunt the London Underground. A 'samantha' is typically a woeful-looking foreign woman with baby-in-arm and an outstretched hand.

Samantha Janus   **Anus**

A British actress gets cast as another example of where the unwanted may be banished to: 'You can stick your job up your samantha' – a want-away employee.

Sam/Sammy Halls   **Balls (Testicles)**

An old piece based on the eponymous villain of a song from the music-hall era.

Sammy Lee   **Pee/Wee**

Yet another of the clan Lee makes the water ejection connection – this time it's an England international footballer of the 1980s who gets to sprinkle the lawn.

Samuel Pepys   **Creeps**

The English diarist (1633–1703) comes in to give you a feeling of unease. A place or a person may give you the 'samuels'.

San Toy   **Boy**

Based on the name of an early 20th-century play, this specifically relates to a member of a gang, one of the 'san toys'.

Sandy McNab   **(a) Cab**

A post-war term for a taxi that is still on the road even though 'bob mcnab' tried to overtake it in the 1970s.

      (b) Crab (Louse)

An early 20th-century example that generally gets used in the plural: 'You keep scratching yourself down there, you got sandy mcNabs?' Probably based on the 1907 song, 'The Wedding of Sandy McNab', sung by Harry Lauder.

Sandy Powell   **(a) Towel**

A northern comedian (1900–82) forms the basis of this 1940s term for a 'drier'. Superceded by 'enoch powell' (qv) in the 1960s.

(b) Trowel

The bricklayer's tool, rarely heard off a building site – and probably no longer there either.

Santa Claus   **Paws (Hands)**

Old Saint Nick arrives with a sackful of presents in his 'santas'.

Santa's Grotto   **Blotto (Drunk)**

A few too many 'christmas cheers' (qv) will get you 'santas'.

Sarah Gamp   **Lamp**

A post-war rhyme from the theatre inspired by a character from Dickens' *Martin Chuzzlewit*. The woman also gave her name to an umbrella.

Satin & Lace   **Face**

No ugly mug this, it would seem.

Satin & Silk   **Milk**

An ad-man's dream of a term to describe the richness and smoothness of cow-juice. 'Kaylimnam' – a backslang milkman.

Saucepan Lid   **(a) Kid 1**

Children are always known as 'saucepans', be they your own little darlings or the pests playing 'knock-down ginger' – knocking on doors and running away.

Kid 2

Applies to deception, whether an innocent wind-up or a lie of a con man, who will try to 'saucepan' you.

(b) Quid (£1)

Example from the 19th century, when a 'saucepan' was a 'saucepan'.

(c) Yid

A not uncommon piece but one of many for a Jew.

Sausage & Mash   **(a) Cash**

A widely used piece although most people don't realise that they are using truncated RS when they state that they 'haven't got a sausage'.

(b) Crash/Smash

Cab-driver's slang for a road traffic accident, how a 'sausage' can close down a motorway or shut a tunnel.

Sausage Roll   **(a) Dole**

Unemployed people have long been 'on the sausage'.

(b) Pole 1

A Polish person, a World War II example reborn at the beginning of the 21st century when a significant influx of Polish immigrants settled in Britain.

Pole 2

All other senses of the word, from the 'sausage' dancer to the 'sausage' vaulter and harassed people can be driven 'up the sausage' by a tormentor.

(c) Poll (Head)

An ancient word for the head took on this piece of RS in 1990s with the hated Poll Tax or 'Sausage Tax' as some people called it – although it has to be said, not that many.

Saveloy   **Boy**

Used to describe a small boy but is sometimes a rival gang member to 'san toy' (qv). 'Yobs and elrigs' – backslang boys and girls.

Savoury Rissole   **Pisshole**

Refers, naturally enough, to a lavatory but not exclusively. Any place that can be justifiably described as a dump or a carsey, be it pub, club, shop, cinema, town or city, can be a 'savoury'.

Say Goodbye   **Die**

As fitting as any term in the book, as it's what we will all do some day.

Scabby Eye   **Pie**

A meat pie, usually a fat-and-gristle job bought from a chip shop.

Scapa Flow   **Go**

Meaning a hasty exit, 'scapa' has long held a place in the annals of RS. It is, however, just as likely to be an example of polari, the theatrical slang based on the Italian language, in which 'Scappare' means to run away. Scapa Flow is a stretch of sea in the Orkney Islands where 71 surrendered German warships were scuttled on 21 June 1919.

Scarborough Fair **Hair**
A 1970s term based on the title of a Simon and Garfunkel song of the period. Two men heard discussing a barmaid:
1st Man: I like her scarborough, don't you?
2nd Man: Yeah, but I wouldn't want it in my dinner!

Schindler's List **Pissed**
A 1990s piece for insobriety following an award-winning film of this title; usually half-cut at 'schindler's'.

Scooby Doo **(a) Clue**
A 1990s example that usually reflects someone's ineptitude or ignorance of a situation – such a person 'hasn't got a scooby'.
(b) Screw
A piece of prisoners' slang for one of Her Majesty's turnkeys. Based on a cowardly cartoon dog on TV since the 1970s.

Scotch Egg(s) **Leg(s)**
Rival to the more common 'scotch pegs' (qv), the difference being this is used in full.

Scotch Mist **Pissed**
An ultra-familiar piece that is never halved, drunks are always 'scotch mist'.

Scotch Peg(s) **Leg(s)**
An example that's been running in the truncated form of 'scotches' since the 19th century. A scotch peg is a thick, triangular block of wood used to keep things from rolling – logs and wheels, for instance.

Scotland the Brave **Shave**
Always reduced to a 'scotland', as in the conversation between a barmaid and a customer who has had a severe haircut:
Barmaid: Not much hair about.
Customer: No, you should scotland more often.

Scraggy Lou   **Flu**

How a woman who normally takes pride in her appearance may describe herself when riddled with flu germs: 'I've got the scraggy lou and I look like her'. Based on a woman of scraggy appearance whose name is Lou.

Scrambled Egg(s)   **Leg(s)**

Typically used in terms of inebriation, when drunks stagger home on 'scrambled eggs'.

Scrap Metal   **Kettle**

An example from the 1950s, which is apt in that it's what old kettles ended up as. Old sculleries were often steamed up because 'the scrap's boiling its intrals out'.

Screwdriver   **Skiver**

A reference to a person who knows just what needs to be done – and how to get out of doing it. Since the contents of a toolbag are a complete mystery to him, the term doesn't seem very apt.

Scuba Diver   **Fiver (£5)**

A piece swimming in the sea of RS as a 'scuba' since the 1950s.

Scully & Mulder   **Shoulder**

Something to cry on, courtesy of the partners in the cult TV series *The X-Files*, although Mulder rarely gets a look in.

Sean Connery   **Coronary**

Used as a mock warning against getting overexcited and having a heart attack: 'Calm down or you'll have a sean connery'. Based on a beknighted Scottish actor.

Sebastian Coe(s)   **Toes**

Since this is inspired by a multi-recordbreaking British runner, it's particularly apt as it refers to making a swift exit. At the sight of the police a villain will have to be on his 'sebastians' a bit lively.

Second-hand Merc   **Turk**

A Turkish person has, for a few years, been known as a 'second-hand'. Based on a used Mercedes Benz car.

Seek & Search   Church

About as suitable a term as you can get, where man seeks salvation in search of the Lord.

Seig Heils   Piles

Another case of haemorrhoids, whereby a nasty 'chute' becomes a Nazi salute.

Seldom Seen   Queen

A reference to our present monarch, which seems reasonably apt – well, I've never seen her.

Selina Scott   Spot

An updated version of 'randolph scott' (qv), whereby sproot-covered juveniles become 'selina'-covered juveniles. Based on a British TV presenter.

Semolina   Cleaner

Applies to a person who arranges dust on a professional basis.

Sentimental Song   Pong (Smell)

Typically used of a young man's living quarters, where unwashed socks, underwear and dishes add to the overall 'sentimental' of the place.

September Morn   Horn (Erection)

If it's your birthday in June, ask your father about this one. Possibly based on a 1912 painting of a nude woman by Paul Chabas (1869–37).

Septic Tank   Yank

If an American is known as a 'septic', is an enemy of Uncle Sam an 'antiseptic'? Taxi drivers use the term as 'seppo'.

Seven & Six   Fix

To be in difficulty is to be in a 'right old seven & six', like getting car trouble and not having the tools to 'seven & six' it. 7/6d was 37½p in old coinage.

Seven Dials   Piles (Haemorrhoids)

An allusion to the painful condition non-sufferers call 'grapes', based on an area of London close to theatreland where the height of the capital's low-life once dwelled.

Sexton Blake   **(a) Cake**

A long-established piece based on a fictional detective of book, film and comic fame.

      (b) Fake

Refers to a forgery or a copy, especially of a painting. Master copier of old masters Tom Keating (1917–84) often referred to his works as 'sextons'.

Shabba Rank   **Wank**

A 1990s example of 'flying solo' based on an American reggae singer. And anything worthless or useless 'ain't worth a shabba'.

Shake & Shiver   **River**

A theatrical piece from the 1930s, rats, snakes and other backstabbing low-life will 'sell you down the shake'.

Shania Twain   **Stain**

A piece of popney that turns a beautiful Canadian singer into soiled goods; clothes, mattresses, carpets, gussets, etc. can all get 'shania'd'. Wonder if this will impress her much?

Sharon Stone   **Phone**

A nineties piece of popney that generally applies to a mobile; inspired by an American actress.

Sharp & Blunt   **Cunt**

Employed only in a vulgar anatomical sense for the vagina.

Sharper's Tool   **Fool**

Given that a 'sharper' is a cardsharp and cards are his tools, this is a sublimely fitting term for one who will always 'find the lady' when there's no money on it. If brains were made of custard, a 'sharpers' wouldn't have enough to cover his spotted dick.

Shaun Spadah   **Car**

A 1920s term based on the name of the winner of the 1921 Grand National, but now a non-runner.

Shell Mex   **Sex**

A sixties example based on the name of an oil company,

whereby to have blagged a bit of 'shell mex' was to have made a successful pull.

Shepherd's Bush   (a) Moosh (Face)

A case of an area of West London representing an area west of the left ear'ole.

(b) Push

Chopped to the 'shepherd's' with reference to dismissal, to get the push.

Shepherd's Pie   Sky

Reduced to the first element, this would appear to have something to do with a red sky at night.

Shepherd's Plaid   Bad

A mid 19th-century rhyme based on the Northumberland Tartan, a material made of small, black-and-white checks. Also called 'shepherd's check'. The term has been obsolete for the best part of a century but if someone sips a beer, pulls a face and says it's 'shepherd's' in a period drama, you'll know what he means.

Sherbet Dab   Cab

A 1990s piece used by taxi drivers in relation to the 'black money box' that they go to work in.

Sherbet Dip   Tip (Gratuity)

An appropriate example since, in cockney parlance, a tip is often referred to as a 'drink' and a drink is known as a sherbet.

Sherman Tank   (a) Wank

The act of 'flogging one's horace' has been known as a 'sherman' since World War II.

(b) Yank

A fitting example since this war machine was an American weapon named after one of their Civil War Generals.

Shillings & Pence   Sense

A very old allusion to a fool, someone who 'hasn't got the shillings he was born with'.

Shiny & Bright **Alright**
A state of satisfaction when all is 'shiny'.

Ship in Full Sail **Pint of Ale**
A term as old as it sounds, a pint was long known as a 'ship'. And when the glass was almost empty, it was said to be 'on the mud'.

Ship Under Sail **Tale**
A line spun by a beggar or con-artist, this is an early 20th-century piece that seems to have sunk without trace.

Ship's Anchor **Wanker**
A low contemptible person, someone who would cause a dung beetle to go 'Ugh!'

Shirley Bassey **Chassis (Body)**
Can apply to the base-frame of a motor vehicle, whereby a car can be written off with a bent 'shirley'. Mostly though, it applies to the shapely body of a woman, much like the one owned by the Welsh diva in the 1960s, when the phrase was coined. Larger women are said to have a 'birley shassey', much like an older Dame Shirley has at present.

Shirt & Collar **Dollar**
A 19th-century term for what is now 25p, which may be responsible for a punter 'losing his shirt'. Sometimes said as 'shirt collar'.

Shirt Collar **Dollar**
Five shillings in old money (see previous entry).

Shiver & Shake **Cake**
A piece from the 1920s, when invitations to 'river' and 'shivers' would have been on a Sunday afternoon in the front room. See also 'River Lea'.

Shoes & Socks **Pox (VD)**
When a known carouser suddenly stops drinking for no apparent reason, be suspicious. Something's afoot! It could be the 'shoes', and he's taking penicillin.

Shooters Hill   **Bill (Police)**

Not necessarily the Armed Response Unit but this has got on the crime scene in the wake of some highly publicised police shootings. Based on an area of S.E. London that stands 432 feet at the summit and was used for public executions until 1805.

Shout & Holler   **Collar**

A piece from a time when collars were detachable, so no longer in vogue.

Shovel & Broom   **Room**

A 'shovel' is a reference to living quarters, not to space. Probably apt as a room the size of a broom cupboard is rentable in an overcrowded city.

Shovel & Pick   **(a) Mick**

Refers to an Irish person, usually a building site worker, which makes the piece wholly suitable.

(b) Nick 1 (Prison)

The 'shovel' has long been a term for one of Her Majesty's guest houses.

Nick 2 (Steal)

Uncommon but shoplifters have been known to 'shovel it and scarper'.

Shovel & Spade   **Blade**

A 1950s term for a knife or razor as carried by gang members. Some things never change: half a century later 'shovel'-wielding young thugs still inflict damage.

Shovels & Spades   **AIDS**

Until they find a cure, the connection is sadly obvious: shovels and spades dig graves.

Shower Bath   **Half**

An example coined on the racecourse, originally for 10 shillings, which was half a pound, universally known as a 'half'. Always called a 'shower', it has made the transition to today's half a quid, 50p.

Shredded Wheat   **(a) Sheet**

A bedsheet. Heard only once in the story told by the uncouth fiend who found farting in bed and pulling the 'shredded wheat' over his wife's head a source of great hilarity.

b) Sweet

This is sweet in the form of 'excellent'. In criminal parlance it's 'shredded wheat' when a plan comes off, or if any kind of merchandise is of good quality. And, presumably, if breakfast is up to scratch.

Sigmund Freuds   **Haemorrhoids**

The Austrian-born grandaddy of psychoanalysis (1856–1939) comes in as 'sigmunds' for the complaint that can drive one round the bend.

Sigourney Weaver   **Beaver**

An example of secondary slang from the 1990s in relation to the pubic area of a woman that has been long known as a 'beaver'. Dammed at the Christian name after an American film actress.

Silas Hockings   **Stockings**

A piece formed in the theatre and probably saw its final curtain there. Silas Hocking was an English novelist (1850–1935), the first author to sell a million copies of a book whilst he was still alive.

Silent Night   **Light (Ale)**

Piece from the 1950s for this type of 'christmas cheer' (qv).

Silicon Chip   **Nip (Japanese)**

A component of the electronics industry comes in for someone who helped develop it. Hoist by their own petard, so to speak.

Silver & Gold   **Old**

From the effect ageing has on the hair, as in the song, 'Silver Threads Among The Gold'. The 'deelo nammow' – the old woman in backslang.

Silver Spoon   **Moon**

The moon was known as the 'silver' long before men stamped their feet all over it.

Silvery Moon   Coon

An abusive term for a black person.

Simon Cowell   Towel

A noughties example, which gives all the other towel terms a wipe-out. Based on an English record producer and panellist on TV talent show, *The X Factor*, many of his rejected hopefuls can take a kind of revenge by drying their bums on a 'simon'.

Simple Simon   Diamond

Applies to the precious stone and the not-so valuable playing card – unless you're holding five of them. Based on the nursery rhyme character, who tried to 'mump' a pie off a pieman.

Sinbad the Sailor   Tailor

An example that was common when most men had their suits made to measure by the local 'sinbad', but less so now that off-the-peg jobs are so readily available. Seaman Sinbad's adventures are written about in *The Arabian Nights*.

Sinead O'Connor   Doner (Kebab)

A piece of 2000s popney that sees an Irish singer getting sliced up in take away food shops.

Sir Anthony Blunt   Cunt

The C-word at its most objectionable since it applies to a 'right scaly-backed reptile' of a person. Someone lower than a suicide bomber in a children's ward. Based on a British traitor (1914–2000), whose knighthood was annulled in 1979.

Sir Walter Scott   Pot

A 19th-century example from the world of the drinking classes as it applies to a pint pot, the norm before pint glasses. Based on the Scottish novelist and poet (1771–1832). 'Top o' retrop' – a backslang pot of porter.

Sit Beside 'Er   Spider

An old piece that was common when houses had outdoor toilets wherein lurked many an arachnid to keep a person company. Inspired by the one that gave Little Miss Muffet the horrors.

Six & Eight   **(a) State**

Applies to a state of agitation or nervousness, the same heeby-jeebies seen at 'two & eight' (qv).

           (b) Straight (Honest)

Refers to anything or anyone who can be trusted; if people or goods are not bent or crooked, they are 'six & eight'.

Six-Inch Nail   **Bail**

A 2000's update on the old and well-rusted 'holy nail' (qv).

Six Months Hard   **Card**

An out-of-date bingo card based on an equally out-of-date prison sentence: a half-a-stretch (six months) with hard labour.

Six to Four   **Whore**

Coined between the two World Wars, perhaps about the odds against catching something from a prostitute.

Skein of Thread   **Bed**

A 19th-century term that probably hasn't been slept in since it was stitched up by 'uncle ned' (qv).

Skin & Blister   **Sister**

An old and widely used piece, often in the first element, whereby in the jargon of burglars a 'two skins' is a dwelling occupied by a pair of ageing sisters.

Skinny as a Broom   **Groom**

Jokingly cut to a 'skinny', as he stands at the altar with his 'fat & wide' (qv). Both terms come from the comic verse made to fit 'The Wedding March'.

Skip & Jump   **Pump (Heart)**

A descriptively accurate allusion to what can do both.

Sky Diver   **Fiver**

A 1980s piece in direct competition with 'scuba diver' (qv) as a reference to a 'ching'.

Sky Rocket   **Pocket**

A widely used example, which is very often used in the first element. A generous man is quick to put his hand in his 'sky', whilst a mean one will enter his under duress. 'Skyer', 'sky-diver', 'skyman' – a trio of pickpockets.

Skylark Park
An appropriate term since a park is where people go to skylark about. Has also been used in connection with parking a car, in which case it may be less than apt especially when you are late because there was nowhere to 'skylark'.

Skyscraper Paper
Applies to all types of paper, including writing, toilet, news – and what chips come wrapped in.

Slap & Tickle Pickle
This is the edible type of pickle rather than a predicament, hence a cheese-and-slap sandwich.

Slapsie Maxie Taxi
A rhyme from the 1930s based on American boxer 'Slapsie Maxie' Rosenbloom (1904–76), a World Light-Heavyweight champion of the period. He later pursued a successful film-acting career.

Slice of Ham Gam (Fellatio)
A rare alternative to the often-mouthed 'plate of ham' (qv). 'Larro exess' – oral sex, the backslang way.

Slice of Toast Ghost
Generally truncated to the first element, as in the 'slice' of Christmasses past, present and yet to come. And who you gonna call? 'slicebusters'.

Slide & Sluther Brother
Sounds like the slippery member of the family.

Slippery Sid Yid
Generally snipped to 'slippery' and may be based on an actual son of Isra-eel called Sid.

Slither & Dodge Lodge
Applies to the branch of a union or society, especially the Freemasons which is sometimes perceived as being somewhat dodgy or slippery, making the term aptish.

Slomvosh Wash
Old piece from the East End that was used when the kids

needed a soaping, the origin of the term probably died with its originator.

Sloop of War   **Whore**
A 19th-century term for a woman of loose morals and even looser knickers, when many a sailor on shore leave would have picked up a 'whore wound' and carried the disease to his next port of call.

Slosh & Mud   **Stud**
Originally a collar stud but there's no reason why the modern ear-stud shouldn't be known as a 'slosh'.

Slowboat to China   **Vagina**
'And Mellors gently opened the lips of the noblewoman's slowboat' – as D.H. Lawrence might have written about Lady Dagenham's Lover. Inspired by the title of a 1940s song.

Slug & Snail   **Nail**
Applies to the finger and toe variety, which sees your 'scratchers' turned into 'slugs'.

Slush & Slurry   **Curry**
A 2000's piece that appearance-wise may be quite descriptive.

Smack in the Eye   **Pie**
Care should be taken when ordering one of these. If the vendor is big and ignorant of RS, *don't*!

Smash & Grab   **Cab**
Either a mini-cab or a black one; probably most apt in relation to the latter as a brick through a jeweller's window is needed just to get inside.

Smear & Smudge   **Judge**
One of several terms for the one who can put a dirty stain on your character.

Smelly Breath   **Chef**
A 1990s term aimed at the proliferation of TV chefs. It's probably apt with all the necessary food-tasting that goes on and it seems that no recipes exist without garlic.

Smile & Smirk   **Work**
Usually cut to the first element, whereby you may be 'smiling' if you are in work. Unless of course you are one of nature's layabouts, in which case you're smiling if you're not.

Smile & Titter   **Bitter (Ale)**
This originally applied to a once-popular mix of mild and bitter, but since mild is now rarer than teddy bear's piss, it has transferred to the other partner alone.

Smoked Haddock   **Paddock**
An example used by the racing fraternity concerning that part of a racecourse.

Snake & Pygmy   **Steak & Kidney**
A 1950s schoolboy's version of 'kate & sydney' and used as a slur on the school-dinner pie filling.

Snake in the Grass   **Glass**
A 19th-century term for a looking-glass, when a mirror was called a 'shiner'. Later it was transferred to a drinking vessel, where it remains as a 'snake'.

Snake's Hiss   **Piss**
Urination, the sound you get when you siphon the python.

Sniffer & Snorter   **Reporter**
Conjures up visions of old Fleet Street, where the intrepid old hack would sniff out a story over a snort of short in The King and Keys. Or it may just be a case of someone who gets up people's noses.

Snog & Fuck   **Dog and Duck**
An inside joke used by City of London workers concerning a nearby pub which allegedly had a reputation for being a meeting place for bosses and secretaries. I suppose I should stress 'meeting place' – much bunking in the snug is not suggested.

Snoop & Pry   **Cry**
The cause of many a sleepless night and midnight row: a 'snooping baby'.

Snoozing & Snoring   **Boring**
An obvious, but appropriate offering which may get reduced to 'snoozing' or 'snooze & snoring'.

Snow & Ice   **Price**
Most commonly applies to a starting price, but a high cost of an article may induce a whining: 'But look at the snow & ice of it'.

Snow Whites   **Tights**
The legwear favoured by women, but not men. Based on the eponymous heroine of fairy story, pantomime and film. The pornographic version sees Grumpy watching Snow White undress until she spots him and he comes over bashful, who gets the needle and thumps him.

Soap & Flannel   **Panel**
A dated reference to being out of work through illness or injury and receiving sickness benefit as a result; this was known as being on the 'soap'. For an explanation, see 'English Channel'.

Soap & Lather   **Father**
For third party use when talking about your old man, it turns the Pope into the 'Holy Soap'.

Soap & Water   **Daughter**
Should be used in full to differentiate from 'soap & lather' (qv).

Soapy Bubble   **Trouble**
Maybe from the story of the sex pest who got into hot water when he approached a plainclothes policewoman and invited her to 'Put it in your palm, Olive.' To which she replied, 'Not on your Lfebuoy. You're nicked!'

Sodom & Gomorrah   **Borrow**
From the Biblical cities of sin comes the expression 'on the sodom', which is fitting because 'Sod 'em!' is the typical reply of a knocker when asked when his creditors can expect payment.

Soldier Ants   **Pants**
A reference to underwear, 'soldiers' for short – or 'shorts'.

Soldier Bold Cold

A 19th-century term for the illness, long known as 'catching a soldier'.

Soldiers Bold Cold

Temperature-wise, 'soldiers' is a rare alternative to the far more familiar 'taters'. See also 'Potatoes in the Mould'.

Solomon Grundies Undies

Inspired by a 19th-century nursery rhyme on the life of Solomon Grundy, who in the space of a week was born, christened, married, taken ill, dead and buried…All seemingly without changing his underwear.

Somerset Maugham Warm

The British writer (1874–1965) comes in for a spell of nice weather. Balmy evenings are said to be 'somerset', as is the glass of beer you left in the sun.

Song & Dance (a) Chance

An example used in full for effect when handing out a flat refusal: 'You've got no fuckin' song & dance!' means you've more chance of buying a bacon sandwich in a mosque.

(b) Nance (Homosexual)

An early 20th-century example from the theatre where it would have been entirely fitting, given the sexual leanings generally ascribed to your average male dancer and chorus boy.

Song of the Thrush Brush

A 19th-century term for any type of brush or broom so maybe a piece from the gutter as used by a roadsweeper. Also, to give someone the 'song of the thrush' is to dismiss them, to give them the brush-off.

Sooty & Sweep Sleep

One to use when putting the nippers to bed, it had a slight currency in the 1960s and is based on a pair of TV glove puppets whose creator, Harry Corbett (1918–89), became rich and famous by squirting himself with a water pistol and bashing himself on the napper with a toy hammer. The luckiest man ever to have pissed in a pot or what?

Sophie Tucker   **Fucker**

The female equivalent of 'tommy tucker' (qv), in that when a little girl plays up she may be a 'right little sophie'. A mild admonishment based on a larger-than-life American star of stage and screen known as the 'Red Hot Momma' (1884–1966).

Sorrowful Tale   **Gaol**

A 19th-century rhyme still appropriate when applied to the tales of misfortune as related by convicted felons. These may range from a deprived upbringing to a flat tyre on the getaway car.

Sorry & Sad   **(a) Bad**

A very well known piece, anything in a bad way is said to be in a 'sorry state'. 'Dabtros' – a bad sort, a backslang git.

                         (b) Dad

'It's a wise dustbin who knows his own sorry & sad' – an entry in the RS book of proverbs. See 'Dustbin Lid'.

Soup & Gravy   **Navy**

Serving sailors have been 'in the soup' since the days of sail.

South of France   **Dance**

Applies to both the physical act of dancing and to a social event, an invitation to which sounds irresistible, but when the music ends so too must the 'south of france'.

South Pole   **Hole (Anus)**

Direction-wise, being at the bottom, this is a more fitting variant of 'north pole' (qv).

Southend Pier(s)   **Ear(s)**

Known as 'southends', presumably in relation to the sticking-out kind. The pier at this Essex seaside town is the world's longest.

Southend-On-Sea   **Pee/Wee**

A term for having 'one up the wheel' that may have been coined on a beano by a bunch of drunken day-trippers, who kept stopping the coach to do just that.

Spam Fritter   **Shitter (Anus)**
A newish term based on an oldish type of junk food.

Spanish Guitar   **Cigar**
An early 20th-century piece generally stubbed to a 'spanish'.

Spanish Main   **Drain**
Money lost or wasted may be regarded as cash down the 'spanish'. Inspired by the historical name given to the North-East coast of South America between Panama and the Orinoco river, a region regularly plundered by Long John Silver and other TV pirates of the 1950s, when the term was probably coined.

Spanish Onion   **Bunion**
Apt in that both may bring tears to the eyes.

Spanish Waiter   **Potato**
As the shoplifter said when the supermarket security guard asked him what he was doing with the stolen joint of beef in his bag, 'I thought I'd roast a few spanish waiters.'

Spare Rib   **Fib**
Fills a hole when a 'pork pie' (qv) is little and white.

Spit & Drag   **Fag (Cigarette)**
An apt example, especially where roll-ups are concerned, when bits of tobacco get dragged into the mouth and spat out.

Split Pea   **Tea**
A piece first brewed in the 19th century – and has all but evaporated.

Sporting Life   **Wife**
An ironic piece based on the fact that for many a young man the sporting life ceased when he took a 'sporting life'. Based on the racing paper published from 1859 until 1998.

Spotted Dick   **Sick 1**
Not necessarily as nasty as it sounds where men are concerned, any illness counts when you call in 'spotted dick'.

     Sick 2
Vomit, often a patch of regurge on the pavement, train or bus after the pubs have turned out.

Spotty Dog　　　　　　**Wog**
Refers to any foreigner, irrespective of colour and particularly, it would seem, from Dalmatia.

Sprasi Anna　　　　　　**Tanner**
An example from the early 20th-century racecourse, in relation to sixpence in old money. In the Shelta language, spoken by some Irish Travellers, 'sprazi' is a sixpence and presumably, cockneys stuck 'anna' on the end to effect a rhyme on a tanner. 'sprasi', by the way, is pronounced 'sprarsey'.

Squad Halt　　　　　　**Salt**
A military piece from World War I, therefore a seasoned campaigner in the service of RS.

Square Rigger　　　　　　**Nigger**
A derogatory term for a black person which originated early in the 20th century, possibly in the docks. Square-rigged ships were the vessels of the slave trade.

Sri Lanka　　　　　　**Wanker**
A useless or worthless individual, an example first seen in a national newspaper with a headline which blazed: 'What a Bunch of Sri Lankas!' – a slight on the England cricket team after it had lost a test match to that country.

St Clement　　　　　　**Lemon**
An obvious connection with the old nursery rhyme 'Oranges And Lemons', based on the patron saint of citrus fruit. Is it?

St Louis Blues　　　　　　**Shoes**
A 1960s term based on the standard jazz song written in 1914 by W.C. Handy (1873–1958). Worn as 'st louis' and first heard in a TV sitcom.

St Martins-le-Grand(s)　　　　　　**Hand(s)**
The extended version of 'martin-le-grand' (qv); based on a street in the City of London and always shaken down to 'st martins'.

Stage Fright　　　　　　**Light (Ale)**
A theatrical piece hinting at the calming effect a bevvy or three can have on the nerves before a performance.

Stammer & Stutter   **Butter**

An old example for bread-spread that serves as a partner for 'needle & thread' (qv).

Stan & Ollie   **Brolly**

Famous more for their bowlers, this great pair of clowns would no doubt have placed their new umbrellas under their coats in a shower to stop them getting wet. See 'Laurel & Hardy'.

Stand at Ease   **(a) Cheese**

An example that grew out of the trenches of World War I, so the first chunk of 'stand at' was possibly a brie.

(b) Fleas

Also from WWI, when itchy soldiers used this ironically: who could stand at ease when there were bites to be scratched? With the sand fleas in Iraq, maybe the term has made it to the 21st century with a new generation of tommies.

Stand From Under   **Thunder**

A warning used by people working overhead that something is to be dropped to the ground, so it's sort of aptish.

Stand to Attention   **Pension**

Originally applied to an ex-serviceman's pension but has found its way to the Post Office in civvy street, where pensioners stand in line for their 'stand to'.

Stanley Knife   **Wife**

A 1990's piece for 'er indoors based on the tool that seems to play its part in every trade.

Starry Night   **Shite**

Used in connection with rubbish or nonsense as 'What a load of starry night!' How someone who knows nothing about art but knows what he likes might judge a Turner Prize winner.

Star's Nap   **Tap (Borrow)**

Based on the bet of the day in the *Star* newspaper, it wouldn't have been uncommon to tap someone for a nicker to back it. A 1940s piece so this *Star* is not the present one.

Starsky & Hutch   **Crotch/Crutch**

Inspired by a popular American cops and crooks TV show from the 1970s, the threat of a 'kick up the starsky' is a deterrent from that time.

Steak & Bubble   **Trouble**

Steak and bubble 'n squeak leaves the noshery to give us a spot of bother.

Steak & Kidney   **Sydney**

Shortened to 'Steak' as one of the few Christian names to enjoy a term of RS. Australians use it as a reference to the city of Sydney.

Steak & Kidney Pie   **Eye**

A piece that hasn't managed to knock 'mince pie' (qv) off the table.

Steam Packet   **Jacket**

Formed on a type of early steamboat, this has been sailing the sea of changing fashion since the 19th century.

Steam Tug   **(a) Bug**

With modern hygiene the term 'steamer' is now mainly heard in old people's recollections of 'the good old days'. Although with indifferent sanitation within the NHS, a range of 'super steamers' are stalking wards and claiming lives.

(b) Drug

A ready-made slogan for keeping kids off drugs: steam tugs are for steamers. See (c).

c) Mug

A piece developed with the shady dealings of the con-artist, a 'steamer' is the gullible fool who falls for a sob story or buys a time share in The Tower of London.

Steamroller   **Bowler (Hat)**

A dying piece simply because the headwear of the typical City Gent is all but a thing of the past.

Steffi Graf   **(a) Bath**

A hot soak served up in the 1980s by a German tennis player, the best of her era and one of the all-time greats with 22 Grand Slam titles.

(b) Laugh

The 1990s version of 'you must be joking'. An overheard conversation in a wine bar: 'So he staggers in at midnight, falls into the bedroom and tells me he wants to be my galleon on a sea of passion. Gawd knows where he heard that! Anyway my romantic galleon was holed below the water-line, if you know what I mean. I said to him, "Call that stiffy? You're having a steffi!" Game, set and match to me, I think'.

Stephen Fry   **Pie**

How this British actor, already a star of stage and screen in the 1990s, got a bit part at the chippy and a lead role in the pie and mash shop. More liquor, Sir?

Stephenson's Rocket   **Pocket**

A wise businessman knows you can't fill your own 'stephensons' without first lining someone else's. Inspired by the train built by George Stephenson (1781–1848), which in 1829 zipped along at a breathtaking 29mph.

Steve McQueens   **Jeans**

Based on a US film star (1930–80) who always had a cool and fashionable image. He lived fast and died young, but unlike a pair of denims, he won't fade.

Stevie Wonder   **Thunder**

A 1990s entry in the RS chart based on an American musician; anything futile is said to be 'Like farting against stevie wonder'.

Stewart Granger   **Danger**

A 1980s rhyme that relates to chance, as in the moan of a long-suffering customer of a slow-moving barmaid: 'Any stewart granger of getting pissed in here today?' Based on a London-born film star (1913–93).

Stewed Prune   **Tune**

The job of the rapidly disappearing pub pianist is to bash out a few 'stewed prunes on the joanna'.

Stick of Chalk   **Walk**

An old piece that's always lagged way behind 'ball of chalk' (qv).

Stick of Rock   **Cock (Penis)**

A piece based on a British seaside tradition, which seems to have been made for the humorous postcard as a double entendre for oral sex.

Stick(s) & Stone(s)   **Bone(s)**

Let's hope we all make old 'sticks'. Nobody can ask for more than a long life and a short death. Hopefully not by choking on a fish 'stick', though. Sticks and stones have a history of collaboration. Both are terms of criticism or abuse by which we can give or get stick, or you can chuck stones, or 'pelters' at someone whilst getting stoned for doing so. For centuries the penis and testicles have been known as 'stick & stones'.

Sticky Bun   **Son**

Makes up a quartet of buns, along with 'cream', 'currant' and 'hot cross' making the male offspring connection.

Sticky Toffee   **Coffee**

A cup of 'sticky' as poured from the pen of a TV scriptwriter.

Stinging Nettle   **Kettle**

When it's tea time in the suburbs they put the 'stinging' on. A 'singing-stinging' – a whistling kettle.

Stirling Moss   **Toss**

Can be used to signify something of little value, whereby an untrustworthy person or a drug dealer in a burger van 'ain't worth a stirling'. Also those who 'don't give a stirling' about something, couldn't care less about it. After the legendary British racing driver of the 1950s – who received a knighthood in 2000.

Stocks & Shares   **Stairs**

A lesser-known alternative to the oft-quoted 'apples & pears'.

Stoke on Trent   **Bent 1**

This potteries town became a 1970s term for a homosexual, who may be a 'stoker'. First heard on a TV sitcom.

     Bent 2

A 1990s example for stolen goods or 'bent gear', anything sold on the cheap is likely to be 'stoke on trent'.

Bent 3

In an increasingly corrupt and crooked world it pays to know who is straight and who is 'stoke on trent' – anyone or anything that can be fixed.

Stone Jug   **Mug (Fool)**

A rare alternative to 'steam tug' (qv) for someone considered to be the filling for a con-man's sandwich.

Stoodeloo   **Stew**

Sort of RS-ish, although it may just be an extension of the word but there's nothing more warming than a nice 'stoodeloo' for dinner.

Stop & Go   **Toe**

A toosie term that pluralises to 'stops' and may be used in full when trouble's afoot, i.e. when someone treads on your 'stop & go'.

Stop & Start   **Heart**

An anatomically relevant piece in that once it starts, it should only stop once.

Stop, Thief!   **Beef**

A 19th-century piece and one that may have been fitting, when coined: food, especially meat, was an oft-stolen commodity amongst the poor of Victorian London.

Storm & Strife   **Wife**

A 19th-century rhyme with more than a passing nod to a tempestuous marriage.

Straight & Narrow   **Barrow**

A wheelbarrow, an example heard on a building site for that which is pushed up a straight-and-narrow scaffold board.

Strangely Weird   **Beard**

Generally shorn to the first element, a piece hailing from the 1950s when beatniks typically had 'strangelys' and and were considered weird.

Strawberry Ripple   **Cripple**

A less-common alternative to the more popular flavoured ice cream 'raspberry ripple'. But no less offensive.

Strawberry Tart   **Heart**
Broken to 'strawberry', possibly because of a resemblance.

Strike Me Dead   **Bread**
A 19th-century term mostly cut to a slice of 'strike me' and spread with a scrape of 'roll me'. See 'Roll Me in the Gutter'.

String Beans   **Jeans**
Often shredded to 'strings', which is just as fitting.

String Vest   **Pest**
A garment worn in full in the company of a nuisance, especially a drunken 'string vest'.

Struggle & Strain   **Train 1**
A World War I railway train, especially a troop train, which may have been fitting if young soldiers sweating under the weight of full kit are considered.

Train 2
Apt 1980s evolvement into physical exertion.

Struggle & Strainers   **Trainers**
'Struggles' are the required footwear for 'struggling & straining'. They are also the overpriced necessity for fashion-conscious teenagers who have to be seen wearing the right names on their feet.

Struggle & Strife   **(a) Life**
If ever there was an appropriate example, this is it – unless you're one of the 'silver spoon in the mouth' brigade. Also, a life sentence is a 'struggle'.

(b) Wife
May be as apt as (a) given the right circumstances, which would probably be the wrong woman.

Stutter & Stammer   **Hammer**
A piece from the carpentry trade banged down to a 'stutter'.

Sugar & Honey   **Money**
A 19th-century rhyme widely used in the truncated form of 'sugar', which is a 'sweetener' when used as a bribe.

Sugar & Spice (a) **Ice**
Mainly employed as a drinks chiller. Ask a barmaid for a couple of lumps of 'sugar' in your vodka and watch the reaction.
(b) **Nice**
An obvious piece – sugar and spice and all things nice, and all that.

Sugar Candy (a) **Brandy**
Time has never been called on this 19th-century piece, so 'sugar candys' all round and a toast to a 150-year-old term.
(b) **Handy**
The major employment for this is in an ironic sense. Heard at a car boot sale: 'You got some electric nutcrackers for Grandad, did you?' 'Well, they'll come in sugar for a man with no teeth!'

Sugar Stick **Prick (Penis)**
Reference to the sex pistol, which may loom large at the talk of licking a 'sugar stick'.

Sunday Best **Vest**
Formed when this garment was restricted to underwear and only slobs ventured out in their 'sunday bests'.

Sunday Morn **Horn (Erection)**
Seems to be based on the one morning a week when a busy working couple can take advantage of one.

Sunny South **Mouth**
A 19th-century term largely unsung due to the common use of 'north & south' (qv).

Supersonic **Tonic**
A 2000's entry in the drinks list, the toppo mixer for gin.

Surgical Truss **Bus**
Obviously made up by one who has suffered the bollockache of public transport.

Surrey Docks **Pox**
Has an identical use as 'royal docks' (qv). Now redeveloped, the Surrey Docks were on the South bank of the Thames at Rotherhithe, S.E. London.

Susie Anna   **Tanner**

An old sixpence, largely unspent rival to 'sprasi anna' (qv), now both reside in the retirement home for obsolete slang.

Suzie Wong   **(a) Pong**

Formed on the title of the 1960 film, *The World of Suzie Wong*, which happens to be set in Suzie's RS rival in the stink stakes, hong kong (qv).

(b) Song

With the popularity of karaoke, more people than ever before are willing to grab a mike and sing a 'suzie', causing more people than ever to leave a pub before closing time and take to drinking indoors.

Swallow & Sigh   **Collar & Tie**

From the early 20th-century theatre, one of a very few examples of double-word rhyme. In backslang they pair off as a 'rallock & ite'.

Swan Lake   **Cake**

A cup of tea and a slice of 'swan', anybody? From Tchaikovsky's 1876 ballet.

Swannee River   **Liver**

Applies to both the living human organ and that of a dead animal reclining on a butcher's slab. Inspired by an 1851 American minstrels' song, 'Old Folks At Home', which begins: 'Way down upon the Swannee river far, far away'. 'Revel and nacob' – backslang liver and bacon, as bought from a 'retchtub' – butcher.

Swear & Cuss   **Bus**

Since millions of people do this every day whilst waiting for public transport, the term couldn't be more pertinent.

Sweaty Sock   **Jock (Scot)**

A very common term for the race, who seem to be taking over television and politics. Like the man at the jellied eel stall said: 'You can't move for sweaty commentators and prime ministers these days'.

Sweeney Todd   **Flying Squad**

A branch of the Metropolitan Police as portrayed by the fictional 'Demon Barber' of Fleet Street, whose contribution to haute cuisine was hair-raising: he would butcher his clients and despatch their bodies to a Mrs Lovett, a pie-maker. On entering his premises, his customers could be said to have had one foot in the gravy and ended up with their fingers in many pies.

Sweet Pea   **Tea**

A nice cup of 'sweet pea' is rarely brewed these days.

Swiftly Flow   **Go**

Originally an Australian piece that is suitable for its sense of movement, especially as 'swiftly flowing' where a rapid departure is intimated.

Swiss Army Knife   **Wife**

The pocket knife with a multitude of attachments comes on board as an example used humorously upon the approach of the other half: 'Look out, here comes the swiss army!'

Sylvester Stallone   **Alone**

Based on an American film star, this is the 1990s version of being alone. A solitary modern youth is more likely to be 'sylvester' than 'on his tod'. See also 'Tod Sloane'.

Syrup of Fig   **Wig**

Only ever used as 'syrup', especially in connection with an obvious wig, which may be termed a 'golden syrup'.

T. Rex   **Sex**

A predatory term from the would-be sexual athlete, who goes out on the pull in search of a bit of 't. rex'. A piece of youthspeak since the youth of the early 1970s based it on a rock band of the day. 'Exess' backslang sex, or 'hoggins' to give it another name.

Ta-Ta Kiss   **Piss**

Only used in the teasing guise of taking the piss, or taking the 'tattar'. 'Teenod eekat the sip' – 'Don't take the piss' – backslang style.

Take a Fright   **Night**

A mid 19th-century piece that probably had something to do with things that go bump in the dark.

Take & Give   **Live**

A 19th-century term that relates to cohabitating, 'taking' together as man and wife.

Take Your Pick   **Thick**

A 1960s example, for someone who couldn't pass a written spelling test, that seems to be inspired by a TV quiz show of the 1950s/60s.

Tale of Two Cities   **Titties (Breasts)**

Dickens' classic novel gets the treatment in the truncated form of 'tale o' twos'.

Tapioca   Joker
A milk pudding comes in for that which runs wild in a pack of cards.

Tar & Feather   Leather
Refers to a leather jacket and worn as a 'tar' by 1960s rockers. It doesn't have to be black, though.

Tartan Banner   Tanner
Redundant term for sixpennorth of our old currency, a sixpenny piece was a small, silver coin. 'Revlis' – backslang 'long-john' (silver).

Tarts & Vicars   Knickers
Ladies underwear gets taken down to 'tarts', leaving the holy men with nothing to do but make the rhyme. Based on a popular fancy dress theme.

Tate & Lyle   Style
Applies to audacity or guiver (swagger). Outrageous liberty-takers need a bit of 'tate & lyle' to get away with the murders they get away with. Based on the sugar company with close connections to the East End.

Taters in the Mould Cold
See 'Potatoes in the Mould'.

Taxi Cab   Crab
The seafood traditionally sold outside pubs on Sundays and eaten at tea time.

Taxi Cabs   Crabs
Refers to crab lice, sexually transmitted little nippers in the 'rubiks' (qv) known as 'taxis'.

Taxi Rank   (a) Bank
In the shortened form of 'taxi' this becomes quite fitting as a London cab is perceived, by those who don't drive them, to be a black money-box – something vehemently denied by those who do.

(b) Wank

A 'taxi' is another example of 'pumping one's percy', which is a bit like waiting for a cab. One will come eventually.

Tea & Cocoa   **Say So**

Unlike 'coffee & cocoa' (qv), this is used in full. So if you want something you had better 'tea & cocoa'.

Tea & Toast   **Post**

The mail, or how your postman brings you your 'tea & toast'. 'Teesop siffo' – a backslang post office or 'stamp-shop'.

Tea Caddy   **Paddy**

A 1990s term for an Irish person that may have its origins in a building-site canteen.

Tea For Two   **Jew**

Generally reduced to a 'teafer', possibly after the 1958 hit for the Tommy Dorsey Orchestra 'Tea For Two Char Char'.

Tea For Two & A Bloater   **Motor**

An early 20th-century term formed as a condescending allusion to the 'newfangled horseless carriage' and now obsolete. The inclusion of a 'tea for two' is simply down to the fact that I like it.

Tea Grout   **(Boy) Scout**

A piece that always rode the crest of the wave behind the one ridden by 'brussels sprout' (qv).

Tea Leaf   **Thief**

The most common term for the sticky-fingered villain and one that is never shortened, thieves go out 'tea-leafing'.

Tea Strainers   **Trainers**

Refers to modern footwear, not necessarily stained and full of holes.

Teabag   **Slag**

A base, untrustworthy person; an informer – someone who may drop you in it and land you in hot water.

COMPLETE COCKNEY RABBIT

Teapot Lid (a) **Kid 1**

Children have long been known in the first element, especially the unruly offspring of other people. 'Wouldn't you think someone would try to control those teapots?' – Grumpy old man at a recent wedding, possibly me!

Kid 2

To tease, or have on; a wind-up merchant will 'teapot' you.

(b) **Quid (£1)**

When this was formed a 'teapot' bought a bleedin' sight more than it does now.

(c) **Yid**

A Jew can either be a 'teapot' or 'teapotish' – Yiddish.

Ted Drake **Steak**

A forgotten example dredged up from the memory of Fred the Ted. Based on an England international footballer, the term dates from the 1950s when, for a decade, he was the manager of Chelsea.

Ted Frazer **Razor**

Not sure if this is in the sense of a tool or a weapon, depends perhaps on whether or not there was an actual Mr Frazer and whether he was a shaver or a shivver. Barbers tend not to be remembered, so my guess is he didn't draw blood by accident.

Ted Heath (a) **Beef**

How a British PM of the 1970s later found employment down the meat market. See also 'Edward Heath'.

(b) **Teeth**

The same 'biters' as at 'edward heath' (qv). And...

(c) **Thief**

...The same 'gonnof' (i.e. one who has 'gone off' with your possessions).

Ted Thakes **Shakes**

Localised term for the morning-after effects of a heavy bevvy; aptly based on a publican of long-standing in the East End, whose long-standing regulars wish he would get some bloody bar stools.

Teddy Bear **Pear**
An old offering from the fruit market but you can also buy tins of 'teddys'.

Teletubby **Hubby**
A retaliatory piece from the long-suffering wife – who for years has had to put up with the numerous pieces of RS thrown at her. Now her awful wedded husband, with his couch-slouch tellybelly gets his comeuppance, based on a puppet from children's television.

Tell the Tale **Daily Mail**
An early 20th-century reference to the paper that does just that.

Ten to Two **Jew**
For whom there are terms in abundance already.

Tennis Racket **Jacket**
Tailored to the first element, which makes it sound as though a sports jacket is indicated.

Tent Peg **Egg**
That whacked with a mallet for one that is cracked for an omelette.

Terence Stamp **Ramp (Bar)**
Refers to a pub counter, when it's your turn up the 'terence', you shouldn't need reminding. Based on an East London-born actor who made good in Hollywood.

Terrible Turk **Work**
Employed by those for whom work is a four-letter word: 'terrible turk in the morning' usually follows a long groan – and has done since World War I.

Terry Waite **Late**
Based on a Briton who, whilst in Beirut to negotiate the release of some hostages of Islamic militants, was himself kidnapped in 1987. He was released in 1991, 'terry waite' getting home by almost five years.

COMPLETE COCKNEY RABBIT

Tex Ritter   **(a) Bitter (Ale)**

British beer based on an old-time Western film star and ordered as a 'pint of tex'. Born in 1905, his last round-up came in 1974.

(b) Shitter 1

A 1950s term for a lavatory, 'shitter' is an old alternative to crapper.

Shitter 2

The anus, only really used in a dismissive, 'tuck it up your tex' kind of way.

Shitter 3

A 1960s example for a promiscuous girl, a 'shitter' is a variation of 'slapper'.

That & This   **Piss**

Only used in connection with water production, no one teases by taking the 'that & this'.

Thelma Ritter   **Shitter 1**

Since the 1940s this American film actress (1905–69) has been on-screen as a lavatory. The 'thelma' would have seen a lot of action when German bombs were dropping.

Shitter 2

The anus and again, during the war years, British 'thelmas' would have twitched at the very sound of an air-raid warning.

Thelonius Monk   **Spunk (Semen)**

A 1940s example that comes down to the Christian name of this American jazz piannist (1917–82).

There You Are   **(a) Bar**

A 19th-century example for a public or saloon bar, which has disappeared along with thousands of back-street pubs.

(b) Char (Tea)

'There y'are, a nice cup of there you are'.

These & Those   **(a) Clothes**

A piece that's never worn short, formal occasions call for your best 'these & those'.

(b) Toes
Pluralistic term for the tootsies for use when a quick getaway is in order, when you need to have it on your 'these & those'.

Theydon Bois **Noise**
Named after a village on the edge of Epping Forest, Essex, which once constituted a day out for the poor children of London. They would be taken there on school or Sunday school outings and given a taste of life away from the slums. Let loose, they would have made a fair bit of 'theydon'. Incidentally, Bois does rhyme with noise.

Thick & Thin **(a) Chin**
On which a big man is expected to take his punishment.

(b) Gin
The spirit of London revisited as a 'drop of thicken'.

Thimble & Thumb **Rum**
Shortened to a 'tot of thimble' as an alternative to the more common 'finger & thumb' (qv).

This & That **(a) Bat**
An early 20th-century schoolboy reference to a cricket bat when the wicket was chalked upon a wall.

(b) Hat
An example always used in full but rarely used at all, 'titfer' rules the headwear department. See 'Tit for Tat'.

Thomas Cook **Look**
A 1990s advertising campaign for this travel agency suggested we should take a 'thomas cook' at their brochure. Mr Cook (1808–92) was a pioneer in the holiday business.

Thomas Tilling **Shilling**
A defunct term for an extinct amount of money based on the name of the Hendon-born founder (1825–93) of a 19th-century omnibus company.

Thora Hird **(a) Bird**
A nineties term from the suburbs that relates to the feathered variety. Time will tell if this Dame of the acting profession (1911–2003) turns back into a 'young lady' type of bird.

(b) Turd

A 1980s example of disrespect to a fine actress, usually as a 'thora' lying in wait for a passing foot.

Thousand Pities   **Titties**

Strange how so much sorrow can apply to things that bring men so much pleasure.

Three & Fourpence   **Reinforcements**

A World War I piece based on three shillings and fourpence in old money. The story goes that by the time the message 'Send reinforcements, we are going to advance' got down the line, it had evolved into 'Send three and fourpence, we are going to a dance'.

Three Blind Mice   **Rice**

An order of chicken curry and 'three blind mice' may be a cause of great confusion to an Indian or Chinese waiter. If it isn't, go somewhere else.

Three By Two   **Jew**

An alternative version of 'four by two' that never really caught on.

Three-Wheeled Trike   **Dyke**

A 'three-wheeler' is a 2000s reference to a lesbian based on a 1900s form of transport.

Threepenny Bits   **(a) Shits**

A double dose of the horrors, a piles sufferer with the 'threepennys'. Or, in basic Poplavian (see 'Trunk & Trees'), 'froopneys'.

(b) Tits

An old piece that still survives even though this coin died of decimalitis in 1971.

Tic Tac   **(a) Fact**

When the world and its brother adopted 'brass tack' (qv), the cockney turned to this, the sign language of the racecourse and dog track.

(b) Sack

Those dismissed from work have got the 'tic tac'.

Tickle Your Fancy   **Nancy (Homosexual)**

A post-World War II piece that may be a corrupted version of a line in the song 'Billy Boy': 'Did (a) nancy tickle your fancy, oh my darling Billy boy?'

Tiddler's Bait   **Late**

Always reduced to the first element, sometimes at the start of an excuse: 'Sorry, I'm tiddlers. I met Cyril on the way home from work and he forced me to go for a drink'. This, however, is not a good excuse and will not stop the sharp edge of the wife's tongue from ripping you to shreds. Often said as 'tiddley bait', especially when alcohol has control of the tongue.

Tiddleywink   **(a) Chink**

A common appellation of a Chinese person, usually known as a 'tiddley'.

                    (b) Drink

Normally shortened to 'tiddley' and widely used in connection with alcohol.

Tidy & Neat   **Eat**

Only ever used in the first element, as in that most futile of instructions to a child: 'Tidy your cabbage'.

Tiger Tank   **Wank**

An act of 'whacking one's wilfred', courtesy of a machine of war.

Tilbury Docks   **(a) Pox (VD)**

The 'tilbury' is an age-old term for being shot down, based on the last working docks on the Thames.

                    (b) Socks

A 19th-century example that originated in the Navy and is worn as 'tilburys'.

Tilbury Forts   **Shorts**

The Army version of 'tilburys' was the khaki leg revealers worn by soldiers engaged in desert warfare in World War II. Based on a Thamesside fortification built at Tilbury, Essex in 1682.

Tin Bath   Scarf

Sometimes shrunken to 'tin' as a partner to 'titfer' in an instruction to keep warm: 'It's freezing out, so put your titfer & tin on'. See 'Tit For Tat'.

Tin Flute   Suit

Sounds like a cheap, off-the-peg job, a 'penny whistle', so to speak'. See 'Whistle & Flute'.

Tin Hat   Prat (Fool)

Worn in full, probably since World War II. It's what's needed to protect someone who may be 'soft in the head'.

Tin Lid   Yid (Jew)

The same tin hat from the same war as the previous example, the piece is often aimed at supporters of Tottenham Hotspur FC. A 'lid' is a cockney hat.

Tin Lizzie   Busy

A 1950s piece from the docks; said in full, dockers were 'tin lizzie' when the boats came in. Based on a slang term for an old car.

Tin Plate   Mate

Would appear to be a less well-off ally of 'china plate' (qv) and is seldom employed.

Tin Tack   (a) Fact

Gained popularity when 'brass tack' (qv) stepped out of the bounds of RS to join mainstream English.

(b) Sack

A common reference to dismissal from work only ever said in full.

Tin Tank   Bank

An inferior version of 'iron tank' (qv) – and sounds like it.

Tina Turner   Learner

A learner driver, that is. Male or female, if you are behind someone with L-plates you are following a 'tina'. Based on an American singer. If you have a driving test coming up, remember this:

Have faith in your ability for the angel did foretell
That you would pass your driving test when he said, 'No L.'

Ting-a-Ling **(a) King**
Applies solely to the ruler in a pack of cards.

(b) Ring
No vulgar associations here, it applies exclusively to an item of jewellery.

Tins of Beans **Jeans**
An alternative to 'baked beans' (qv), which is rarely used but when it is, it is cut down to 'tins'.

Tiny Tim **Flim (£5)**
A 'flim' has been a slang term for a fiver since around the time Dickens was writing about this famous crippled child in *A Christmas Carol*.

Tit For Tat **(a) Chat**
A 1990s example that remains unshortened so as to avoid confusion with (b). Neighbours may drop round for a 'tit for tat', but if you turn the telly off and keep quiet they'll soon go away.

(b) Hat
Always shortened to 'titfer', this is one of the few pieces of lowspeak to hit the heady heights of everyday language. If you can't fight, wear a big 'titfer' – a piece of useless advice.

Tit Willow **Pillow**
Based on a Gilbert & Sullivan song, this rarely used piece is never truncated. It doesn't sound seemly to rest your head on a 'tit'. Nice, but not seemly.

To & Fro **Snow**
An old term heard when it's been 'to-ing & fro-ing'. When else?

To & From **Pom**
An Englishman, according to Aussie servicemen of World War II; may be said of our cricketers, who went to and from the crease a bit too swiftly in the 2007 Ashes series.

Toasted Bread   **Dead**

A slice of black 1990s humour from a crematorium?

Toblerone   **Phone**

Based on a chocolate bar, this 1990s rhyme has followed in the wake of the mo-pho (mobile phone) boom as a 'tobler'.

Toby Jug   **Mug**

A soft touch, a gullible fool based on an ornamental drinking vessel. A 'toby' would buy a 'genuine' Ming one.

Toby Jug(s)   **Lug(s) (Ears)**

A reasonably well-known example, particularly in relation to noise funnels of the FA Cup handle variety. Clipped to 'tobys'.

Tod Sloane   **Alone**

Extensively used in the first element, everyone likes to be 'on their tod' from time to time. After an American jockey (1874–1933), who rode in Britain around the beginning of the 20th century.

Toe-Rag   **Slag 1**

Since the early 1960s this was lads' talk for a female of easy virtue, often said of the girl who had given the lad a knock-back: 'I wouldn't touch her anyway, she's an ol' toe-rag'.

Slag 2

A despicable nerk, someone said to be lower than a snake's belly down a pothole. A 'dratsab' – a backslang bastard.

Toffee Wrapper   **Napper (Head)**

'Napper' is an old term for the head and here gets dislengthened to the first element. I could be accused of nit-picking by insisting terms should be used in specific ways, but as Confucius would no doubt have said, had he come from the Limehouse branch of Chinatown: 'Man who don't pick nits, end up with itchy toffee'.

Toilet Roll   **Dole**

May be wistfully employed by the long-term unemployed when asked if they have found a job yet: 'No, still on the toilet'.

Tokyo Rose   **Nose**

Based on a radio broadcaster of Japanese propaganda of World War II, this is always cut to the first element: 'Why do I keep calling you sinex? Because you get right up my tokyo!' 'Tokyo Rose' was the name given to Japanese-American Iva Toguri D'Aquino (1916–2006).

Tom & Dick   **Sick**

Applies to any form of illness, not just the physical act of vomiting. Also to be on the 'tom & dick' is to be off work and drawing benefit.

Tom & Jerry   **Merry**

A reference to being happily drunk and would appear to be based on the cartoon cat and mouse double act on TV. But in the 19th century a tom & jerry was a low drinking house and to 'tom & jerry' was to behave riotously.

Tom Cat   **Mat**

Usually a doormat, or the one in front of the fire that gets monopolised by a pampered pet.

Tom Cruise   **Booze**

A 1990s piece based on an American film star, one of whose starring roles was as a barman in the 1988 film *Cocktail*. Whether this has any bearing on his inclusion here is debatable, I'd say it's just because it rhymes.

Tom Dooleys   **Goolies (Testicles)**

Based on the eponymous murderer of a 1958 hit record by Lonnie Donegan, amongst others, in reference to the spot where a kick will cause a man to hang down his head and cry.

Tom Finney   **Skinny**

The legendary England footballer, now Sir Tom, gets on the pitch as someone with little meat on his bones. A 1960s put-down of a pencil-like girl was: 'Nice face, a bit tom finney, though'.

Tom Hanks   **Thanks**

A 1990s piece based on the Oscar-winning US actor; it was in use amongst the young as 'tomanks'.

Tom, Harry & Dick **Sick**
An extended version of 'tom & dick' (qv), which then gets cut back to 'tom harry'.

Tom Mix **(a) Fix 1**
Originally applied to a state of difficulty, being in a 'right tom mix' meant you were in trouble.

Fix 2
If it ain't broke, don't 'tom mix' it.

Fix 3
In the sordid world of drug abuse, a 'tom mix' is an injection of a narcotic.

(b) Six
Based on an American star of early Western films (1880–1940), this applies to anything to do with the number six. It is common as £6, odds of 6/1, a big hit by a batsman, a playing card and it's a stalwart in the call of a bingo host.

Tom Noddy **Body**
Given this example hails originally from America, it probably applies to a corpse. Inspired by a slang term for a simpleton or fool.

Tom Sawyer **Lawyer**
Apart from those employed in the legal profession, this often relates to a bar stool know-all whose freely given advice is seldom heeded or needed. Based on a character of Mark Twain's creation.

Tom Thacker **Tobacco**
Pipe or rolling 'bacca', an archaic piece that probably went up in smoke years ago.

Tom Thumb **(a) Bum**
An early 20th-century piece, when schoolkids who mis-behaved could expect six of the best across the 'tom thumb' with either slipper or cane.

(b) Rum
Possibly the term most often used by rum-drinkers over the past century as it fittingly applies to a tot. Based on the three-

foot tall 'General' Tom Thumb (real name Charles S. Stratton) (1838–83), an American who gained fame whilst touring the world with Barnum's Circus.

Tom Tit   **Shit**

A well known piece which actually means to defecate, rather than the resultant mess. Pluralised, the 'tom tits' is an attack of diarrhoea.

Tom Tripe   **Pipe**

An extinct term for an almost extinguished tobacco burner first recorded in the mid 19th century. Based on the stage name of Arnold P. Barnoldswick, a music-hall offal juggler.

Tom Tug   **(a) Bug**

A very old term for a parasite, based on an even older name for a waterman.

(b) Mug

A dupe, someone easily stitched up, a person the used car salesman 'sees coming'.

Tomato Purée   **Jury**

A 1990s piece that explains how '12 good men and true' collectively form, or are asked to sit on a 'tomato'.

Tomato Sauce   **Horse**

Usually refers to a racehorse, often one so far behind it'll never ketchup.

Tomfoolery   **Jewellery**

Mainly an underworld term popularised by countless TV cops 'n' robbers and always as 'tom'.

Tommy Cooper   **Super**

Based on the legendary British comedian (1922–84), this 1970s example used, as an expression of excellence, often comes with an f-word prefix: 'This bitter's fuckin' tommy cooper'. Never shortened, the term is used just like that.

Tommy Dodd   **(a) God**

A 19th-century euphemism for The Almighty that was used in phrases like 'If a man is judged by the company he keeps, then

Tommy Dodd help us all'. Tommy Dodd's garden – a cemetery or churchyard.

(b) Odd 1

The opposite of even from a mid 19th-century coin-tossing game. The Song of Tommy Dodd from the period contained the line, 'Heads or tails are sure to win, Tommy Dodd, Tommy Dodd'.

(c) Rod (Gun)

An early 20th-century piece that originated in America.

(d) Sod

A term of mild abuse for a git or, less scornfully, for a rascal. And when the wife and kids are playing up: 'Tommy dodd this for a game of mothers & fathers!'

Tommy Farr　　　　　**Bar**

Formed on the name of a British boxing champion (1913–86), it's that part of a pub with the elbow prints where the drinks are served.

Tommy Guns　　　　　**Runs (Diarrhoea)**

Probably inspired by the effect on the faecal factory when staring down the barrel of one.

Tommy O'Rann　　　　　**Scran (Food)**

An old example of RS for an even older piece of slang for 'noshery'. Oh, there's another one!

Tommy Rabbit　　　　　**Pomegranate**

A piece from a late-Victorian fruit stall.

Tommy Rollar　　　　　**Collar**

A 19th-century term for what would have been a detachable one. Now detached from RS usage.

Tommy Rollocks　　　　　**Bollocks**

The testicles, whereby a let-down is a 'kick in the tommys' and a load of rubbish is a 'load of tommy'. 'Skollobs' – backslang goolies.

Tommy Steele(s)　　　　　**Eel(s)**

Applies to the jellied variety, the great cockney delicacy based on a South London-born entertainer.

Tommy Trinder   **Window**

An example based on a London-born comedian (1909–89), who used aggression tempered with charm in his act. A master ad-libber, he had a reputation for never being stuck for an answer. This would appear then to be a perfectly fitting term as he had all the attributes required to be make a blinding double-glazing salesman.

Tommy Tripe   **Pipe**

To look at, to observe: 'Tommy, the geezer in the golden syrup'. See Syrup of Fig.

Tommy Tucker   **(a) Fucker**

Normally said without malice in reference to a spirited or mischievous person. An overactive child can be a 'right little tommy tucker' to a harassed parent.

(b) Sucker

An underworld term for a mug, someone easily sucked in. The type of person who is willingly sold the biggest dummies outside the Land of the Giants branch of Mothercare.

Tommy Tupper   **Supper**

A 1950s reference to an intake of evening food.

Tomorrow   **Borrow**

To be on the 'tomorrow' usually means a small loan between friends or neighbours, meant to be paid back the next day.

Tonka Toy   **Boy**

A 1970s rhyme based on a brand of hardwearing toys, which mainly relates to 'one of the lads' or 'one of the tonkas'. The piece was latched onto football hooligans of the period.

Tony Benn   **Ten**

A 1970s example from the City of London, where a tenner became a 'tony benner' and is based on a long-standing MP, born Anthony Wedgwood Benn in 1925.

Tony Blair   **Hair**

Ex-PM Blair comes in on a wave from the suburbs and time alone will tell if it's to be permanent. Personally I can't see it cutting down on 'barnet's' majority, although a 'tony' can be a single hair, where 'fred astaire' (qv) will probably dance rings around him.

Tony Cottee   Potty

When toddlers want to do 'ucksies' sit 'em on a 'tony', a 1990s nipper-crapper inspired by an England international footballer of the period.

Tony Hatch   Match

A 'striker', the original fag-lighter, based on a British composer of many a hit record and TV theme.

Tooting Bec   Peck 1

Food – for which 'peck' is an old slang alternative. Nibbled down to the first element whereby a quick bite to eat becomes a 'speck of tooting'.

                    Peck 2

A little kiss, as in 'a little tooting on the hide & seek' (qv).

Top Gun   Ton (£100)

A 1980s piece from the financial types in the City of London based on a popular 1984 film.

Top Hat   (a) Prat (Fool)

An old term for a pillock that's never shortened and may be based on the annual upper-class pose-in at Royal Ascot.

                    (b) Rat

Applies mainly to the rodent, but has been used in connection with an untrustworthy character. Either way, give a 'top hat' a wide berth.

Top Joint   Pint

As with 'roast joint' (qv) this would once have effected a rhyme and has similarly disappeared.

Top of the Form   Warm

Rarely heard since its formation on the name of a popular radio quiz of the 1950s–60s.

Torville & Deans   Beans

A piece that surprisingly wasn't recorded when Jane Torville and Christopher Dean became the Olympic ice dancing champions in 1984. In 2008 they made a comeback for TVs *Dancing on Ice* and a new expression was heard in a Greenwich café, 'torvilles on toast'.

Total Wreck   **Cheque**
Perhaps one from an insurance company after writing off a car.

Touch & Tap   **Cap**
Both elements are slang terms meaning to borrow, so the connection may be in passing the hat round.

Touch Me on the Nob/Knob   **Bob (Shilling)**
An obsolete piece from the days of our previous currency when it was considered lucky to touch the head ('nob/knob') of certain people. To touch is to borrow and the phrase 'Can I touch you for a touch me?' used to be quite common.

Touched by the Moon   **Loon**
Which is precisely what a lunatic is. Said of someone thought to have a 'rafter loose in the attic'.

Tower Bridge   **Fridge**
How a London landmark got into the cold storage game, but these days it's only perishables that get bunged in the 'tower'.

Tower Hill   **Kill**
Aptly based on the place where executioners once wielded their choppers and Royal heads did roll: 'Slow down or we'll all be tower-hilled' – a plea to a speeding driver.

Town Crier   **Liar**
Everyone knows a 'town crier', a person of whom you disbelieve 50% of what he says and are dubious of the other half.

Town Halls   **Balls (Testicles)**
A piece that doesn't get halved, dirty fighters aim their boots at the 'town halls'.

Towns & Cities   **Titties**
An old term which was never as popular as its meaning.

Trafalgar Square   **Chair**
Only sits comfortably when shortened to the first element of this London landmark.

Treacle Tart　　　　　**Fart**
A 'treacle' won't produce a sweet smell.

Treasure Hunt　　　　　**Cunt 1**
A fool, much in the way of 'berk' (see also Berkshire Hunt), so the next time someone calls you a 'treasure', make sure they're smiling.

　　　　　　　　　　　　Cunt 2
The vagina; the booty of the sexual adventurer.

Treble Chance　　　　　**Dance**
A 1950s example for the boy-meets-girl activity of pre-disco days, the term relates to a wager on a pools coupon, but you had more chance of scoring at the local palais or dancehall.

Trick Cyclist　　　　　**Psychiatrist**
An old and well-known piece although I'm not sure if it's RS – but it is slang and it does rhyme, so here it is.

Trilby Hat　　　　　**Prat**
Hard to believe that pratt has become so widely acceptable relating as it does to the vagina and to a fool in the same way as 'cunt'. Still, a clot is a 'trilby' and has been for some time.

Trolley & Tram　　　　　**Ham**
Generally sliced to the first of these two forerunners of the modern bus.

Trolley & Truck　　　　　**Fuck**
Used in reference to the sex act since the early 20th century. And, if you're caught on the job with someone you shouldn't be with, you're 'trolleyed'.

Trollywags　　　　　**Bags (Trousers)**
An obsolete piece from the 19th century that may have some bearing on why the shortened version, 'trolleys', has come to represent underpants. Then again, it may not.

Trombone　　　　　**Phone**
People have been making calls on the 'trombone' since the Jazz Age.

Tropical Fish　　　　　**Piss**

A Scottish example of a 'drain-off', where a leak is a pish.

Trouble & Fuss　　　　　**Bus**

Given the transport problems in London, this is a very appropriate piece and likely to remain so forever.

Trouble & Strife　　　　　**(a) Life**

For many this is about as apt as RS gets.

　　　　　　　　　　　(b) Wife

The 'trouble' is by far the most familiar of terms for the woman who, in ideal circumstances will be wooed, won and wed. Very often though, it's a case of bed, bun and brood. Sometimes she may be 'the trouble at home'.

Troubles & Cares　　　　　**Stairs**

A seldom-climbed alternative to 'apples & pears' (qv).

Trunks(s) & Tree(s)　　　　　**Knee(s)**

An example that appears to have developed in Poplar, E. London, where in the 1950s worked a Mr Davies, a Welsh teacher who insisted on calling the cockney dialect 'Basic Poplavian.'

Tug O' War　　　　　**Whore**

A woman often pulled.

Tumble & Trip　　　　　**Whip**

A collection, a whip-round and always gathered as a 'tumble'.

Tumble Down the Sink　　　　　**Drink**

In the shortened forms of 'tumble' or 'tumbledown', this is solely used in connection with alcohol. To go for a 'tumble' is to go down the pub.

Turin Shroud(s)　　　　　**Cloud(s)**

The Heavenly sunshield based on the shroud that reputedly covered the body of Christ. From the suburbs, this is heard as often as the Holy Shroud is seen.

Turkish Bath　　　　　**Laugh**

Anyone having a 'turkish' at your expense is on a wind-up or taking the 'wet stuff'.

Turkish Delight   (a) **Shite**

Anything deemed to be rubbishy or crappy is said to be 'a right load of turkish'. And the full-of-bowel will sit for a 'turkish'.

(b) **Tight**

A 'turkish git' is the stingy littleworth who 'wouldn't give his shit to the crows'.

Turpentine   **Serpentine**

The lake in London's Hyde Park has been known by generations of taxi drivers as 'the Turps'.

Turtle Dove   (a) **Glove**

From a lightweight fashion glove to an industrial protector, anything worn on the hand is a 'turtle'. Boxers 'touch turtles' and come out fighting – and criminals won't touch anything without them.

(b) **Love**

An old term from the pens of romantic balladeers in search of a rhyme for love. They didn't know they were composing a piece of RS.

Tweedledee   **Pee/Wee**

One of the twins of Lewis Carroll's creation comes in as a term of lavatorial relief, when men 'point percy at the porcelain' and women 'take alice to the chalice' – in the form of a 'tweedle', of course.

Tweedledum   **Cum (Semen)**

Not to be outdone, the other twin comes in for another type of relief and, like his brother, often in men's toilets, where there may be 'much tweedling in the bog'.

Twelve-Inch Rule   **Fool**

A pre-metric buffoon, being known as a 'twelve-incher' may not be as good as it sounds.

Twist & Twirl   **Girl**

Descriptive of what a young lady can do to a smitten swain. Around her little finger goes he. 'Doog elrig' – a backslang good girl, one who keeps her hand on her ha'penny.

Two & Eight **State**
Nearly always said as being in a 'right old two an' eight' in reference to being in a predicament or a state of agitation.

Two & Three **Key**
An old term, one the number may be up on. Can be misplaced as a 'bunch of twos'.

Two by Four **Whore**
A prostitute from around the time of World War II. When the bombs were dropping, so were the 'two-by's' drawers.

Two Eyes of Blue **Too True**
An extension of 'eyes of blue' (qv) – same tune, different arrangement.

Two Thirty **Dirty**
Refers to uncleanliness rather than rudeness. An overheard description of a dirtywack's feet: 'His plates are so two thirty you could grow spuds on 'em'. See Plates of Meat.

Two-Bob Bit(s) **Shit(s)**
'Two-bobs' has been a common expression for diarrhoea since before this coin was replaced by a 10p piece. In the singular it's defecation and the produce of that function, so a 'two-bob bit' on the footpath may be best left alone.

Two-Foot Rule **Fool**
Another measure of stupidity, presumably twice the idiot as the one seen at 'twelve-inch rule'.

Ty-Phoo Tea **Pee/Wee**
A urinary outpouring inspired by a brand of tea that for years ran an advertising campaign stating 'Ty-Phoo Puts the T in Britain'. This in turn inspired a piece of graffito seen on the wall of a hospital toilet in Plaistow: 'If Ty-Phoo put the T in Britain, who put the Cunt in Scunthorpe?' This little snippet has just re–entered my memory and is totally irrelevant to this book.

Typewriter **Fighter**
Can apply to a boxer but mainly refers to strength of character. Anyone who keeps fighting through illness or adversity is said to be a 'real typewriter', as was my late pal Johnny Skeels.

Tyrannosaurus Rex   **Sex**

An extension of the older 't. rex' (qv) that gets reduced to the first element when there's nookie to be had.

Tyrone Power   **Shower**

A 1950s term for a shower of rain that, via the Merchant Navy, moved into the bathroom. Sweating seamen took regular 'tyrones'. Based on an American film star (1914–58).

Ugly Sister   **Blister**
That which painfully appears on the hand after a bout of unaccustomed tool usage or on the foot as a result of wearing ill-fitting shoes or glass slippers.

Umbrella   **Fella**
Normally used in reference to a husband or boyfriend: 'How's your umbrella these days?'
'He's OK as long as he doesn't leak'.

Uncle & Aunt   **Plant**
As sold at a garden centre, whereby your prized blooms may become your 'uncles'.

Uncle Ben   **Ten**
Eyes down, look in, it's another rhyme from Johnny Bingo-caller.

Uncle Bert   **Shirt**
A rare, but old substitute for the frequently-worn 'dicky dirt'.

Uncle Bertie   **Shirty**
Annoyed or angryish; you are well entitled to get 'uncle bertie' when you've been queuing and someone pushes in and gets served first.

Uncle Bob   **(a) Job**
The unemployed seek work at the 'uncle bob centre' and if they find it, bob's your uncle.

(b) Knob (Penis)

Sometimes used vulgarly by a less than smooth operator: 'Come on, darlin', come and meet my uncle bob'. 'Bonk' – a backslang knob, which may account for the verb 'to bonk' – to have sex.

Uncle Dick   **(a) Prick (Penis)**

Not to be confused with 'uncle bob'. Same pipe, different bacca really.

(b) Sick

Very common in relation to being physically sick or in general bad health and often reduced to the second element, as in 'dicky minces' – bad eyes, or the well-known 'dicky ticker' – weak heart.

Uncle Fred   **Bread**

A comical example whereby children are encouraged to eat up their 'uncle fred'.

Uncle Lester   **Molester**

A child-molester; a paedophile. A 1990s kiddie-fiddler.

Uncle Mac   **Smack 1**

Corporal punishment 1950s-style based on the working name of Derek McCulloch (1897–1967), presenter of radio shows *Children's Hour* and *Children's Favourites*.

Smack 2

A 1980s example for heroin. If you hear a whirring sound coming from the grave of the above Mr McCulloch, it'll be him spinning in it.

Uncle Ned   **Bed**

This enjoys extensive employment, generally in its full extension: the tired and weary can 'Hear their uncle ned calling them'.

Uncle Sam   **Lamb**

Applies to the animal as sold by the butcher, a leg of 'uncle sam' goes down well on a Sunday.

Uncle Wilf   **Filth (Police)**

A 1980s example of the 'narks' used derogatorily.

Uncle Willie   **(a) Chilly**
A pre-World War II example that accompanies a shiver and a flapping of the arms as in: 'uncle willie, innit?'
                                   (b) Silly
An allusion to anyone acting in a manner that suggests substandard mental equipment.

Uncouth   **Youth**
A well appropriate piece relating to a boozing, farting, swearing young man.

Unicorn   **Horn (Erection)**
Shortened to 'uni', this stands up well as an appropriate example based on a fabled beast with a horn.

Union Jack   **Back**
Anatomically employed, usually in connection with an aching back and its role in getting you out of heavy lifting: 'Sorry I can't lift that, I've got a dodgy union'.

Up & Down   **Brown**
Used to describe all things brown, especially brown ale.

Up & Under   **Thunder**
During a violent middle-of-the-night storm many nervous people are known to get up and go under the stairs.

Up a Tree   **Three**
Eyes up, look out, there's another bingo-caller about!

Uri Geller   **Stella (Artois)**
A popular French lager based on a TV psychic from Israel, famous as a power-of-the-mind metal-bender. Eight pints of 'uri' and you're on a bender of your own!

Uriah Heep   **Creep**
An untrustworthy, snot-grovelling, toady type of person and appropriately inspired by the 'ever-so 'umble' creep in Dickens' *David Copperfield*. Pluralised, this slimy character may give you the 'uriahs'.

Valentine Dyalls　　　　**Piles**

Haemorrhoids, the so-called 'ring of fire' gets the treatment by way of a British actor (surname Dyall, 1908–85), who was famous as 'the Man in Black' on wartime radio. Known as 'valentines', the term dates from the 1940s.

Vampire's Kiss　　　　**Piss**

To urinate but mainly used as 'taking the vampires', getting a laugh at someone's expense. Often light-hearted or jocular (after the well-known Scottish vampire), but usually it's going for the jugular with a bit of spiteful fun-poking.

Vancouver　　　　**Hoover**

A 'suck-dirt'; no matter what the brand of vacuum cleaner, they are all known as 'Hoovers', or 'Vancouvers'.

Vanilla Fudge　　　　**Judge**

An underworld term from the 1970s either based on the sweet or a US rock group of the period; whichever way, the accused stands before the 'vanilla'.

Vanity Fair　　　　**Chair**

On which people have sat and read this book by William Makepeace Thackeray (1811–63) for many years.

Venetian Blind　　　　**Mind**

The workings of the nut get reduced to the first element of a sunshade; often takes the form of an Italian dwarf when an idiot is involved, as in: 'You must be out of your tiny venetian'.

Vera Lynn   **(a) Gin**
Named after the East Ham songstress, who won the hearts of fighting men of World War II. The forces' sweetheart is still a favourite with gin-drinkers.

(b) Skin
A modern piece for a cigarette paper used for rolling a 'drugfag'.

Veronica Lake   **Steak**
A tastier version of 'joe blake' (qv), based on a Hollywood actress of the 1940s (1919–73), who was known as the 'peek-a-boo' girl. Once considered top tottie, she's now a piece of top rump.

Vicar of Bray   **Tray 1**
The number three for which 'tray' is a common substitute, especially for the playing card, and inspired by an 18th-century ballad about a popular, but Machiavellian man of the cloth. A case of never trusting somebody that everyone likes.

Tray 2
The plate-carrying implement of the waiter or how a couch-potato has his dinner on a 'vicar' whilst watching TV.

Victoria Cross   **Toss**
The couldn't-care-less type couldn't give a 'vc'.

Victoria Monk   **Spunk 1 (Semen)**
An example for 'baby gravy' that stretches back to the days of music hall, of which Victoria Monks (1884–1972) was a star.

Spunk 2 (Courage)
The girl who first pleaded with 'Bill Bailey to please come home' is now silent in this guise.

Victory V   **Pee/Wee**
A sign perhaps made by one on the point of bladderburst, but just made it to the lavatory?

Vincent Price   **Ice**
Frozen at 'vincent' in respect of that which chills a drink and based on an American actor (1911–93), whose film roles chilled many a spine.

Vincent van Gogh Cough
Based on the Dutch painter (1853–90), there are two ways of shortening this. You either have a 'vincent' or a 'van gogh', never the full monty.

Vindaloo Poo
To defecate and also the ejected outcome of it, based on the curry dish that often generates an 'urge to purge', it's said in full or reduced to 'vinda': 'I had a vindaloo last night and three vindas this morning'. Nice!

Virgin Bride Ride
A rare term for sexual intercourse based on an even bigger rarity, although this was probably not the case in the Victorian era when it was formed in connection with travel. It made the jump to its present meaning during World War II and if a soldier said he'd just had a 'virgin', it's likely he paid to get his end away.

Virginia McKenna Tenner
Based on a British actress, a 'virginia' comes well down the cast list of terms for £10.

Vivien Leigh Pee/Wee
Known as a 'vivien', this 1940s piece is based on the British actress (1913–67), who found fame as Scarlett O'Hara in the 1939 epic movie, *Gone with the Wind*.

Von Trapp Crap
To defecate; a 1960s dump by way of the name of the family from the 1965 musical, *The Sound of Music*.

Wait(s) & Linger(s)   Finger(s)
Who knows where points the fickle 'wait' of fate?

Wallace & Grommit   Vomit
The Oscar-winning duo that made a big splash in the world of
animation now score a hit on the pavement. Anything that ever
made you sick will now make you 'wallace'.

Wallace Beery   Query
In the betting shop, a dispute over a settler's calculation is
known as a 'wallace' – at least it was in the 1960s. After an
American actor (1885–1949), who appeared in early films.

Walnut Whip   (a) Kip (Sleep)
Based on a chocolate sweet, all an insomniac wants is a good
night's 'walnut'.

     (b) Snip
A vasectomy, laughingly called 'the walnut' by everyone but
the bloke with the sore nuts.

Walter Joyce   Voice
From an 1887 ballad called 'Tottie' by George R. Sims, with no
clue to the identity of old Wally.

Wanstead Flats   Spats
An obsolete term for a long-departed fashion based on an area
of East London.

War & Strife　　　　**Wife**
Another piece for 'er indoors, which portrays the marital home as a battlefield.

Warrior Bold　　　　**Cold**
A cold; the illness that causes you to call in sick with a 'warrior'.

Warriors Bold　　　　**Cold**
Applies to low temperature, from a cup of tea that's gone 'warriors' to cold weather.

Watch & Chain　　　　**Brain**
Cut to the first element when speaking a dullard or a quick thinker, whose 'watches' may be slow or fast.

Waterbury Watch　　　　**Scotch**
Time was called on this century-old piece years ago. The Waterbury Watch Co. of Waterbury, Connecticut, with an office in London, mass-produced quality watches from 1880–98.

Watercress　　　　**Dress**
The garment and the donning of it; to get dressed is to get 'watered'.

Waterloo　　　　**Stew**
Always a bowl of 'waterloo' – a bowl of 'water' doesn't sound particularly hearty.

Watford Gap　　　　**Map**
Based on the service station on the M1 – which you may need a 'watford' to find.

Wayne Rooney　　　　**Looney**
An England international footballer takes over the nutter's mantle from the much older 'mickey rooney' (qv). A piece of youthspeak from the 2000s.

Weasel & Stoat　　　　**Coat**
Commonly cut to the first element. Only in RS can a mink be a 'weasel'.

Wee Georgie Wood　　　　**Good**
Formed on the name of a midget British comedian (1897–

1979), which sees the good stuff as being 'wee georgie' and the dreck as 'no wee georgie'.

Wee Willie Winkie　　　　**Chinky**
A Chinese person is known as a 'wee willie' as a result of a kid in a nursery rhyme, so Chinese men need not feel offended.

Weekend Pass　　　　**Glass**
A National Servicemen's term for drinking receptacle, which would have been apt since a weekend's leave would have seen more than a few raised 'weekends'.

Weekend Passes　　　　**Glasses**
Spectacles – 'weekends' for weak eyes.

Weep & Wail　　　　**Tale**
An apt example that relates to a sob story as told by a beggar.

Weeping Willow　　　　**Pillow**
A piece well used in the first element since the 1914–18 War. Bad news from the Front would have seen many a weeping widow crying themselves to sleep on their 'weeping willow'.

Weigh Anchor　　　　**Wanker**
Always used in full, whereby the useless and valueless are a pair of 'weigh anchors'. Either a seaman's or a docker's term for anyone seen to be 'as useful as an inflatable anchor'.

Well Hung　　　　**Young**
Sounds like an older woman's idea of the perfect toyboy.

Wellington Boot　　　　**(a) Root**
A 1990s example for sexual intercourse that sounds as unromantic as you can get, unless you're a rubber fetishist.
　　　　(b) Fruit 1
Fresh 'wellington' may go down well after the 'waterloo' (qv).
　　　　Fruit 2
How a homosexual becomes a 'welly'.

West Ham Reserves　　　　**Nerves**
Used in connection with irritation, annoyance and exasperation, apt when you're a West Ham supporter. A pest may get 'right on your west hams'.

West India Docks   Pox

A relevant old piece in that the entrance to these docks was in Limehouse, a sleazy part of East London where prostitutes and seamen mingled and a lot of people were 'wounded in action'. Or caught with the 'west indias'.

Westminster Abbey   (a) Cabbie

May be derived from the complaint of an American tourist that, 'Wherever I went in London by taxi, I seemed to go past Westminster Abbey'. Actually it was a Japanese tourist, but I can't write in that language.

(b) Shabby

A run-down building or a scruffbag of a person may be 'westminster'.

Wheezy Anna   Spanner

A 1950s term still used by elderly motor fitters and inspired by a song by British variety double act, The Two Leslies (Sarony and Holmes).

Whip & Lash   Tash

A moustache that's shaved to a 'whip'.

Whip & Top   Strop (Masturbate)

You don't have to be a masochist to 'whip' yourself. Just alone.

Whiplash   (a) Rash

Possibly one picked up from a dodgy bird in the pursuit of S&M.

(b) Slash

A rare piece but if you wish to popularise it, crack away! It means to 'water the weeds' – to urinate.

Whippit Quick   Prick (Penis)

A 1950s rhyme based on a character from British radio that may allude to a swift act of masturbation. See 'Whip & Top'.

Whisper & Talk   Walk

A 19th-century term that's reduced to going for a 'whisper', for which you need soft shhhoes.

Whistle & Flute   Suit

The most common term for a suit of clothes, always cut to the first element as in a 'three-piece whistle'.

Whistle & Toot   Loot (Money)

An old piece that is unusual in that it is most familiar in the second element. Post-war spivs and wide-boys made a lot of 'toot' from the black market.

White Cliffs of Dover   Over

Said as 'all white cliffs', meaning the end – a symbolic term, given their position.

White Mice   Dice

A 1940s example that's used in full, you're in luck when the 'white mice' are running for you.

Whitechapel   Apple

Named after an infamous area of East London, renowned for its grisly murders, generations of immigrants and aptly, Spitalfields fruit and vegetable market before it moved across London to Leyton in 1991.

Wicked Rumours   Bloomers

A reference to women's underwear of years gone by and a feature of many a seaside postcard. Big drawers are now likely to be called after the eponymous heroine of a 2001 film: 'Does my bum look big in these bridget joneses?' 'No love, it's just wicked rumours'.

Wicked Witch   Bitch

An obvious piece for a malicious, spiteful woman: the mother-in-law from Hell may be so-described.

Widow Twanky   (a) Hanky

Decreased to the first element, which means that blowing one's nose on a 'widow' isn't so bad as it sounds.

(b) Yankee 1

Based on a character from the pantomime, *Aladdin*, a 'widow' is an old theatrical term for an American tourist.

Yankee 2

A rarely used piece in relation to a type of bet made up of four selections in six doubles, four trebles and an accumulator. Therefore a £1 'widow' costs £11.

Widow's Mite   Light

A 19th-century rhyme for a light for a cigarette or pipe, the term has probably been extinguished but the parable of the Widow's Mite is still there for all to see in the Gospel of St Mark.

Widow's Wink   Chink

A Chinese person; a 1970s example from the theatre.

Wilbur Wright   Flight

A totally suitable piece relating to air travel always trimmed to the Christian name of this American pioneer of aviation (1867–1912). Seems a bit unfair that Brother Orville (1871–1948) doesn't get a mention seeing as how he's equally responsible for the the headache of airports, packed planes and delayed 'wilburs'.

Wild West   Vest

A dated term for underwear that's worn in full.

Wilkie Bard(s)   Card(s)

A 19th-century term formed on the name of a music-hall artiste – any type of card can be a 'wilkie' – and has long been heard in the plural as playing cards. This British comedian was on the billboard of life from 1874 to 1944.

Wilkinson Sword   Bald

This 1990s piece relates to the 'cultivated spamhead' look – the shaved head. Based on a brand of razor blade, which makes it a pretty sharp example.

Will O'The Wisps   Crisps

Crisps of any flavour, texture or shape are 'willers'. Based on the common name of ignis fatuus (see 'Jack-a-Dandy').

William Hague   Vague

A piece from the late 1990s based on the then leader of the Conservative Party. He resigned after his party lost the 2001 election. The term may survive, it may not – it's all a bit 'william hague', really!

William Hill   Pill

A well-known British bookmaker lends his name to a drug, generally an amphetamine.

William Joyce   Voice

A World War II example based on the most reviled 'william' of the conflict: Lord Haw-Haw. Born in America in 1906 to English and Irish parents, fascist Joyce was hanged as a traitor in 1946.

William Pitt   Shit

Not sure if this is based on Pitt the Elder (1708–78) or his clever dick of a son, Little Pitt (1759–1806). But then who gives a 'william'? As far as RS is concerned, one English statesman is much the same as another, especially when they share the same name. The term applies to defecation and its product. In plural, it's diarrhoea: 'Don't take that out-of-date laxative, it'll give you the william pitts'.

William Powell   Towel

A 1940s term for a 'wipe' that has its roots in prison and is based on an American film star of the period (1892–1984).

William Tell   Smell

How the legendary 14th-century Swiss hero became a 20th-century British pong.

Wills Whiff   Syph(ilis)

Based on a brand of small cigar, this came to represent any of the anti-social diseases.

Willy Wonka   Plonker (Fool)

A piece heard in a 1980s sitcom and based on a Roald Dahl character. The original meaning of the word 'plonker' is the penis but a willy's already a willy, so a 'willy wonka' is a twerp.

Wilson Pickett   Ticket

Inspired by an American soul singer (1941–2006), this was valid in the 1970s, when a 'wilson' applied to anything from a bus ticket to a Cup Final one.

Win or Lose   Booze

An old example from the racecourse, from whence comes the rhyme:
Win or lose, we have our booze
But when we win, we have gin.

Wind Trap   Flap

A flap is that piece of hair that semi-bald men pull from one side of their heads to the other in a vain attempt to cover up the bare facts. A totally apt term, as in breezy conditions the wind tends to get under the strategically placed locks, causing them to behave in an unruly manner, often like a demented squirrel's tail. Also known as a comb-over.

Wind-Jammer   Hammer

An old carpenter's term, one that's based on a type of sailing ship.

Winds Do Whirl   Girl

A 19th-century term that seems to have been blown away.

Windsor Castle   Arsehole

The 'brown windsor' as it is sometimes known is yet again the designated orifice up which the unwanted may be consigned. To confuse even further, instead of 'work it up your windsor', try saying, 'stick it up the queen's gaff'.

Winklebag   Fag

A 1970s cigarette curtailed to a 'winkle' and based on whatever a winklebag is – perhaps a condom?

Winona Ryder   Cider

One from the young boozing classes of the 1990s and based on a US film actress of the period.

Wise Monkey   Dunkie (Condom)

What's needed to keep the 'old chap' from evil; fitting also that condoms traditionally come in threes, as do wise monkeys.

Wishbone Ash   Cash

The British rock band have been around since the early 1970s. This was heard in a pub off Tottenham Court Road in London, in 2008 when a customer complained that he didn't have enough 'wishbone' to pay for four pints.

Wooden Heart   **Fart**
A piece that became common for a time following Elvis Presley's hit record of this title in 1961.

Wooden Leg   **Egg**
Interesting to see the reaction of a waitress when asked for a 'wooden leg on toast'.

Wooden Peg   **Leg**
As old and outdated as a peg-leg.

Wooden Plank   **Yank**
An American, especially a tourist in Britain – after 11 September 2001, London cabbies were seen crying into their cocktails over the lack of 'wooden planks' in town.

Wooden Spoon   **(a) Coon**
The prize for coming last is a term of abuse for a black person.

     (b) Moon
Heard in prison, where a 'woodener' is a month's porridge.

Woody Herman   **German**
Extension of the famous Herman the German – which is how a Deutschlander became a 'woody'. Based on the legendary American jazz musician (1913–87).

Woolly Mitten   **Kitten**
A baby pussycat, but mainly how one feels after an illness: 'As weak as a woolly mitten'.

Woolly Vest   **Pest**
Apt in that a nuisance can be as irritating as an itchy undergarment. A grouch may claim that a friend in need is a 'woolly vest'.

Woolly Woofter   **Poofter (Homosexual)**
Barely admissable in RS as 'woofter' and 'poofter' have the same meaning. Still, they do rhyme and what difference does it make anyway?

Woolwich & Greenwich   Spinach

A brace of boroughs in South-east London give us a piece with its roots in the greengrocer's trade.

Woolwich Ferry   Sherry

A fairly common example based on the famous Thames river crossing.

Woolwich Pier(s)   Ear(s)

An old term for nature's audio equipment that hails from the docks, where the teeth of the wind gets sharp enough to bite your 'woolwiches' off.

Working Class   Glass

A common-or-garden term for the receptacle, in backslang an 'esslag' or 'slag'.

Working Classes   Glasses

Spectacles, worn by the near- and far-sighted as 'workings'.

Worm(s) & Snail(s)   Nail(s)

A useful piece to get children to stop biting their fingernails, which bears a resemblance to the old warning: 'Don't bite your nails, you'll get worms'.

Worry & Strife   Wife

The 'worry' is an infrequent variation of the oft-mentioned 'trouble' (& strife) (qv).

Wrigley's Gum   Bum

A shapely backside of a woman may be known as a 'wrigley's' due to a well-known chewing-gum manufacturer.

Wyatt Earp   Burp

A 1960s term based on the famed American lawman (1848–1929), who may (or may not) have suffered with indigestion.

X Files   **Piles**

Based on a cult TV series about a team of FBI agents who try to get to the bottom of paranormal activity and the horrors of the supernatural. Unfortunately for the sufferer, the pain of *anus horribilis* is only too real.

X-Ray Specs   **Sex**

Piece shortened to 'x-ray' that had a short currency in the late 1970s when a British group of this name had a few hit records.

Yankee Doodles   **Noodles**

A 1990s example heard on a building site in relation to pot noodles, a favoured snack amongst site-workers. How to confuse a Chinese waiter: ask for some crispy 'yankees' with 'goldie hawns' (qv). From the song, 'Yankee Doodle Dandy', made famous by US actor James Cagney.

Yard of Tripe   **Pipe**

Not exactly an ad-man's dream of a term: 'Live in peace with your yard of tripe?' I don't think so! Just as well pipe-smokers are on the Endangered Species list.

Yarmouth Bloater   **Motor**

A piece harking back to a time when only toffs had cars and Yarmouth had a major fishing industry.

Yellow Pages   **Wages**

The modern update of 'greengages' (qv) and turns 'greens' into 'yellows'.

Yellow Silk   **Milk**

A piece used by milkmen of a century ago, who substituted the word 'pint' with 'yard', hence a pint of milk became a 'yard of yellow silk'.

Yet To Be   **Free**

An early 20th-century piece that relates to the word in all its senses, but mainly to free of charge.

Yiddisher Mama　　　**Bummer**

Either based on a Jewish mother or the song about her, 'My Yiddisher Mama'. Either way, a disappointment or a let-down is a 'yiddisher'.

Yogi Bear　　　**Chair**

A 1960s rhyme based on a popular cartoon character; for a while kids were pulling up a 'yogi' to watch him on TV.

Yorkshire Rippers　　　**Slippers**

A 1980s term inspired by the media nickname for mass-murderer Peter Sutcliffe.

Yorkshire Tyke　　　**Mike**

Referring to a microphone, this had its beginnings in the entertainment industry and was picked up by those doing a turn down the pub.

You & Me　　　**(a) Flea**

A piece from the 19th century that may still be scratching around somewhere…At the vets, perhaps.

(b) Pea

Fresh, frozen, tinned or dried and blown through a peashooter, they're all 'you & me's'.

(c) Pee/Wee

'Let's you and me go for a you & me' – sounds like one for the girls, who tend to visit the 'rosie's' in tandem. See 'Rosie O'Grady'.

(d) Tea

…With which to wash down all English troubles: a nice cup of 'you & me'.

(e) Three

Wonder how many people have yelled 'Bingo!' after 'you & me, the number three' has been called.

You Know　　　**Snow (Cocaine)**

The term for cocaine ('snow') has been around for a century or so and its rhyming equivalent almost as long; RS at its most secretive.

COMPLETE COCKNEY RABBIT

You Must   **(Bread) Crust**

A term used by parents when trying to get their offspring to eat all their 'buppy'.

Young & Frisky   **Whisky**

How one may feel after a few – but in the morning? Old and fragile, more like.

Yours & Mine   **Nine**

Markers out for another piece from the bingo hall…

Yours & Ours   **Flowers**

A piece that grew in the flower market at the beginning of the 20th century.

Yul Brynner   **Dinner**

A 1960s example that's never shortened: you always break for 'Yul Brynner'. After a famously bald Hollywood actor (1915–85).

Yuletide Log   **Dog**

An uncommon alternative to 'christmas log' (qv) in reference to a greyhound, although both are left in the traps by 'cherry hog'.

Zachary Scotts   **Trots (Diarrhoea)**
The 'squitters' or 'zacharys' 1950s-style after an American star of stage and screen of the period (1914–65). Often a villain, aptly he's now appearing with breathtaking regularity in NHS hospitals across Britain.

Zasu Pitts   **Shits**
Co-starring with 'zachary scott', this Hollywood actress (1898–1963) is currently on a tour of NHS isolation wards, and appearing in a bedpan near you. Superbug victims are plagued with the 'zasus'. 'Don't stand for diarrhoea' – a piece of graffiti seen in a hospital toilet.

Zola Budd   **Spud**
A 1980s example based on a controversial South African athlete of the period. New or old, jersey or king edward, they're all 'zolas'.

Zorba the Greek   **Leak (Urinate)**
A 1960s term based on a 1964 film title, which had young drunks dancing off to the gents for a 'zorba'.

Zsa Zsa Gabor   **Whore**
A 1960s example based on an oft-married Hungarian-American actress. If she wants to sue, she should know that I'm a compiler, not a composer.

Anatomically Bubblin'

He passed his medical exams in Delhi
And immediately he was London bound
He tried to learn the language from the telly
Then he got a practice down in Canning Town.
He couldn't get the jargon of the cockneys
Who came to him about their aches and pains
He couldn't tell a dodgy loaf from knock-knees
Then an educated barrer boy explained

Let us start with your Crust o' Bread
Which is covered in Barnet Fair
Unless of course you're Madame Tussaud
Then a Syrup you can wear.
On the sides are your Southend Piers
And in the middle of your Chevy Chase
Are your Fireman's Hose and two Mince Pies
So you can Butcher's right into space.
Then you've got your North an' South
Where all the River Ouse goes in
With your Hampstead Heath and Jimmy Young
It's just above your Gunga Din
And don't forget your Fish an Chips
For kissing Lemons if you ain't an Iron
And on either side of your Gregory Peck
Are your Granite Boulders for a China to cry on.
Now on the ends of your Lucky Charms
Are where you'll find your German Bands
Clench your Melodies into an Oliver Twist
To belt the bully who fills your Boat with sand.
We now come to your East an West
The ladies have their Moonlight Flits
They're just above the Derby Kelly
Upset that you'll get the Eartha Kitts
Then there's parts of the anatomy
You keep cased up in your smalls
Always look after you Hampton Wick
Not to mention your Coffee Stalls.
And round the back is the Penny Black
It's nice to stick it to your Uncle Ned
And when it gets windy round the Khyber Pass
It's fun to pull the sheets over your Trouble's head
And if you should get Mozart and Lizst
And unsteady on your Scrambled Eggs
Try to keep your Plates o' Meat
Or you might fall down and crack
Your Crust o' Bread
Which is covered with Barnet Fair...